WITHDRAWN

REASON AND THE CHRISTIAN FAITH

VOLUME I

Faith and Reason

Faith and Reason

by

NELS F. S. FERRÉ

Abbot Professor of Christian Theology
Andover Newton Theological School

HARPER & BROTHERS PUBLISHERS

New York and London

FAITH AND REASON

Copyright, 1946, by Harper & Brothers
Printed in the United States of America

A-Y

To Katharine

in that "love
which is the bond of perfectness"

Contents

Author's Note

I have, indeed, been gratified by the response to the early printings of *Faith and Reason*. At this time, however, I should like to correct two rather common misunderstandings of my analysis. The first is to the effect that when I have gone to the limit of rational analysis, I suddenly advocate a leap from reason to faith, because of the fact that reason as such can never reach the ultimate. This would mean no more than that all human beings are finite and must, therefore, recognizing the prescribed conditions of their thinking, live more adequately beyond it in the realm of vital faith. To others this "leap" is considered to be due to the fact that the ultimate cannot be proved by anything less than itself, for the terms in which the ultimate would in that case be proved would be more dependable than the ultimate, which is, of course, a contradiction in terms. Both of these statements are, of course, true and are accordingly used for their worth in the book, but they are not at all the nub of what I am saying. I stress, rather, that every understanding of the ultimate is existential in the sense that reason is inevitably involved. There is thus no artificial or arbitrary leap from reason to faith; but simply a question whether or not the reason used within man's inescapable faith judgments concerning the ultimate is the best possible, both from the point of view of validity and adequacy. Nor is this relation between faith and reason true only because man's reason is part of faith's inevitable whole-response, but because we live in a dynamic process where the evidence is not all in, and where inevitable tension must, therefore, exist between faith's fullest seeing in line with the pointing of process and reason's true seeing of the difference between this ideal and the process as it now actually is. The fuller relation between the either/or and the both/and aspects of this problem are carefully worked out in Appendix B of *Evil and the Christian Faith*. Reason as systematic interpretation based on empirical observation is thus both partially fulfilled and yet at the same time partially rejected by faith. How this takes place, to what extent, and in what contexts is the main burden of this book.

The second common misunderstanding is to the effect that my insistence on the most high as the principle of interpretation is basically a Platonic analysis of the relation between time and eternity. Several reviewers have interpreted my analysis in this way, but to do so is to forget that what is central to my finding is the meaning of history for the problem of knowledge. Process points. In Platonic thought history as such has no unilinear, cumulative significance. The upshot of my whole understanding is that if history as a whole has no meaning, there is no reason at all for seeing the historic process in the light of an eternal Purpose. Then we are without a doubt needlessly multiplying essences! But this Purpose of the Most High is demanded precisely by process in order for it to find meaning in the light of the fullest possible truth. Thus even a formal analysis would take basic exception to the Platonic approach. As I continue with the content of my analysis in succeeding volumes the difference will become even more clear. But I see no point in differing; only in finding the truth. What actually has happened in my analysis is that *epistemology* has been brought into living and essential relation to *eschatology*. The more I ponder the relation between faith and reason the more I realize that the Christian presuppositions have not been adequately used to illumine this subject. This work explores a trail that leads to very rich territory.

Preface

Our age is experiencing a crisis of faith. We hear everywhere that we must return to faith. But to what faith? To the Christian faith? How can we return when among Christian leaders there are basic disputes as to what constitutes Christian faith? Nor can we return wholeheartedly until we are convinced that this faith is the truth that we and the world need, that this faith, indeed, is true. Our age is thus also a crisis of reason. We have lost our common language. Reason has been so abused and has come to mean so many things that we have no sure way of talking to our own contemporaries. We have a hard time even to discuss meaningfully whether or not our faith is true.

Our basic problem in thought is, indeed, the meaning and the relation of faith and reason. Everywhere I go I meet people who keep asking about these matters. Many discussions, serious searchings about what to believe and to do in an age like ours, at last land in the problem of faith and reason. People want to know what they believe and why. Ministers of every faith are getting more and more determined to get down to something basic. My students keep asking for more definitions of terms, more careful analysis. They, at least the best of them, want something solid that will stand up. One of the ablest and most thoughtful students in my seminar recently expressed his problem thus: "If I simply accept faith and then reason out what follows from there I cannot feel sure of myself. How do I know that I am not just rationalizing? If, however, I insist on justifying my faith by reason, it seems to me that I have no faith. In one case I am arbitrary and have nothing to say to all the people who start with another faith and refuse to examine it. In the other case I have no hope and driving power for a world like this." This student came from a conservative background and had just taken his master's degree under an outstanding philosopher. He could see and feel the truth in both positions. His case is that of many.

The tendency to split faith and reason apart is harmful to both. The tendency to absorb one into the other either way is equally dangerous. The present study is an attempt to analyze the terms, give them definite meanings, and to show in what sense they may be for or against one another. I have greatly profited by the controversy between the liberals and the neo-orthodox. The issue between the objective and the existential use of reason is basic. We shall not get far until we get hold of their right combination. This work tries to suggest one that will give a real place to both, separately and together.

Our age must also get to work on the question as to what extent theology can be scientific. The chapter on our knowledge of truth through science may cause an explosion in certain circles. I have sat for hours and hours and discussed these problems with sincere seekers after truth who have thought that they cannot be honest if they go beyond what "science says" and who have had no message because they have mistakenly starved their faith in order to be honest. Those who simply denounce science cannot help us. Nor can those who have not won their freedom from it through honest seeing. As I write this I can see tensely white faces, some older, some younger, of men who have had to wrestle hard with these problems in order to be freed by the truth. There is no easy short cut to insight and power to deal with these issues. Yet those who have awakened to the problems cannot be free from them by merely turning their back on them. Suppression never strengthens the soul. They can become free only by the understanding of the problems and their solutions.

Another question that keeps coming up everywhere is that of the finite God. If reason is accepted at all, how can we escape the fact that God is finite? There is evil in the world. How can a perfectly

wise, good, and powerful God have created it? Many feel strongly
that we have no right to evade the challenge of philosophy to the
Christian faith. I agree with them. The most difficult sections of
this book are on the relation of philosophy to religion. They should
not be read fast but with a good deal of pondering. They will help
prepare for the section on evil in the next volume. That problem
which haunts us more than ever can only be dealt with effectively
after the problem of truth has been explored and answered to the
best of our ability.

The final chapter deals with the standards which are peculiarly
those of religion and the reasons why these standards are accepted.
I have given faith both objective content and subjective meaning
without forfeiting, I feel, the highest use of reason. We need desperately to ground our faith solidly. American theology has been
weak in method, in basic principles. Every year I go through the
same experience with my students. They are often surprised at
having to spend six weeks on faith and reason. They want to assume faith and go right on. At the end of the year, however, they
come around and thank me especially for this part of the course,
and as they come back in later years from their churches or from
the chaplaincy they keep telling me: "Stress method; that's what
helped me the most."

This volume is in the same way quite necessary to the volumes
which I hope to write. *Faith and Reason* is the first volume of
"Reason and the Christian Faith." Volume II will be *Evil and
the Christian Faith,* in which I intend to analyze the meaning
of the Christian faith and its relation to the practical problems
which face us as individuals and as society. Especially I hope to
come to the problem of evil with some suggestiveness. Volume II
is already completed in its first draft. The chapter on evil is, in
fact, already in final form and promises at least to affect my own
life and thought more than I had foreseen.

I am indebted to *Christendom* and to *Theology Today* for the
use of two of my articles as appendices to this book. I am grateful
to Professor Albert C. Outler of Yale Divinity School and to Professor Roger Hazelton, my own colleague at Andover Newton The-

ological School, for reading the manuscript and for their constructive suggestions. I am thankful to my wife, to whom this book is
dedicated, for her unflagging interest and for preparing the manuscript for publication. I am thankful to the Andover Newton Theological School for my Sabbatical leave which gave me opportunity
to work uninterruptedly on this book. Most thankful, however, I
am to God who has let me have the health that I needed. When I
started to write this volume the days were for me the darkest in
years; as I end they are the brightest.

NELS F. S. FERRÉ

Newton Centre, Mass.
October 13, 1945

CHAPTER I

Religion and Reason

It is time for constructive thinking all around. Not only is there wide longing and deep need for it. There is also good chance for it.

Our present state is unusually ready for the positive approach. In science, philosophy, and religion alike past methods and conclusions are being questioned. Honest and competent thinkers in all fields realize how self-defeating the dogmatic attitude is. New and misspent knowledge join insistently to demand that we criticize each field first of all from within itself, and that then we criticize our criticisms. "To acquiesce in discrepancy is destructive of candour, and of moral cleanliness."[1]

Beyond such self-criticism, searching thinkers reach out to relate their own fields to fields of common or similar interest and to the whole field of human knowledge. No method which is on the defensive can be adequate. Isolationism has no place in the world of knowledge. During his last years of lecturing Alfred North Whitehead made a theme of the fact that one of our greatest needs now is to re-examine all methods of knowing in the light of all that we know.

Such re-examination is greatly needed purely from within our modern problems of knowledge. Truth to tell, however, many have come to see this need for honest and thorough re-examination of how we know, what we know, and why we know, and for a more constructive and co-operative thinking all around, because of the confusion, the moral weakness, the misguided energies, and the revolting destruction of our kind of civilization. Most of us know

[1] Whitehead, *Science and the Modern World*, p. 265.

with tragic trueness that the questions of what is true, right, and good will not down. Two basic needs for the modern world are adequate authority and intrinsic motivation. We need, that is, to agree on common truths for common ends to which we must bow because these are not of our own making, are for the common good, and rule out partial thinking and divisive conduct. As we see the truth of that common good, moreover, we need also to discover and to obtain the power to do it. Our common impotence, confusion, and suffering have led many to surrender their defensive thinking in order to reappraise their own proper methods both from within themselves and in the light of our total needs and overlapping problems.

Along the lines of such working together the Conference on Science, Philosophy and Religion hews a rough trail and deserves much credit. Each field, however, generally and naturally assumes too much that its own approach is basic and co-operates mostly by viewing common problems from its own present perspective rather than by studying the presuppositions and the relations of the several methods as the primary task with a view to enlarging and correcting its own. Adequate methodology is a basic need of both modern research and creative thinking. Method cannot give us a new spirit, but it can free the spirit from confusion and false burdens. Critical thinking is generally supposed to destroy. What, however, if we become more critical of the adequacy of the kind of critical thinking that we have kept assuming to be the final method? Our conclusions, whether positive or negative, follow in large measure from what we are in the habit of taking for granted and generally forget to present for common inspection. In the field of method we assume far too much that our customary ways are good enough. The three chapters following this seek to examine the methods of science, philosophy, and religion in order to establish what is the proper sphere of each, how they are related intrinsically in the common task of knowledge, where and how they differ, and how they can best co-operate by means of both community and difference. Whitehead's way of putting what we are after is that we ought to examine each individual method in the light of the general consideration of method in order to establish the proper limit of efficacy of each method.

In general, method must be determined by the nature of the object to be investigated. We must be careful, however, to avoid drawing neat boundaries around arbitrarily surveyed fields, for by so doing we shall artificially limit other fields. We must rather assume all possible common ground. Good fences do not by themselves make good neighbors. Good neighbors may use accurate landmarks and stout fences, but always for the sake of convenience and proper responsibility. In the field of human knowledge responsibility for the common task precedes the division into separate tasks. It must also succeed such division. Happy and creative working together requires that all be interested in the larger undertaking, big enough to see it, and while expertly disciplined in their own fields at the same time actively concerned with their neighbors' work and ready to offer at all times all the help that they can gather from the experience of carrying out their own special task.

It is time, we repeat, for constructive thought all around. Our common civilization needs the co-operation of science, philosophy, and religion. All have in common the whole field of human problems, interests, and knowledge. By field and function they have separate work to carry out but this work cannot be satisfactorily rendered except by a sense of common goals and a converging understanding of that fuller perspective of truth which can be arrived at by no one way. Naturally such constructive thinking must nevertheless not be guilty of belittling the genuine strains and tensions which arise not only from the divergent logical tendencies inherent in difference of method but even more from the human limitations of mind and spirit which corrupt and enlarge these tendencies into defensive attitudes and controversial contents. Our aim is to be as positive as possible without blurring even the edges of actual difficulties. Only such a solution can stand.

The following discussion, although it is definitely from the religious perspective, attempts to be within the clearest possible focus of the full perspective of truth. We know of no perspective in general without concrete content. All perspectives are from some concrete point of selected facts. We know no presuppositionless thinking. Even self and consistency become problems as soon as they are used as standards for interpreting either the actual or the ultimate world. The whole field of human knowledge is occupied territory. Our task is to understand our neighbors' point of view in order to correct and enlarge our own by means of what they see. That is what we mean by subordinating our religious perspective to the full perspective of truth.

In order to discuss to advantage from the point of view of religion the relation of science, philosophy, and religion we need a clear definition of religion. Such a definition must be both adequately descriptive of the whole range of religion and yet distinct enough from other fields to afford a definite and usable perspective. Our working definition of religion, which we shall explain bit by bit, is this: Religion is our normally necessary whole-response to what is considered to be most important and most real. This definition is at the same time as wide as human experience and yet different in essence from both science and philosophy. It also provides a common formal basis for all religions while allowing amply for their concrete differences. Religion as such is not presupposed to be true or false, good or bad. The definition makes no claim to establish one Religion with a capital R. It does not decide whether religion is cultural or cosmic in content, or both. It is not a definition of an ideal religion even formally. It is simply a formal definition of actual religion. All these problems we leave to be explored in their proper place. All we want to do here is to give a general idea of our approach to serve as a makeshift tool while we discuss science and philosophy.

It may even help to state our formal definition of right religion as follows: Right religion is our fully positive whole-response to the complete combination of what is most important and most real. The rest of this section will be devoted to a serious searching of the truth of this definition. First we shall investigate the bearing upon it of science and of philosophy. Then we shall test it against the requirements of its own field. The second section of the book will in turn try to find and to test the concrete content which best fulfills the requirements of the definition.

Our claim that religion is a necessary form of experience in general may seem arbitrary. Naturally we have said "normally necessary" because there are human beings so limited or damaged that they seem to us to have no capacity for interpreting that to which they respond. God only knows the depths in the deranged and they come under the problem of evil rather than under the normal function of religion. Yet the nature of religion itself is such that no normal person can escape it. At least the more we search and ponder the more true this seems. Our very word probably comes from the Latin *religare,* "to bind." Cicero uses the term *relegere,* "to reread." Religion would then be that which comes out of our deepest reflection. *Religare* seems to have the broader meaning and also to be the more commonly accepted derivation. This derivation is generally used by later Latin writers.[2]

Religion is, then, no option. It is our inescapable boundedness with the universe or with what controls the universe itself. It is our basic hanging together with that upon which we most fully and finally depend. We might possibly escape gravitation, but religion, never. We can deny or defy religion in the way that we can deny or defy the rules of health. But in both instances our denial is only verbal and our defiance, destructive. Religion, moreover, is not merely passive. We are bound up with a universe in which to live is to react. We are acted upon and we, in turn, react to that which acts upon us. We all hang together with the universe but how depends in great measure upon ourselves.

Nor are all our reactions religious. Religion is our whole-reaction to what we consider to be most important and most real. It has to do with what is most vital. Religion is the pattern that regu-

[2] Both Webster's *New International Dictionary,* Second Edition, and the *Oxford English Dictionary* agree on this. The latter claims that most modern scholars have now accepted this derivation. The *Columbia Encyclopedia* gives a definition of religion which is partially like ours: "Religion has to do with what is most vital in the feeling, belief, and performance of every human being."

lates our lives. It is the pattern of our response. It is the basic way we choose. It is the very character of "the repetition of the reactions" which constitute our experience.[3] Quite simply: to live as a human being is to react to what we most deeply want in relation to our chance of getting it. We cannot settle here, at any rate, what chance we have of getting what we want, or what we need. The two may be very different, yet what we want is always in depth relation, rightly or wrongly, to what we need. If we had no chance at all to get what is most important to us it would be totally irrelevant. And it is hard to see how what is totally irrelevant could be most important. As we shall see later, need within involves conditions without. In any case, what is most important and what is most real are inseparably connected both in experience and in all actual religions. They may not be one and the same; they may even seem far apart, especially in sophisticated theories. But even to be thought about and to be talked about they have to be that much together. And actually they are much more so. How far together or apart they are, are known to be, and must or need not be is a matter that we must discuss under our ideal definition.

An agnostic may deny religion with his mouth but he cannot deny it in his life. A man who hung on a rope over a chasm could deny hanging on. That would not alter the fact. But he could let go. In religion even that is impossible. We cannot let go of the universe. We cannot live without all the time passing on what we think to be most important and most real. To live is to keep deciding. Perhaps we seldom consciously choose. We may seldom "reread" or ponder. Even so, all the time we make whole-responses as to what for us is most important and most real, in whatever way these may then hang together, whether in us or outside us in their own nature and being.

Religion, we have said, is our normally necessary whole-reaction to what is considered to be most important and most real. Whole-

---

[3] "For experience is based on the repetition of the reactions." F. H. Heinemann, "The Analysis of 'Experience,'" in *The Philosophical Review*, Nov., 1941, p. 577.

reaction is an important word. Man is an organism who reacts as a whole whatever disharmony there may then be within that whole. "The totality of our existence is at stake, and thus the totality of our personality must participate in the search."[4] Our emotions are our likes and dislikes of the world to which we respond. Reason is the way we recognize, remember, and interpret that world and our relation to it. Our will is the steadiest way[5] that we react to it. It has structure, content. To call the will simply the self in action is to forget that sometimes we act "against our will." We may be forced to do so or have a feeble will. The self, in any case, always responds as an organic whole over and above drives within it, like emotions, reason, or will, whatever their degree of harmony or conflict.

Sometimes the self yields unwisely to the emotions in their desire for immediate satisfaction. Sometimes it follows them wisely. Sometimes it controls them and acts according to reason contrary to inclination. Reason itself, of course, is based on remembered observations, more or less digested, previous choices, examined and unexamined, and all the content of its training, formal and informal. Sometimes, moreover, neither emotions nor reason are in the saddle of the self but rather conscience, the light of the will, based on the urge to consistency of conduct along the line of some ideal or purpose; and conscience may ride the self, because the self lets it into the saddle, contrary to both present inclination and seeing. Ideally they ought all to co-operate. And even though there is seldom complete co-operation there is yet a strong tendency based on our organic need for wholeness bringing constant pressure to bear on all the differing aspects of the self in order to make them act in harmony.

There is never an act without also an idea and an emotion, however small and unrecognized, which to some extent accompany it. There is never an idea which does not prompt the self to some

---

[4] Kroner, *The Function of the Religious Imagination*, p. 63.

[5] The formal division into ideation, affection, and conation has a place yet in discussing actual man it is better to use the will in the sense of dominant content rather than of pure conation.

response, whether expressed or repressed, and which is not surrounded with emotional color. There is never an emotion without some small idea and call to action. This is the more true on the level of religious experience. There is no simple separation of any of these aspects of the self. They baffle us in their depth relations. They go so deep that it is necessary to say that "it is not the mind which thinks but man,"[6] it is not the will which wills but man, it is not the emotions which feel but man. Man himself, the person, the spirit, is deeper than all these aspects in his depth decisions. He is led by them and also refuses to be led by them. He is molded by them and is himself also remolding them. Thus no act is without some positive will, feeling, or thought though the major drive of some of these aspects may be suppressed or inhibited in any whole-response by the self to his dynamic environment.

This fact is important for our definition of religion. Religion is whole-response which always involves yet which can never be reduced to thought, emotion, and will. Sometimes in our experience, or in certain religions, thought may be the dominant drive while the emotions are thwarted and the will is inhibited in their major drives. Sometimes the emotions may be the leading factor and reason and will may be thinly positive and thickly thwarted. Sometimes will may have the upper hand and the self may keep responding as a whole in spite of starved emotions or slighted reason. We shall shortly analyze these several aspects in their wrong and right functions. But the steady tendency of the self is to unify its several aspects. The ideal response of the self is naturally a whole-response with full harmony of all organic aspects of the self.

Wieman's definition of religion in this regard is both good and to the point: "Religion at its highest and best, is the devotion of the total self, through search, service and adoration, to the highest cause of which one is now conscious, provided that cause is deemed worthy of the devotion of all men, and is symbolic of ever higher unexplored values."[7] Such surrender of the total self to truth and

---

[6] M. C. D'Arcy, in *Revelation,* edited by John Baillie and Hugh Martin, p. 195.

[7] Wieman and Wieman, *Normative Psychology of Religion,* p. 38.

value also discovers how hard and long the road to it is. Right religion even according to our formal definition demands the full measure of devotion and sincerity. Otherwise the reaction of the self to its own problems within itself darkens and confuses its clear and immediate reaction to what is acting on it. Even as we begin this search we must therefore constantly bear in mind that we shall get nowhere unless both the writer and the reader keep finding the fuller truth in their own fullness of life in response to the complicated world which always meets up with us. Baron von Hügel has ably expressed this fact:

We get to know such realities slowly, laboriously, intermittently, partially; we get to know them, not inevitably nor altogether apart from our dispositions, but only if we are sufficiently awake to care to know them, sufficiently humble to welcome them, and sufficiently generous to pay the price continuously which is strictly necessary if this knowledge and love are not to shrink but grow. We indeed get to know realities in proportion as we become worthy to know them—in proportion as we become less self-occupied, less self-centred, more outward-moving, less obstinate and insistent, more gladly lost in the crowd, more rich in giving all we have, and especially all we are, our very selves."[8]

Every aspect of the self is needed at its highest pitch of energy and discipline. Whole-reaction always includes reason. For the whole-reaction to be right, reason must then also be right. Trouble comes in when aspects are neglected, suppressed, or perverted. Then partial paralysis or tension sets in. No whole-reaction is ever right without full use of right reason. Right religion and right reason in this sense are inseparable. The anonymous author of "The Epistle to Diognetus" well states this necessary relationship between religion and reason:

Nor do I aim at anything inconsistent with right reason. . . . For in this place the tree of knowledge and the tree of life have been planted; but it is not the tree of knowledge that destroys— it is disobedience that proves destructive. . . . For neither can

[8] Baron von Hügel, *Essays and Addresses on the Philosophy of Religion,* p. 104.

life exist without knowledge, nor is knowledge secure without
life. Wherefore both were planted close together. . . . Let your
heart be your wisdom; and let your life be true knowledge inwardly
received.[9]

Whether right reason and right whole-reaction actually do or
can go together will be the central problem in this book. Obviously
our definition is of an ideal relationship. It states a formal requirement. We have to wonder whether reason can tell us what the most
important and the most real are, and what the relation between
them is. In order to summarize intensely two theses which are scattered throughout the whole book we have added at the end of
this section two appendices. Their pointed style tries to bring out
into bold relief two main ideas which will form part of the general
background. In this way they can be both quickly isolated for inspection and tested throughout the whole book.

Formally, then, right religion and right reason go together. A
right whole-reaction must necessarily include right reason. The
content of experience which constitutes the criterion of right
reason, however, is in no way determined by the fact that formally
right whole-response and right reason must go together. The answer to what is most high and real, or most important and most
true, cannot be had from a mere examination of the reason itself.
Reason is on the side of man's response to that to which he reacts.
Truth is the right interpreter of that to which we respond. Truth
must never be reduced to method. The right processes in man must
not be substituted for the right interpretation of what is outside
man. If reason itself as such is made the standard we have merely
admired the threshing machine and not threshed any wheat. The
spider may spin its thread from within itself but to live it must
catch something with it. Our capacity for rational thought must
not short-circuit its task by accepting reason as the most high and
the most real. To do so is at least arbitrarily to make a noun out
of a verb, reason out of reasoning. Truth probably is as much of a
verb as a noun, an acting as a being, at least some combination of

[9] "The Epistle of Mathetes to Diógnetus," in *The Ante-Nicene Fathers*,
Vol. I, pp. 28–30.

the two, since what we meet is action. Truth is what we must tell concerning that to which we react. But the truth we are after is the thing we meet and we must never presuppose that this is the same as our process of interpretation. To say that like can only know like and that therefore what meets us is of the same nature as our organ of interpretation is to prejudge our case. It is worse than that, for we are not primarily reasons but persons. We interpret through whole-response. Reason is not the same as the will or the emotions, and certainly not the same as the depth of whole-response.

The formal requirement that right religion and right reason go together involves no necessary content within rational discourse. It presupposes or precludes no definite criterion. What we are guarding against at the outset is that false intellectualism that separates reason from man and treats it as something independent of him. Alfred North Whitehead in writing *The Principles of Natural Knowledge* confined his theme to "the coherence of the known" but he began by admitting that in so doing he was isolating for purposes of observation one part of the whole of knowledge and admitted that to deal with the full truth you have to pay attention "to the consideration that there is a mind knowing it."[10] And around the mind always pressing on it are all of man's emotional and volitional drives. But some do not see how what the mind knows is affected by the mind knowing it, with all its inclinations and prejudices already acquired; nor do they see the important effect on knowledge of the organic stresses and strains of adjustment that are always taking place in relation to new reactions. Such people sever reason from the whole man thinking. They think of reason as possible apart from right emotions and right actions. They even sometimes claim that these hinder clear thinking. But there is no such detached reason. Reason cannot be taken off man like a spare tire. Reason is a necessary part of the whole man. It is an organ that in this life at least dies apart from the whole life of man, spirit, mind, and body. It cannot even, as we said before, be rightly treated as apart, for there is no such actu-

[10] P. vii.

ality. Right reason is always *the whole man* thinking rightly. Wrong reason is reasoning apart from the needs and the situation of the whole man.

We naturally want to think that detached reasoning is possible. Then we can dodge our responsibility for living truth. There are areas of investigation with such settled and measurable content that little of emotion and action are involved apart from the obligations of honesty and carefulness. In these areas there is little personal risk because the conclusions do not affect living decisions directly. To avoid the demand of full depth response we tend to take these areas as the model of all truth and to say that the less emotion and the less action are involved the better. But all truth is living. The closer it comes to the center of life the more alive we find it. It is found in the fullest, purest whole-surrender to what is most important and most real. Truth is of "the inward parts." It requires the fullest possible combination of what is most important and what has the most power of being to make this central, or "to come true." Truth is seeing what is really there. Truth is seeing how what is really there really acts. What is really there can change what is actually here, can "come true." Truth is refusing to hide one's eyes from the real difference that there may be between what is most important to us here and now and what is really there acting as it really does. Truth is an active right relation of whole-response. Whole-responses, obviously, are not right merely by being whole, since we must all make whole-responses. Truth is wholeness and sincerity before whatever is really there. Because we want what is most important and most real to go together the way we need them to go together we must never try to see them as being more together than they really are the way they really act. To do so is to court moral blindness, whole-blindness. Yet unless we respond as wholes without exception to what is really there, including in the fullest unity all of our being, unless we act in wholeness before God, we shall not see what is really there as it really acts as rightly and as fully as possible.

When we make too much of reason to the neglect of the emotions or the will we invite a dry, academic attitude which is both artificial and false to the main areas of knowledge. Intellectualism is the absence of living truth. It is the denial of whole-truth. When we dodge sympathy and action we must necessarily reason falsely in the most vital areas of truth, in the areas of whole-response. Our very defense of our dodge, that we must be above the battle of life to think clearly, is a rationalization, an unconscious lie to protect us from accountability. All our thinking in the vital areas of knowledge where value and choice are involved is consequently spoiled by this dodge.

Religion must have right reason and therefore requires the reason of the whole man thinking in whole-surrender to find truth —in thought, appreciation, and deed. We can also see this fact in the case of the other aspects of the self. Emotions are needed for both enjoyment and drive. We are powerless to effect the good without strong emotions. Yet emotions for their own sake, or undisciplined by reason and unused in action, make for unhealthy emotionalism. "Our emotions are our response to the call of the inner life of the cosmos."[11] Yet these emotions must be within whole-response, tested and directed by reason and salted by action. William James made too much of "our passions" when he held that they "fix our beliefs beforehand." He claimed that they force the logical reason to "find arguments for our conviction."[12] But reason is rather part of whole-response and should be used to interpret rightly that "inner life of the cosmos." Emotionalism never finds depth of truth, but depth of truth cannot be had apart from a full and free emotional response. Man can hide from truth and what truth requires by indulging in emotionalism or, on the other side, he can starve out truth by refusing right emotions.

The same thing is true in the case of the will. Action for its own sake is activism. That is bad, a running away from the task of reason or the deeper call of emotion. Yet without the right action we cannot find truth. To think about value and choice and yet not pay the price for them is soon to think falsely about them. "It is

[11] Julius Seelye Bixler, "A Phenomenological Approach to Religious Realism" (especially dealing with Max Scheler), in *Religious Realism*, p.76.

[12] William James, *Varieties of Religious Experience*, p. 436.

only as we become more and more personally moralized by faithful performance of already known duties that the full demand of duty upon us is progressively disclosed. . . . Clear knowledge does not precede performance, but follows upon it."[13] "If any man will to do his will, he shall know of the doctrine." Before we discuss reason further, or even enlarge on our definition, we want to stress as of utmost importance that, whatever be our later conclusions or remaining problems, reason must always be within whole-response. Reason must be the whole man thinking.

By reason we mean any and all ways of understanding. Our definition of right reason will come later. Our definition of reason now needs to be as inclusive as possible. It is any interpretation at all by any means whatever of that to which we respond including the interpretation of our own reaction. We know no self except as a reactor and therefore we know no self in itself and prior to all reactions. Such a self we may isolate by thought but we can never experience it. Reason cannot be prior to self but must be within it and within the total relations of the self. We include under reason more than our capacity for logical reasoning. That might rule out the depths of some experience that fails to fit in with our ordinary patterns of consistency, or which even refuses to be told in present language. Every interpreted sensation, either through special attention or through the interpreting activity of the whole self, participates in the reason of the whole man thinking. We also include any revelation by whatever method, by voice, intuition, inspiration beyond common experience, or even the coming into history of a unique person. In so far as such revelation forms part of that to which we respond, the interpretation of it is by means of reason. Even if the understanding is "in and by the Spirit," if the self can understand it at all that understanding, although not from, is yet through reason in the inclusive sense. To define reason, for instance, as that which we can know apart from Christ's having come into the world is at least to be arbitrary in defining terms. Reason, at its broadest, is any and all interpretations of our reactions. In this general sense reason and revelation cannot be in con-

[13] A. E. Taylor, *The Faith of a Moralist*, Series I, pp. 158–159.

flict because they are on different sides of the gap: revelation is part of that to which we react while reason is part of our reaction. Conflicts can come only because of false or limited instruction to which we react, because the whole-self wants to interpret falsely or interpret away something which acts on us, or else because the whole-self wants to put something outside itself to react to what is not there.

The trouble is, however, that what we interpret does not always go together, that we get different ideas about the same thing as we get more experience or are changed by some radically different experience, that other people often interpret the same stuff differently from us, that they differ among themselves, and that they, too, keep changing. We therefore need some standard for right reason. Such a standard can be arrived at promisingly only through taking into account our neighbors' understanding of that to which they react. After all, they are very much like unto us and they meet pretty much the same world as we do. Beyond what we can interpret rather clearly there is, moreover, a whole realm to which we react vaguely striving to understand. And through and beyond both our clear and our vague, vast realm, there is yet another realm to which we have to react without reason's giving us a complete answer. That is at least the report of many people. It is also our own experience. Some have seen, furthermore, that the way they react to all these areas in their interrelations has in turn a vital effect on their ability to think them through further and even on the kind of interpretation which in the light of this new insight they must give even to those realms which they thought that they understood fairly well. The third realm to which we react is that of faith. From the point of view of reason as any interpretation of whole-response faith must be included under reason. Nor can right faith ever be contrary to right reason, the best that we can know about what is truest in this world. Yet faith may not fit fully under a careful definition of what we can know legitimately about this world as it now is. What we can know rightly about this world here and now may perchance fit well under a larger point of view that would include right reason.

Right reason we may think of as that which can be stated clearly to ourselves, told meaningfully to others, and then tested by them in some manner open to all people. By clear statement we mean any idea simple or complex, easily acceptable or baffling, that can be isolated, identified, and recalled. Even though reason formally thought of is the capacity for logical inference based on free ideas,[14] we must be careful not to make formal clarity the standard of right reason. By so doing we shall shut out the richness of experience which refuses to be coined into words. Words convey but only miserably contain meaning. They signify more than they say. Even what exact meaning they contain we cannot confine. Books are written to explain one or a few words and beyond the books the fuller meaning haunts us. Words are symbols to suggest our experience to others. The meaning of the symbol depends upon the hearer as much as, and perhaps more than, upon the sayer, or upon the reader as upon the writer. The value of the coin varies with the reserve stock in the bank of both parties. It is most flexible. Two people hear the same sentence and gather astonishingly different meanings from it. What we think with, the reserve stock, is usually more important in understanding than what we think of, the exact present coin. The rich man seldom uses all his riches at once. Words, to change the figure, are isolated soldiers; sentences are battalions; a book may be a whole division; but the strength of any fighting force depends upon the vast reserves, upon the total armies in use, or available for use if necessary.

We must therefore be wary of too strong longing for clarity of statement as an end in itself lest we also be tempted beyond our strength to forfeit the depths of truth. Clarity may be the sign of much strength. Lack of it may mean failure to examine and ponder, "to reread" our experiences. Clarity may have cost years and years of depth and devotion. Because sentences are clear they need not be shallow. Because a thought is simple it need not be superficial. There are many today who cry against clarity as a

[14] For an excellent statement on reason in this respect compare Brand Blanshard, *The Nature of Thought,* 2 volumes.

sign of light-mindedness. Such judgments may be true but they are often shallow prejudgments. They can be the excuse for hard thinking. Yet clarity, on the other hand, may be due to an insecurity in our lives which makes us want to see everything clearly beyond despair or doubt. Clarity may be an attempted short cut to truth, but just as Mr. Hypocrisy in *Pilgrim's Progress* instead of arriving at salvation ended by taking the road to destruction, even so those who seek clarity in order to be completely sure of what they see and to hold it fast beyond doubt of losing it find, not saving truth, but destroying thinness. Descartes made "clear and distinct ideas"[15] a final standard of truth. That way lies intellectualism and not truth through whole-response. Depth of insight, where experience is not peeled but pondered by reason, keeps defying ordinary clearness and flees for its life from all easy clarity.

Jesus seems so clear to many; yet the disciples failed to follow what he said. It has in fact taken ages to understand him and some of us think that it may still take ages to see what he saw. Truth always says, "Woe unto you when men follow easily." Depth, however, must seek all possible clarity. Language should be a help and not a hindrance. We must therefore try and try again to state the interpretation of what we experience as clearly as we can without thinning out what we see any more than we can possibly help.

We must never forget that what we can state and what we can experience are two different things. Our depth experience is far fuller than what we can grasp by reason. After that, what we can grasp in whole-thinking is richer than what we can isolate and identify in definite ideas even to ourselves. Then after that, again, what we can get across to others even of that which we can grasp and formulate seems but a sorry crust. Every deeply searching soul must consequently be lonely save as he rests in God, who understands him better than he understands himself. We must ever

---

[15] *Oevres de Descartes,* Méditation Troisième, p. 81: "et partant il me semble que déjà je puis établir pour règle générale que toutes les choses que nous concevons fort clairement et fort distinctement sont toutes vraies."

be thankful for the truth that Paul Minear has stressed, namely that for us, as for children, it is more important to be understood than to understand. In our human situation we neither understand nor are understood. The very problem of knowledge thus cries for a reality beyond the limitations and frustrations of human life.

Our second standard for right reason is what can be told to others. John Dewey points out that "we affirm only that which we take to be capable of *con*firmation."[16] Right reason is always capable of becoming a social affair. It depends for its deep roots, for its solid strength, upon what the ages have thought into some degree of clearness. We must all start with a history of ideas going back thousands of years. No one can start afresh. No one can start by himself. Being human in any normal sense at all means depending upon a historic heritage. Neither depth nor newness of significant knowledge can be attained except by some deep baptism into the history of knowledge at some point or other and by some means or other. Personal freshness in knowing is mostly a matter of recapitulation, of reliving the past; only in part is it the experiencing for oneself immediately those depth responses which gave the ideas we have to others in the first place and which have gradually become common enough knowledge to be constantly shareable through language. "We *learn* our conceptual interpretations largely through imitation and co-operation."[17] If we are careful not to commit the genetic fallacy by the "identification of process and product"[18] we can even see the truth in Boodin's contention (summarized and cautiously reviewed by J. A. Leighton) to the effect that "personal minds arise only through social interaction. The group is genetically prior to personality."[19] Language itself is perhaps the greatest factor in this learning from the past and in the living of our lives by largely reliving the past. Here, however, enters a very subtle temptation. The past did not stand still else language could never have grown. The present must

[16] John Dewey, *Logic,* p. 187.
[17] Clarence I. Lewis, *Mind and the World Order,* p. 114.
[18] Dewey, *op. cit.,* p. 67.
[19] J. A. Leighton's review of *The Social Mind,* by John Elof Boodin, in *The Philosophical Review,* May, 1941, p. 333.

not stand still. History must be a help and not a burden. Knowledge must never thrust itself athwart the fresh desire to search for the new. Skill must not quench imaginative creativity. We must not reduce what others have said in the past to what was said before them. There is newness in history. Nor must we equate what has already been told with what can now be told to others. New experiences can give new meaning to words and can invent new words. No man has the right to be as small as his own past. No age has the right to become of a fixed age.

What can be told to others also depends upon them. Words speak only to those who hear. "He that hath ears to hear, let him hear." John Dewey insists that "a universe of experience is the precondition of a universe of discourse."[20] Some cannot "hear" because what is spoken registers no meaning to their minds. Their experience is thin and limited. Yet what is most important is open to all and more have in fact experienced it than have interpreted it fully enough to state it or to understand it if stated. We are all human beings in a common world. The stuff of experience is generally the same. What is quite apart can hardly claim to be essential. Therefore if we are as simple and as clear as we can be and keep paying the cost for such simple clarity as is consistent with depth we should be able to make ourselves at least partly, perhaps even generally, understood, if people would only be willing to go to the trouble of really trying long and patiently to understand. There are different kinds of soil. We know that; yet that need not become our excuse. For whether or not people will try to understand, and how long and patiently, depends also in large measure on the importance of what we have to say.

Two obstacles always block the way. One is that words are likely to be filled with different meanings. And important words, even positive value words, have gathered up unpleasant as well as pleasant overtones. That is true of even the best of words like reason, Christ, faith, virtue. People may even rebel against the word truth, being afraid of what may be involved, or fearful that something is being "put over" on them. We poor creatures are too

[20] Dewey, *op. cit.*, p. 68.

much afraid. We are foolishly on the defensive. Yet we long to learn, and in good measure we dare to trust. Therefore words are no final obstacles if we elicit good will and faith. We can tell others meaningful ideas by trying patiently and humbly to understand what they believe and to avoid at the outset their deepest prejudices, by being sincere, and by using simple language in a precise and consistent manner. We have, in fact, the obligation to establish our own authenticity.

The second obstacle to understanding is that all of us are tempted to acquire a position. Such a position may become fear's defense. We may become eager not to know anything that will pierce our armor of supposed intellectual security. We may even have developed a system. A system tends to be closed seeing. We need to live in a locus rather than in a position, in a moving rather than in a fixed point. Our search must not fence us into a finished system, but rather open out into further consistent seeking. Perhaps we had better take a good look at this problem of consistency. Consistency is both a necessity and a danger. Some consider consistency the hallmark of truth; others treat it mostly as the sign of a defensive system.

We must have consistency as a standard of truth. Not only do we need to aim at the greatest possible harmony within our own interpretation. We must also correct and enlarge our own view by comparing it with others' to find out to what extent and in what ways it agrees with their findings. But consistency is no easy task and offers no easy answer. We have said that mere formal consistency is not enough. That is substituting the process for the product, the tool for the work, the inner relation for the outer result. We can nevertheless all agree that in so far as thought is not thereby thinned out or falsified the more consistency we have, the better.

The trouble comes when we try to take any actual content other than the form itself (in so far as that is also a content of experience) to serve as a standard for what truth is. As soon, in any case, as we begin to say what is most important and most real in that to which we react, we generally begin to see differently. Reason as capacity for logical inference must be fully honored in its innermost nature. Yet it must work in a world which is far more than a logical network. Reason must tell us, as far as it can, what is true out there and important; more than that, reason can to some extent handle that world, which is at least enough like reason to be partially understood by it, stated by it, and tested by it.

Self is no immediate standard. Self is, of course, more than reason and is, therefore, a better standard for truth than reason is. Personalism is bigger and truer than rationalism. Yet the self is also, like reason, on this side of the equation of our response situation. Self is the reactor, not necessarily what acts on us, although, to be sure, what acts on us may be other reason or other self. We know, at least, that each reactor reacts to other reasons and selves. But to start by assuming self or assuming reason as the final standard of truth is to start our task with a presupposition, if not necessarily a prejudice. Such a standard merely proceeds to measure all by itself and to conform all to itself. It thus ends with some system of reason or self a bit enlarged and enriched but basically spun out of its own web. Unless, as it looks out, it becomes aware of its false position and gives up its starting point, it will fail to find truth—unless perchance it actually finds nothing but a reason or a self out there in all things like itself and thus happens to be right in spite of its assumed starting point.

Our real question is what content of experience out there, what aspect of that to which we react, is to be rightfully considered the standard of truth. Aquinas wrote that "truth is in the intellect in proportion to its conformity with the object understood. . . . Truth is the equation of thought and thing."[21] Whitehead calls truth "the conformation of Appearance to Reality."[22] Truth must be the right reading of what is out there and such reading must be by means of ever closer conformity in all our living. But yet what is there, really there, in the way it really works, that is most important and most real? It would be easy if we could say that all out there is equally real. If we could only say that "the truth is

[21] Aquinas, *The Summa Theologica*, Vol. I, question XVI, Art. 1.
[22] Whitehead, *Adventures of Ideas*, p. 309.

the whole"[23] and leave it there! Then we should only have to describe what is there accurately and fully. There would be no need to explain it, to ask why it is there. Consistency and wholeness would be standards enough. Our problem would still be immense in this baffling world of ours but it would be easier than it actually is. We shall find later that all that is here and now actual, the totality of temporal events, gives no full reason for the occurrences which we know have come into history. Hegel, of course, subscribed to no static actual and to no closed here and now. For him the whole was "the essential nature reaching its completeness through the process of its own development."[24] Yet one wonders if his theory of "self-becoming, self-development"[25] by which the Absolute was to be what it becomes in the end is any more adequate than most descriptions of the actual which include possibility and development. What the Absolute "is in very truth"[26] may become evident at the end of process, but it is very difficult to see why and how such an end is to be expected from what we now see unless it already is equal in wisdom and power to that end.

The fact that what is now actual has not always been actual, that we have had a series of different actual worlds, an actual world, for instance, in which there was no life, makes it necessary, in any case, to discuss especially the meaning and nature of this actual world. Close reasoning may show us that what is now and here actual as a whole points to probabilities beyond itself. We shall find that what is most important and what is most real do not go completely together out there and that therefore religion to be right and full cannot rest with the finding of reason. Reason itself carefully used will show us that it points beyond itself.

Perhaps we had better define right reason as the fullest and most consistent explanation of what is now and here actual based on the most thorough description of it and such reasoning beyond it as may be warranted by the facts found within what is here and now actual. This we may call rational knowledge. This definition

[23] Hegel, *Phenomenology of Mind*, p. 82.
[24] *Ibid.*
[25] *Ibid.*
[26] *Ibid.*

of right reason leaves the door wide open to any creative thinking beyond the present and to any illumination of reason by means of faith as whole-surrender to truth. We include also prayer, inspiration, revelation, or any other means by which ideas can possibly be had to light up more fully all that we can truly know of this world of ours, and concerning this world of ours. The point even here is to make no artificial exclusion from right reason but to include every way whatever in which what is here and now actual as a whole can be stated to ourselves and told to others. Arthur E. Murphy has well stated a demand for whole-reason which we hope to heed. Any faith that is true ought to be indicated negatively or positively by our best use of reason.

> What we need now, with peculiar urgency, is the wisdom to find a faith that can maintain itself in practice and in the open, as the spokesman for a good that is in fact what it purports to be and can perform what it promises, and what its disciples profess. For the attainment of such a faith we shall need the best use of all our powers, those of rational discrimination and comprehensive understanding not least among them. While, therefore, we shall welcome any aid that faith can bring to reason, we shall have to ask that faith to identify itself and present its credentials.[27]

Our definition of right reason accepts both reason and experience as standards of knowledge. Both must be combined as fully as possible. It makes no claim to confine full truth to right reason. Truth may go beyond right reason even while using it as fully as possible both critically and creatively. We shall have to contend with the limits of reason and with the problems of faith in the search for the fullest possible truth. Such faith, however, has no business at all with knowledge and can lay no claim to truth unless it springs inescapably out of the knowledge situation itself. In that sense we could include faith as part of reason, and indeed from the perspective of whole-response we do. We know neither of any specially religious brain cells nor of any religious area fenced off from reason. Faith is open to inspection and must be required by the right analysis of knowledge.

[27] Murphy, *The Uses of Reason*, p. 12.

Our preference for this definition of right reason is that many almost naturally think of reason as backed by the evidence of what we can now and here see as actual. Anything beyond that they feel is not within the province of reason. We could otherwise say that reason is all that we interpret in any way whatever of that to which we react including our own reaction; while right reason is that which can be stated, told, and tested by others according to the demands of the subject matter. In that case, right reason would include faith. If a distinction were to be made between what can be said and tested about what is here and now actual and all that the self can interpret beyond that from the very facts offered within that actual and its history, we could call the former knowledge and the latter reason, the powers of reason outstripping what we can know. Reason would then be seen in its dynamic, searching, creative nature as well as in its critical and systematic capacity. Yet many want to confine the scope of reason to what we can know in terms of present process. These, however, have seldom thought of the problems connected with the nature of the actual, usually take it for granted, and will therefore be little better taken with this distinction. They want to stop with reason as knowledge and truth will not let them. Even the term knowledge, however, gives a false impression since what we know of that which is here and now actual itself brings up vital questions which make a faith-judgment about itself, the content of what is called knowledge, or reasonable, in the end necessary. Our analysis will show that reason to be whole must become religious. The two appended papers will analyze this theme from slightly different angles. What matters is the truth situations, not words.

Instead of saying that reason must become religious because it must interpret whole-response, we can say that all whole-responses to truth include emotion and action and are therefore better called faith.[28] Then right reason and knowledge as we have defined them are necessary aspects of faith's total inquiry. Right

[28] This definition is, of course, formal only. Later we shall contrast the contents of faith and reason. The crux of the contention between the two usually lies in the selection of critical contents.

reason, then, we define advisedly as whatever can be clearly stated to ourselves concerning what is here and now actual, meaningfully told to others, and tested by them for wholeness and consistency in any manner whatsoever.

We have already discussed the testing to some extent under the telling. The very fact of there being numberless other thinkers made the desirability of a common story a test in itself. But the testing cannot be limited to the two standards of consistency and wholeness. By so doing we arrive too easily at systems which satisfy. We cannot agree with Emerson that "with consistency a great soul has simply nothing to do."[29] Yet what we know is surrounded by ever receding mysteries. The day comes not yet without the night. Our little history is a drop in the eternities. For us being hangs over the great abyss of non-being. Over, beyond, and all through our best wrought systems are the mists of ignorance. "The wind bloweth where it listeth." Every new becoming speaks of the endless forms of God's wisdom. Of all men, they say, no thumb prints are alike. Whence this vast differentiation; whence all newness? The laboratory gives us one kind of test. Only part of what we know can be so tested. Reasoning about the things we know gives us another kind of test which outstrips the exact measurement by the tools of our hands. The world of values is a yet more complicated realm of testing and yet we cannot but live in that world. The problems of spirit are deeper still. As we go into the analysis of knowledge in chapters which follow we shall make the issues as clear as possible.

We have, in any case, to accept testing of that which can be stated clearly to oneself and told to others by any manner whatsoever. But it must be open to all. Open does not mean common. The highest reaches of music appreciation may be known to only a handful of people, or at least to only a small number of gifted and trained individuals. What they truly know may not be common knowledge. Yet apart from the natural variations of native ability such testing must be open to anyone. Only to those who

[29] Ralph Waldo Emerson, "Self Reliance," in *Essays*, p. 43 (Burt & Co. ed.).

are qualified, however, can it be common knowledge. In the realm of spirit there may be insights so compelling that they become necessary knowledge to disciplined, trained depth response of the whole man thinking. We may see relationships with complete compulsion. All we can do is to report what we see. These truths may be stated in words or symbols enough to tell others. And when they see they know. Yet often the real seers are few. A. E. Taylor is most decisive about this sense of seeing. "The whole of what can properly be called 'theory of knowledge' is contained in an answer to the question 'How does knowing differ from opining and believing?' And the true answer to this question can be given in three words, 'By being vision.' "[30] Wholeness and consistency confirmed by all in thought based on whole-experience is the ideal of rational knowledge but must never be the ravager of it by the reducing of it to the common average attainment. Consensus of opinion is no sure test of knowledge. There would be no advance of knowledge if *"securus iudicat orbis terrarum"*[31] were true. The general judgment of mankind is *not* "sure." Therefore we have a Jesus and a Copernicus to correct it.

Two questions might as well be taken up right away. They are road-blocks to the unwary and to the easily persuaded that often make them turn back discouraged from the road to truth. The first is this: Is reason competent at all, being so limited by our natural ignorance, to deal with truth, particularly the higher reaches of it? The second is like unto it: Is not reason hopelessly perverted by our pride? To the first question we may use Hegel's response to Kant's insistence that reason itself must be examined before we can accept its conclusions. Hegel answered with telling simplicity that even such an examination of reason must be by an act of reason: "The examination of knowledge can only be carried out by an act of knowledge."[32] We may find, of course, that reason reaches limits beyond which it cannot go.

It is possible to know that we do not know. It is even possible

---

[30] A. E. Taylor, *Philosophical Studies,* p. 398.

[31] Augustine, *Contra Epist. Parmen.,* iii, 24.

[32] *The Logic of Hegel,* translated by William Wallace, p. 17.

to know in general the regions we do not know by their relation to what we do know. A map of discovered territory drawn in white could leave a definite outline in black of what was not discovered. The unknown would not be shapeless. That is a sort of knowledge. But it is not right to call it true knowledge. It is, to be sure, more than a lack of knowledge. It is the knowledge of a limit. Knowledge must go beyond that limit in some way in order to fix it. Ignorance thus known is an invitation to appetite for more knowledge. Hunger is not food but it implies and seeks for it. Knowledge of ignorance may be the grace of creative mystery. It may be more important in the long run than that which we think we know. Whitehead says that "not ignorance but the ignorance of ignorance is the death of knowledge."[33] Glimpses of light may tantalize our imagination and may make us want to see through and out. The knowledge of ignorance means that the forms of knowledge reach out both potentially and actually beyond what we now know, beyond present content. Thus reason is bigger than knowledge and we are bigger than we know. We can know ignorance because our depth knowledge and whole-relation reach far beyond our conscious knowledge and chosen relations. Or we can say that faith is this depth relation of whole-decision. In that case reason is, as Tennant says, "leavened with faith."[34] It awaits the whole lump being leavened. Tennant defines faith as "venture dictated by human interest."[35] We could say that it is living according to our deepest needs beyond present knowledge according to the truest nature of that we find to be truly out there. We prefer to define faith as dynamic whole-response, with reason that aspect of the interpretation which can be known in terms of what is here and now actual, rather than to reduce faith falsely to one aspect of knowledge. Yet even in depth-living courting mystery reason has at least one arm around the beloved object. And in the wedding of faith and truth reason is always the best man. Without that best man there simply can be no wedding. Still, as we shall clearly see,

[33] Alfred North Whitehead, lectures.
[34] F. R. Tennant, *Philosophical Theology*, Vol. i, p. 299.
[35] *Ibid.*

we must never confuse the best man with either of the wedding party.

We shall not prove that reason knows. Reason is all we have in the interpretation of whole-response and he who doubts all and everything ought to begin by doubting his own doubts. "In the course of our thinking we come to know more, but we should never come to know more if we did not *know* what we start with."[36] Thus far at least we agree with George P. Adams that "there is no road from an initial substantive isolation of ideas to any subsequent cognitive intercourse with real things."[37] If human reason in general is not trustworthy all is anarchy. And it is not. Convention is a smart word to stigmatize the common base of knowledge. Those who do not grant reason any competence contradict themselves by trying to persuade us that they are right. They have no right to a voice in the matter at all. They are parasites on the human plant of intellectual inquiry, enjoying their own skepticism because they live on the bounty of accumulated intellectual inquiry seriously undertaken and laboriously carried out.

But does not our pride distort reason in the higher realms of knowledge? Are we not constantly told that sin has rendered our reason useless at least in the matter of religious knowledge? If the whole man thinking is so utterly corrupt that there is no good in him, this is indeed true. But then we are hopeless, for revelation, too, is no help. An authoritarian revelation externally imposed without any relation to our actual state could never evoke a genuine whole-response from within a real self. There could be no understanding, no willing acceptance, no real reason or religion. Whitehead defines the practical reason as "the enlightenment of purpose."[38] If between us and the universe there is no understandably organic relation practically as well as speculatively, religion in the sense of depth- and whole-response is as incidental and unimportant as reason itself.

The same thing holds true of the unconscious as the deter-

[36] Sir W. David Ross, *Foundations of Ethics*, p. 145.
[37] "Naturalism or Idealism," in *Contemporary American Philosophy*, p. 72.
[38] Whitehead, *The Function of Reason*, p. 29.

mining fact of experience. No one wants to deny how utterly important the unconscious is. But however deep the roots in self of our response may be, religion as whole-response involves reason not only as the understanding of that to which we respond but also as a help in the directing of our response. Ideas vitally affect our decisions. We all know that. And we know that we have to hold ourselves responsible for our decisions and that society surely does. We have been told that even a hospital for the mentally ill depends upon the sense of responsibility as far as possible in its patients. The unconscious is a no-man's-land which can be appealed to with only limited credit. We must be careful to include all genuine evidence in so far as it can be established within rational discourse, but we must be equally careful not to fall prey to blank checks without credit drawn by careless men on insufficient funds of investigation. Those who appeal to nothing but external credulity of any kind, for or against anything, those who reject, in short, all rational discourse with weight to know, are not yoke-fellows with us in the serious investigations of mankind. Literally we cannot afford to bear them who will not bear with us. Our only fellow travelers are those who confidently accept that those who seek shall in some measure truly find.

Religion we have defined as our normally necessary whole-response to what is considered to be most important and most real. The phrase "what is considered" may seem unnecessary because what we react to in the final fact is what is actually there and what is constantly acting on us. To some we might seem to be falling into some sort of subjectivism. The fact is that the writer has only recently added this phrase because of the kind criticism of thoughtful students. He has done so because they are right in insisting that the definition we are using now is after all a descriptive and inclusive definition of actual religion; and what we actually react to on our part is always colored and directed by our understanding of what is there. Our reaction, that is, is always influenced and mediated by our understanding. Actual reason is ever part of whole-response. Our own reason, too, is cradled and nurtured by what the ages have thought. It can hardly escape all false whole-responses and false interpretation of whole-responses. Our reaction and reason are also floated in the stream of constant thinking by others apart from which we should hardly be human at all. Thus individually and socially we react through the mists of partly clear and partly clouded seeing.

If a stranger far different and better than we were to come to help us out of our many troubles we might upon seeing him run away or try to defend ourselves against him. What we considered him to be might be far different from what he was. Our understanding of him would influence, indeed direct, our reaction. Actually we would act according to what we considered him to be. We could, of course, have learned of his intention and yet run away or hide ourselves from him. We could determine to have none of him, not to understand him, in fact to misunderstand him, and in talking to others to misrepresent him. In our foolishness or false selfishness we might deem the present plight more pleasurable than the deeper satisfactions and the fuller life which he told us about, and which, at that, we knew deep down in our hearts to be better.

Yet if that stranger were the ultimate, if he had inescapable control over us for our own good, if our actual condition always related itself inevitably to the way that we reacted to what he wanted of us and told us to do, even our actual reactions according to what we considered to be our most good and most true would still in fact be our reaction to the inescapable stranger. For in running away we should only be running away from one whose footsteps followed faster down life's way. Religion is the way we react to what we cannot evade. We react always to that with which we hang inseparably together. The farthest edges of the wildernesses of what is most bad and least real are impenetrable. There only starvation is offered to those who cannot stop being driven by hunger. Even there they find that from what is most important and most real there is no full escape. Simply we can say that the ultimate is that to which all must react; and whole-response according to its own nature can find no realm apart from all being and meaning.

We may be felt to be using what is important and what is real together and thus prejudicing the whole case in our favor to begin with. In our actual experience they are together, and yet not totally so. That is the main problem. If we simply equate them we do violence to the fact of evil. There is no broad highway open to comfortable travel from the tangled field of our actual situation and actual religions to our ideal definition where the most high and the most real are merged. The facts demand, however, that we include both in some way. Then we can go on to explore in what way they go together and to what extent. Both the nature and the history of religion demand that we couple them together.

What is most important to whole-thinking is what most fully satisfies our deepest needs. What is most high is what meets our deepest needs. We do not mean our actual wants. They may be like a child's craving for sweets even while its mouth is festered with sores from lack of the proper vitamin diet. Does it then not rebel against the orange juice the physician knows it needs? We mean, rather, that which truly can reach our depth needs and fulfill them with increase of life and satisfaction. Those needs of whole-response must naturally include the needs of the mind for truth, of the heart for high emotion, and of the will for right and satisfying action—and of the whole self for the fullest and richest harmony within and the truest and most deeply rewarding relation to what is without.

To make need the criterion of what is most important is not to be unduly man-centered. We cannot think as gods or as mice. We must think as men. That is the very necessity of whole-thinking. All other points of view are part-thinking. All else is artificial. If there be truth at all it must be truth for us as men, as whole men thinking, as men thinking as fully and as truly as we can from the place where we are put. Yet this does not necessarily make man central in religion. He is central as the reactor, as the thinker, yes. Religion is whole-response and we cannot escape the perspective from which we must look. We are human and must accept that basic fact. It is simply nonsense to try to evade starting from the human standpoint. We have no other. That does not mean, however, that we must end with humanity as the central factor in what is most important and most real. For we start with man as a re-actor interpreting the prime reality to which he reacts. What we are after is the truth and the reality of that prime reality. What we need cannot be drawn out of our definition. What we want actually and what we need may be so different that the one might make man central and the other might make him face a center outside himself.

This much is implied. Man is part of the total reality of action and reaction. He is organically involved in it and cannot be ex-plained at all apart from it. There is, therefore, a necessary gen-eral sameness of source between man and the rest of the world to which he reacts. There is enough similarity so that his life is in-extricably involved in it, and so that he can partly understand it, use it, and feel at home in it. Whole-thinking cannot escape this fact. To deny this is simply to set him apart falsely from the wholeness within which he reacts. We may not arbitrarily separate man from the organic relations of his constant reactions. Experi-ence itself is constituted by the repetition of those reactions and truth must be found within the whole context of man's experience. We can put this bluntly by saying that we only make fools of our-selves if we try to find what is most important and most real apart from the repetition of our accumulated reactions, in history and in ourselves, which forms the core of our development, which as a matter of fact is our only source of knowledge. Again we agree with Murphy as far as he goes:

> The ultimate realities *for us* will have to be those that can make good their claims in the whole course of experience and action: the standards of truth and practical importance, those which we can stand on and stand by in the further conduct of life on the highest attainable level of human excellence.[39]

If man is, in any case, a total accident within the universe de-void of rhyme or reason for being there, or if he is a puppet ma-nipulated by a being entirely external and radically unrelated to the world, we know that we cannot organically and compellingly

[39] Arthur E. Murphy, *The Uses of Reason,* p. 304.

know even this. The whole history of man and his cultures in their constant interrelations to the world to which he reacts suggests, however, that we can start with courage; and he who naturally has reached the end many times before he started this beginning, while still looking for the simpler way to the better and fuller end, has already found that as far as our knowledge is competent the cumulative evidence of organic interrelation is overwhelming.

From the beginning the most real cannot be altogether separated from the most important. Somehow what is real and what is important are enough together out there to enter together in whole-responses and to be thought together in whole-thinking. They are part and parcel of the world to which we react. When we separate them we must already have done so in thought for they do not knock on separate doors or enter at different times. What is most real, truly there really acting on us, must be defined in terms of its steady power, its stubborn streak, its independence of character, its refusal to be thought away at our convenience. If we can make ourselves think that we have dismissed the real to our advantage the real, because it is real, takes revenge on us by making us pay for our illusions. The real is the power out there to affect us, to determine our destiny, to condition or to control in an inescapable way our actions so that even our choices of what is contrary to the nature of the most real show this finally determining nature of reality.

Since the important and the real come in together from out there the basic question is simply to what extent they are the same or different. We can think of it this way: Our deepest needs as human beings, the needs of our whole-responses, are organically related to what is out there. Need itself is the adjustment in the organism to its environment in its vital and dynamic dependence upon it. We know, then, that what is truly out there is related to some extent in the form of need to what is within us. Need is the organic interrelation between ourselves and that on which we depend. Needs bind us (*religare*) to the universe beyond the fact, and more intimately, that we simply are in the universe and have nowhere else to go. The basic question is to what extent that which is truly out there, that with the permanent stubborn streak, that which we cannot think away since it keeps acting on us decisively, that which is most real—is also of such a nature as to meet our deepest need. To what extent will what is truly out there allow us to have what we most basically need? That is the primary relation between what is most important and what is most real.

Some think that the solution is inherent in the nature of the whole-response. Yet a rat's whole-response might find more than rats (could the rat have free ideas and a capacity for rational inference) out there in the world it observed, and what was real to the rat might be far beyond that which was directly important to its own needs. It might need water and grain and to perpetuate its species, and yet it might also find human beings out there far beyond it in certain respects and yet not necessary to its ratness. Perhaps, of course, if the rat knew its deeper relations over the whole of time it could find still deeper needs into which the presence of human beings might be related.

Be that as it may, we cannot think truly without struggling as far as possible, even at the furthest reach of thought, with the fact that we human beings have certain basic needs and aspirations and that what is out there contains many problems which must be solved before we can truly see and respond to the highest claim of religion, namely that what is most important is also most real. The extent to which these are known to be the same and by what kinds of knowledge are the central tasks of our whole work. We want to know as truly as possible what we know, how, and why. Such a knowledge can facilitate our whole-response in depth. For many people are most importantly confused and bewildered in this whole area of living. They dare not believe because they are afraid that what they most deeply want is not true. Faith can be strong if truth has made us free from groundless fear. Our will to believe is often awakened if we see our right to believe. To trust truth is a necessary preliminary to strong faith.

Wieman indicates a limiting method when he writes: "Love uses glowing words; but accurate thinking demands cold, abstract terms."[40] But even here what he has in mind is that faith must be willing to give reasons for its claims. And these must stand the tests of truth. Faith must be a way of seeing within believing. He may be right that for many, at least, "the symbols of religious devotion do not fit into the instrumentalities of intellectual inquiry,"[41] and that "therefore we have reached a time when philosophy rather than theology must do the intellectual job of setting forth the realities of religious concern."[42] Yet we propose to examine not only the adequacy of symbols to satisfy religious devotion but the adequacy and validity of our very "instrumentalities of intellectual inquiry." People have been blocked off from much truth by false obstacles. Truth can never be merely grasped, in any case, by "cold" and "abstract" thought unless religion is decisively wrong in its affirmation that what is important is also real. The important is always a matter of interest, of value, and that can never be grasped for itself except by means of whole-thinking including appreciation, seeking for the important, and all the time the greatest possible acceptance of it.

Historically the two aspects of religion have always gone together. We might say that the modern stress on value as all-important to religion is only a matter of unbalanced emphasis. It springs from a theoretical way of thinking where reality and value have been allowed to fall apart. William A. Christian, in line with much modern thought, defines religion entirely in terms of what is important: "Religion is interest in what is regarded as most important in the universe."[43] He wants to include the humanists. Yet the humanists exist, and in them importance and existence are organically joined. They too, moreover, have to struggle with the problem of the status of value. Value simply cannot be without any status of existence. Even possibility is a mere verbal evasion of this problem, or else it must have meaning with reference to

[40] Wieman, *Religious Realism*, p. 155.

[41] Wieman, *The Growth of Religion*, p. 239.

[42] *Ibid.*

[43] W. A. Christian, Jr., "A Definition of Religion," in *The Review of Religion*, May, 1941.

reality and actuality. Besides even the humanists have to struggle
with the problem of appreciation, acceptance, and actualization
of the most important, and as we shall see, they cannot even avoid
the problem of origins except by default. Edgar Brightman says
that to him "the what" of God is much more important than "the
that"; yet who more than he is showing us that value and nature
cannot be artificially torn apart? Much of this kind of thinking,
even in religion, was furthered by Ritschl, who kept value and
existence largely in two separate categories. Before him Kant had
pointed out the difference between the theoretical and the practical
reason. One dealt with the realm studied by the natural sciences
and mathematics while the other dealt with the realms of duty.
Kant's thinking is itself evidence of a false splitting apart of
whole-thinking; even though in justice to Kant we acknowledge
that some scholars feel that he meant all ways of knowing to be
leading to the one whole realm of truth, nevertheless his method
has misled many, or at least has been the occasion for unfortunate
emphases on one aspect or another of truth. The turn to value
apart from existence, to what is most important apart from what
is most real, is due to a falsity of method which we shall examine
in the next chapter.

In general, however, there can be no question that the great
historic religions have held together, even though in different ways
and different stresses, what is most important and what is most
real. In the Chinese *tao* truth and goodness are joined. Buddhism
may insist on its "not this, not this," on the complete separation
between our ordinary thoughts and actual desires, and salvation
in Nirvana. Yet salvation is by illumination of what is really real,
which shows us the nature of the illusions of our selfish desires.
The contrast is thus really between the untruth and unreality of
our actual wanting and thinking and the truth and reality which
lie on the other side of such wanting and thinking. What is most
important is this illumination and this salvation. Thus truth and
importance are most indispensably joined. Hinduism combines
existence, knowledge, and bliss in its very concept of the ultimate:
saccidananda. Judaism defines righteousness and truth in terms of

the central being of God. The Platonic religions identify being with goodness and even define evil as non-being. In Islam the Asherites and the Mutazilites may debate whether the good is simply because God wills it or whether God also wills it because it is good but in either case they must go together. Christianity has even defined God, the true being, as love, the highest form of goodness. As a matter of fact the great Christian theologians have identified the two aspects of religion almost as unconsciously or easily as the great classical tradition in philosophy, as Arthur O. Lovejoy ably demonstrates in *The Great Chain of Being*, has simply assumed the basic identity of thought and being.

Both from the nature of experience and from the witness of history we can see that being is inseverably connected in some way with what is important. Hazy thinking on this score has resulted in destructive or confused prescriptions for whole-response. Our age is suffering acutely from a lack of careful whole-thinking on this subject. The modern critical temper is all to the good to whatever extent we are forced to be thorough and trust nothing but truth. Nothing else will stand the test of our day, let alone the test of time. If the truth is that what is most important is thoroughly rooted in what is most real, then we can be more and more delivered from whole-responses which are divided and insecure. Then we can make ready for a new age of creative zest. We have analyzed our problem only enough to show the meaning of our definitions. Do the facts indicate any way in which we can pass from our definition of actual religion to our ideal definition of it? Is the highest claim of religion true, and should it guide our individual whole-responses and our social living? From now on we must test our ideal definition that right religion is our fully positive whole-response to the complete combination of what is most real and most important against the facts of knowledge and of actual life. Our very first task will be to analyze the nature, competence, and limits of the scientific method from the general point of view of co-operative inquiry. Then we can go on in succeeding chapters to philosophy and to religion.

CHAPTER II

The Circle of Science

Science is the golden word of modernity. A large section of mankind has fervently hoped from it both the discovery of truth and the victory of the good. With good reason the scientific spirit and method have been thought to be the key to human progress and happiness. After all, to be scientific in the deepest sense, do we not need to be calm, intelligent, well trained, careful, and co-operative? To find the truth we must see each field in the light of its own highest ideal. By thoroughly appreciating that ideal we can the better shave off the false face which the actual situation presents. By seeing the distinction between the ideal method and the abuse of it we render a service both to the specific field involved and to the whole field of human knowledge.

Science has the right to awaken high hopes. It has touched and helped almost every phase of life. In the material world it has more and more conquered drudgery and want. As far as science is concerned, we could even now have almost the golden age. There are many who are both ungrateful and unseeing. They do not thrill at the vast difference which modern technology has made to man's total welfare. What of modern hygiene, modern medicine, modern general education, modern communication, and the endless helps and comforts that modern man enjoys? It is a sad experience to hear someone denounce science as the cause of modern chaos and destruction. Our technological advance may be abused and make of what could be a near heaven a near hell, but that is surely not the fault of science as such. Science has not failed man, but man has failed science.

Besides its material achievement toward a better world, science has helped decisively to introduce and to develop disciplined investigation in all branches of human knowledge. Naturally we must be careful at this point. Science, philosophy, and religion have grown up together and profited from each other's labor. Disciplined thinking antedated the rise of modern science, and this is itself greatly indebted to other kinds of thinking. Who can read Plato and Aristotle, or Augustine and Aquinas, and not recognize this? Whitehead continually stresses the mutuality of knowledge, particularly the importance to the rise of modern science of the development of the speculative reason in the Middle Ages. George Sarton, professor of the history of science at Harvard, puts weight on the importance of the whole culture which surrounds or precedes concrete scientific advance. In a pregnant phrase he defends the Middle Ages as important even from the point of view of science. To him it is "the time of gestation of modern science."[1] Dampier-Whetham in *A History of Science* gives numerous examples of this fact of mutuality: For instance, a type of Platonism went through Galileo and Kepler to the mathematical system of Newton;[2] nominalism before it blossomed out in induction was preceded in its speculative development among others by Berengarius of Tours and Roscellinus with regard to the problem of the elements in the sacrament of the Eucharist;[3] and Pascal's study of the games of chance underlies much of recent science and social statistics.[4]

Albeit this mutuality is true, particularly with regard to the creation of novel hypotheses and perspectives, nevertheless we come back to our second main claim that modern science has since the time of Roger Bacon had profound effect on modern civilization through all its branches of development. The whole rise of the modern historical consciousness is perhaps largely to be attributed to the creation of scientific canons of criticism. Von Ranke is, of course, symbolic of this beginning, but many students of "the

[1] Sarton, *The Study of the History of Science*, p. 26.
[2] Dampier-Whetham, *A History of Science*, p. 190.
[3] *Ibid.*, p. 87.
[4] *Ibid.*, p. 155.

science" of history, both of research and of creative interpretation, have best understood the method of history through Langlois and Seignobos, *Introduction to the Study of History*. A careful comparison of the principles advocated in this great classic with the principles of the natural sciences will show how utterly close together these authors try to make them. That is both the strength and the weakness of the work; but the fact is that for a long time it had enormous influence on the ideal of modern history. The same is true of philosophy and of religion. Who can understand the development of philosophy since Descartes, since Kant, or since Brentano and Husserl, without seeing this? Who can study the history of logic, for instance, the most theoretical of subjects, without seeing the influence on it of science, for example in Aristotle (if we may go back beyond the rise of modern science) and Kant, or in inductive and symbolic logic? Religion, too, has been feeling the earthquake of scientific method both in the application of scientific history to its sacred writings and in the constant challenge of its claims by men who have introduced the "scientific method" in the study of religion. They would, indeed, be less than farseeing who could not be genuinely thankful for the exceedingly important service science has rendered high religion. In perhaps all fields of knowledge science has been the catalytic agent which has changed their contents. If the change has not always been for the better, it has not been the fault of science; it has been due either to the use of a false science or to the use of science falsely. As far as the whole realm of the intellect is concerned it is hard to be thankful enough for the purification brought on by the wholesale challenge of science to disciplined thinking.

We have not even mentioned the almost endless vistas of new truth, moreover, which science has made possible by delivering us from our little earth-bound perspective toward the realms of the infinitely great or the infinitely small. We live in a radically changed intellectual climate from that of a few centuries ago. It is hard to adjust to it, but the growth of knowledge is a challenge to the growth of spirit. The fact is that science has made possible an all-around better world. Science cannot make a better world. Man must. Though science has made life more complicated, the more developed the organism is, the more complicated it becomes. The physical should be a help rather than a hindrance to the moral and spiritual life. Spiritual decline and moral decadence often point a finger at science. But Irenaeus long ago knew the right relation between body and spirit when he wrote that "the flesh . . . is not destitute [of participation] in the constructive wisdom and power of God."[5] Physical knowledge by itself never thwarts spiritual growth. We are going to say a great deal about false science and the false use of science in this chapter. Be it understood, however, that we want no part with the religious writers who suffer from nostalgia for past centuries, for that simplicity of life and for that childlike spirit that had not yet been awakened by historical criticism and scientific scholarship, and for that whole unity of life which, they feel certain, characterized the world before the development of the modern scientific method. He who does not appreciate the contributions of science to truth and to life is a traitor to both.

Because of this great hope in science, and because of its central position in the development of modern civilization, it is proper to begin our investigation by carefully trying to define the nature of the scientific method and to see whether, and to what extent, it can throw light on what is most important and what is most real. Beyond the praise or the blame of science this investigation is especially important for two reasons: (1) Because of its central position in modern civilization science itself is now undergoing a searching period of self-examination; (2) science is being used defensively by insecure people who dare not, or by insincere people who will not, face the responsibilities of life.

First, science itself is today in a state of self-examination in an exceptional sense. This self-examination is due to both practical and theoretical considerations. Practically we see that mere science cannot save. The mere discovery of new realms of facts and relations cannot assure growth in human assurance and welfare. Man may fail science. Yes, man may use science to bring hell to earth.

[5] "Against Heresies," in *The Ante-Nicene Fathers*, Vol. I., p. 529.

The facts of science make possible such use of them as to prostitute science itself, to divide and to destroy both men and their treasures, and finally to force the scientists themselves either to support such destruction or else to suffer the consequences of their loyalties. Science rises as a specter before our eyes, as a possible monster that may be led unresistingly to destroy civilization. We may be on the verge of such discoveries in destruction that a few individuals can hold out against the world. Who knows what fantastic weapons beyond our concrete imagination may become known to the scientists and used by men filled with hatred and thirsting for power and revenge? Science may develop explosives capable of destroying civilization.[6] Practically we must have much more than an academic discussion of scientific method. For those in positions of responsibility not to be practical and alert on this score is to be a traitor to mankind. We must have some way of converting men to intelligent good will. We must find ways to creative and co-operative conduct. We must win people for social adequacy. We must give men something compelling to live for outside their narrow self-interest, however magnified or extended. Or else men in order to lose themselves and in order to find something to live for will serve any charlatan who offers certainty and a demanding cause to live for—even though they may half suspect, or even half know, the evils involved in his partial cause. We have no right to stop with description; we must go on to adequate analysis and prescription, and a prescription that can be filled. Fortunately men of science are themselves, as a whole, much more co-operative and concerned about all of life and civilization than they were in smoother days.

Scientists are also going through a period of self-examination

[6] Since the writing of even the last draft of this chapter our surmise has come true. We now can destroy civilization with far greater ease than ever before. Scientists, too, have turned to the practical tasks of politics. That is to the good. They must assume social responsibility. They also discuss values, but to our knowledge, are still limiting themselves to safeguarding civilization from the wrong use of science. There will be no solution on that level. Scientists as *men*, not science as a *method*, must face the relation of science to spirit, to the ultimate. Apart from this basic level the problem of force has no adequate solution.

because of theoretical difficulties. The swing of science for a period of time has been more and more toward the laboratory method, to a scientific positivism, that is, to a pure description of facts, relations, and operations. Modern physics, however, has brought up theoretical problems as to the nature of the ultimately small, non-Euclidian space, and relativity which involve the whole question of the relation of the limited laboratory technique to rational discourse. Eddington, in *The Philosophy of Physical Science*, claims, for instance, that the root problems of physics, such as relativity, involve epistemology. Whitehead has long been repeating that if science is now to advance it must do so by an examination of the method of each science in the light of the general consideration of method. In his last years of lecturing he never tired of pointing out how between 1890 and 1920 all certainty as to the adequacy of past methods and results in scientific inquiry was swept out. Science, he held, may be on the brink of a new and better day if it will only be big enough and patient enough to reexamine its basic presuppositions in the light of all we know. Sarton points out that

. . . any branch of science may be completely revolutionized at any time by a discovery necessitating a radically new approach to the subject. Chemistry today is essentially different from chemistry in the eighteenth century. The fundamental notions are different, the methods are different, the scope is indescribably larger, and the contents are infinitely more varied. We may safely assume that the chemistry of the twenty-fifth century will be as unlike that of the present as that, in turn, is unlike that of the fifteenth century.[7]

In psychology the swing to the laboratory method once went toward the kind of investigation typified by Watson's behaviorism; but today men like Allport come out with a fuller view of the subject as, for instance, in *Personality, a Psychological Interpretation*. In sociology Sorokin seeks new ways in books like *The Crisis of Our Age*. Einstein in mathematics, as well as Russell and Whitehead, quests for further depths in grappling with our ways of

[7] Sarton, *op. cit.*, pp. 7–8.

thinking. George Birkhoff, one of the country's leading mathematicians, in his presidential address to the National Academy of Sciences stressed this larger dimension, "the aura of faith" which it must have if it is to be increasingly creative and productive. In biology Joseph Needham advocates considerations of the larger organic context to escape past limitations.[8] Although these men may be dubbed "religious," "mystics," "metaphysicians," "unscientific" by men who cling to the narrower past, it is significant that the men of science in large number both for practical and for theoretical reasons are themselves open-minded to a thorough self-examination of their own methods.

We have said that science is today peculiarly open to self-examination for two main reasons: the practical and the theoretical problems which it faces. This is our first thought under the suggestion that science needs, particularly today, to be appraised with regard to its ability to show us what is most important and what is most real. Secondly, science is being used as a cover for moral, social, and spiritual irresponsibility. That is natural enough. Men are insecure and know very little. Our galloping history is leaving behind old securities, usually long before new ones are found. A consequent general attitude is this: Science has already swept away from under us so much and so fast that we hestitate to commit ourselves to anything lest that, too, be swept away tomorrow. Men must have some security and they seem to prefer to know the worst rather than to be sure of nothing. That is the one thing intolerable. The one thing that seems to stand is scientific method. To embrace that no matter what is at least one form of certainty. Even though this trust in the stability of the scientific method may be unwarranted, even though a great historian of science like Whitehead can say that science has changed more than religion, even though right now science is itself in great ferment, nevertheless the burden of thinking and knowing is hard and men see that of late science seems to have been in the saddle; the exact hows and whys and wherefores do not matter. Science is the child of

[8] Needham, "A Biologist's View of Whitehead," in *The Philosophy of Alfred North Whitehead*, edited by P. A. Schilpp.

modernity. The child has grown big and dangerous enough to frighten its own parent; suddenly modernity appeals to its own child to give to it the protection of a parent. Science is supposed by many to have banished every realm of the sacred; and behold, science becomes the sacred cow!

Science helps us. Why, then, should we be wary lest it hurt us? Because science is in the service of man, and man is far too much in the service of evil. The defensive attitude is bad enough when it makes people afraid to believe that there is anything important and real. The defensive attitude hurts us enough when men are too paralyzed by past discoveries, as they assume they affect the realms of morals and the spirit, to dare to commit themselves wholeheartedly and feelingly to the more personal, social, and spiritual sides of life. We no longer laugh at the possibility of a moral vacuum sucking in despair and destruction. We have already in our day seen the first fruits of false science and science falsely used in tearing down civilization. Moral and spiritual leaders, being stunned by science, have failed to build better and truer habitations for men's spirit. We must not blame the scientists. Nor must we dread destruction of what can be destroyed. The scientists have done their job well. Would that philosophy and religion had built with equal vision, confidence, and success! But we have been stunned into defensive thinking. This defensive attitude is bad enough.

But there is a worse side to this defensive attitude: It has become a convenient hiding-place for men who dare not or will not face their social, moral, and spiritual responsibilities. Our age is one of unbelief and individualism. Men would find fellowship but they dare not or will not enter into it. Alcohol, artificial social stimulants, and a pumped-up reliance on sex give the semblances of a "good time" to a jaded age. The business house and the mart give one sort of living and working together. But life as an inner unity is falling apart, and even its innermost fellowship, the family, is splitting wide open. Men are bewildered and look wistfully at every kind of remedy, including religion. But they cannot find full fellowship, peace, and power. Men are generally individualists, living mostly for themselves, and when they then build together somehow the structure reminds them all too much of the tower of Babel. A lostness and a wistfulness characterize our age. Men would be saved but dare or will not. One reason for this lack of daring and willing is the lack of a compelling faith in anything good and real; but another reason, and a stronger one, being even in large part responsible for the lack of faith, is that when the light of what is good and real comes with challenge and power bidding men to forsake their selfish ways and to lose themselves in the larger discipline, responsibility, and concern for the common life, *they will not*. They see the way. They give it a nod, for the general public. But too many want to be the exception to the rule, and to walk in their own irresponsible way. Life at a creative and satisfactory level cannot go on without trust, honesty, responsibility, and self-giving concern; when each one is faced singly with the problem of surrender to this fact, however, he fights shy of it, if he can, or else he fights it. Few open up wholeheartedly to it. If this surrender of the selfish part of us, moreover, is not made with complete sincerity, it might as well not be made at all. Without complete surrender of such self-concern the self which destroys society and which hinders the social self from finding fellowship is still in the saddle. A sad fact about the modern world is that many hide behind science in order to escape from the fuller truth and the fuller duty. They say, "Science says that all things are relative." "Science says that we cannot even know whether Jesus lived." "Science says that there is no god." "Science says that inhibition is bad for us." "Science says . . ." From leading scientists, philosophers, students, to the man in the street, people hide behind a general phrase. Speak of what must be if we are to have a better world, and in more or less true statements, in more or less relevant statements, men will hide from their responsibility for this better world behind what science "says"— often though it does not say so at all, and even makes no claim or pretense of saying anything about the subject. If we are to be honest and are to face the facts that can help us, we must understand how utterly emotional the subject of science is. This is not the fault of science. It does not claim to be either a philosophy or a religion. It claims to describe accurately such truth as falls within its competence. Yet science has become a popular idol. All men of good will who want to know the full and saving truth must therefore dare to examine their whole-response. They must ask themselves if for them science is a "sacred cow." Justin Martyr is right: "Sound doctrine does not enter into the hard and disobedient heart."[9] As we examine scientific method we shall delve deeply into its problems, trying constantly to weed science from science so-called; and in so doing we shall help both those scientists who have never seen the problems clearly and all those who have been kept from individual and social and spiritual adequacy by science so-called. For those who will not see, however, there is no solution except a change of heart. When they accept "the knowledge which is according to godliness," that knowledge which is for the common good and which is anchored beyond their individual isolating desires, they shall find that they shall know the truth and the truth shall make them free.

Before we go further we must define the term "science." Historically the term meant two different things during two different periods. Classically, science meant any disciplined, examined, and organized knowledge. Today, the term refers generally to the method used by the natural sciences. The broad meaning of the term simply stands over against superstition, opinion, external authority, arbitrary faith, and all knowledge so-called that is not rationally examined. If the first meaning of science is used we must include under it all disciplines of knowledge; if the second, we must distinguish, for instance, among science, philosophy, and religion. Trouble comes when a thoughtless or invidious definition is allowed to take the place of a careful, honest use of the term, when the broad definition is confused with the narrow or vice versa. Sarton, for instance, defines science as "systematized positive knowledge, or what has been taken as such at different ages and in different places."[10] whereupon he goes on to say that "the history

[9] Justin Martyr, "Fragments," in *The Ante-Nicene Fathers,* Vol. I., p. 302.
[10] Sarton, *op. cit.,* p. 5.

of science is the only history which can illustrate the progress of mankind."[11] Science to him is plainly the method of the natural and historical sciences and this is then equated with all system-atized positive knowledge. He then even illustrates this exclusive point of view by showing that "charity" is "unprogressive." He probably does not know enough of the history of the term or the attitude, and does not consider the fact that once upon a time neither the word nor the reality was even present in history, nor was even conscious life. This is not his field and he is under no obligation to know it. These unfortunate, dogmatic statements, nevertheless, although doubtless devoid of evil intention, are what make co-operative inquiry difficult.

Yet we all make mistakes. What we must do is to keep terms straight, trying to be well informed even outside our own use of them and outside our own general professional competence. In this volume we shall never use science in the broad sense. We shall take for granted that all fields that ask to be heard have accepted disciplined rational discourse. If we are to get anywhere at all with one another, and if we are to arrive at knowledge in our own field, we must surely use careful, critical methods open to public understanding and inspection. We must all abandon recourse to ignorance, appeal to relativism, and refuge behind external revela-tions. The human heart is fickle. It longs for relativism to escape unavoidable responsibility. It also longs for infallible authority to obtain permanent security. It dreads both restlessness and rest. It dreads both knowing and not knowing. In the realm of our ultimate values and hopes open inquiry may involve anguish of soul. Yet history affords no city of refuge from such anguish. Theology in the future must dare to face the test of organized in-quiry or lose its hold on the great body of intelligent people of the world. On this score we again agree with Wieman: "If our science-informed civilization survives, no religion, which repudiates reason . . . can survive along with it."[12]

In the broad sense of "science," of critical and organized in-

[11] *Ibid.*
[12] Horton and Wieman, *The Growth of Religion,* p. 256.

telligence, we stake out carefully the field of inquiry making certain that all relevant facts are included and that all irrelevant facts are excluded. We then proceed patiently to survey all the facts and their relations or functions. We thereupon try creatively to find hypotheses that will subsume, relate, and explain the nature and relation of those facts. We may at any stage of the inquiry pursue inferences that follow from our conclusions. Our next step is to test our hypothesis according to the nature of the field of inquiry and the particular subject matter at hand. Then, finally, we are anxious to have many competent observers or participators check our findings and, if possible, to do so also in the light of other theories in this or in other fields. This is the method of critical and organized intelligence, of all public knowledge. The natural sciences, to be sure, have helped immensely to develop and popularize disciplined knowledge and attitudes, but, as we have said before, this total way of knowing is a joint product of civilized man. Civilizations, moreover, have been cradled and reared by religion. Perhaps today again the further advance in knowledge and civilization waits on new impulses and power from religious thinkers who can interpret adequately by the method of critical and organized intelligence our whole-response to what is most important and most real.

By scientific method in the proper modern sense we mean something more specific than the general method of critical and organized intelligence which we have just stated, and which we have touched upon at greater lengths in the preceding chapter. Science stresses minimum hypothesis. To be sure the hypothesis is supposed adequately to explain the facts. But the stress is strongly on minimum hypothesis. This we shall find leads to important logical and psychological results. Science also needs to go back to end referents in sense-experience, particularly in terms that can be accurately measured. Science deals basically with quantitative sense-experience. Here we have to be most careful because the whole life of science revolves around hypotheses, theories, and laws; and all these are concepts and not objects of sense-experience. Surely no one senses directly any hypothesis, however much he may sense the facts and perhaps even the relations. "Science," says Whitehead, "is in the minds of men. . . . Science therefore is nothing but a confident expectation that relevant thoughts will occasionally occur."[13] Similarly Lewis points out that "concepts are of the mind. All knowledge is in terms of concepts."[14] Yet granting this, science is nevertheless particularly concerned with the simplest explanation of quantitative sense-data. All else must somehow be brought back or be reduced to this basis. The scientist makes perception and mathematical reasoning central, "continually checking one by the other, a method which forms the essence of induction. . . . The scientist only believes in perception; his belief in inference is only very partial."[15]

Even the narrow meaning, however, is hard to mark out precisely, for scientific theory is not so much a speculative product as a general growth alongside of the development of physical research. It would be much easier if it would be authoritatively defined with completely clear-cut divisions, with a signpost bearing the inscription, "Here begins scientific method by unanimous agreement and enactment; see the next signpost for the exact place where it ends." There would not then be this pull between those who want to stick to laboratory science or its equivalent and those who want to use inference far into the realms of speculative philosophy in order to throw larger lights on its problems. Yet for our purposes we accept the following general assumptions as characteristic of the scientific method.

Truth increases as we approach the highest point of public verifiability; public verifiability depends upon exact measurement; exact measurements are to be found almost exclusively within the formal and the physical realms, that is, in mathematics and sense-experience. Whatever extensions be allowed must ultimately rest on this base, must be translated into its terms, and must be traced back to these end referents for their scientific standing. Certainty is to be limited to this kind of test and reasoning and does not

[13] Whitehead, *Principles of Natural Knowledge*, p. 10.
[14] Lewis, *op. cit.*, p. 345.
[15] Acharaya Ananda, *Brahmadarsanam*, p. 47.

extend, as far as science is concerned, to the systematic wholeness demanded by the speculative reason or to direct personal experience. This certainty of science is to be found at its maximum at the two opposite poles of experience: the regularity of form and the regularity of physical fact. One pole is mathematics; the other is laboratory science. At the pole of physical fact certainty is the highest in a laboratory experiment where we have the testing of one carefully isolated fact in terms of its most relevant function under the maximum controlled conditions and tested by the largest possible galaxy of recognized experts in the field. Even this result is only approximate, since any change in the understanding of the conditions surrounding the fact of the fact itself, or of the testing of the fact, or any new element introduced concerning the adequacy of the tools, and any new perspective or relation of any kind whatever, might, of course, change the result. At the formal pole of experience, on the other hand, certainty is at its highest in pure logic and in pure mathematics. Formally speaking, we agree that A is not non-A. Six and four are taken to be ten wherever rational discourse obtains. The metaphysical problems of the nature and implication of physical fact or of the numbers are irrelevant to scientific method until they come within the scope, at least, of immediate use. The speculations of Nicholas of Cusa have no relevance to science except as they lead into the discovery of calculus. But in general, mathematics and laboratory science are the ideal limits of scientific method and constitute the poles toward which it continually gravitates.

Right here enters one of the basic problems connected with scientific method in connection with our main purpose to find through the adequate interpretation of whole-response what is most important and most real. This problem exists to a limited extent even within scientific method. It is the tension between full explanation and exact verifiability. In physics, for instance, experimenters may agree on the exact results of limited experiments and yet keep disagreeing on the fuller interpretations of the results. Under definite conditions the behavior of light may be agreed upon while at the same time the nature and function of light may still be the occasions of different theories. Even though Hamilton, Lloyd, Arago, and Foacalt, for instance, seemed crucially to have settled the case between the emission and the wave theory of light in favor of the latter, the experiments satisfied only certain conditions, and other experimenters still looking for the fuller truth came upon facts that led to the quantum theory. Yet even since 1910 have there not been continual searchings for the fuller understanding of the nature of light even though the exactness of certain significant experiments is accepted? Or the forces measured at the end of sense referents may be agreed upon and yet there be different theories as to the nature of submicroscopic physics; there is at least the continual urge for the fuller truth in that region, which may be discovered, not very likely by the finding of inaccuracy in certain previous experiments, but by the finding of new angles to the problem. Thus, although exactness is the ideal and although minimum hypothesis is exalted, both are constant beggars at the table of the fuller truth which as yet evades exact formulation and of the larger hypothesis which will include the aspect which outmodes the old experiment, however exact. Or again, while all may agree that atoms behave according to statistical averages, some hold to the principle of uncertainty or indeterminacy while others from the very same facts conclude that what is indicated is the principle of incomplete predictability. With the same facts at hand some will incline in the direction of Bridgman's operationalism while others will take the turn toward Eddington or Whitehead, who hold that each science can best advance by the study of the philosophical implications of its method. If this happens to the green tree of physics, what must happen to the dry? Physics is obviously a more exact science than biology, psychology, or economics. Thus even in science proper there is this tension between exact measurement and adequate whole-explanation.

We may put this tension, which makes for a healthy condition of growth in science but which ever threatens to become pernicious anemia beyond the proper limit of scientific efficacy, in this way: The more exact public verifiability tends toward its maximum, the more adequate interpretation tends toward its minimum. We may also look at it from the other point of view: The more adequate interpretation tends toward a maximum, the more exact proof tends toward a minimum. The more objective demonstrability in terms of exact physical measurement tends toward a maximum, the more full accounting for the facts in all their interrelations and implications tends toward a minimum while the more fully a total area of knowledge is completely explained in all its involvements the less possible it is to put this total explanation to exact proof. This basic fact of knowledge must be carefully observed in the relation of scientific method, properly speaking, to the interpretation of whole-response with respect to what is most important and most real.

Before we assess scientific method with regard to the thirteen logical and psychological tendencies which have to be watched carefully all the time if we are to let science contribute its fullest amount of truth to whole-knowledge, we had better define them. These tendencies put no final limit on science. Science should be used as far as it can possibly be profitably used in every field of knowledge and in every sphere of life. Comity and co-operation will not come by the drawing of official lines of demarcation, but rather by the patient understanding of the nature of all methods and of the full claims of truth.

By a "logical tendency" we mean the pull on the investigator of the ideal of the method which he must ever watch lest, in succumbing to it, he do injustice to the actual nature of the object of inquiry. The logical tendency is the direction toward which, because of the nature of the method and the nature of the field of inquiry, the investigation naturally gravitates. We could call it the methodological tendency of each field of inquiry. Empiricism, for instance, means simply the taking of experience as a base of truth. Yet since sense-experience can best be tested and objectively discussed, the natural pull of empiricism has been toward sensationalism. Those who would call themselves empiricists and include the whole reaches of spirit have to go against the main currents within the field. And to refuse the sensationalists the use of the term on the ground that they obviously are using it only in a

partial sense would strike many as a most highhanded procedure.
Obviously some of the greatest empiricists have not been sensationalists; but the natural pull has been toward this position. A
logical tendency is the natural pull of the method toward its ideal
operation, clearly and distinctly, which unless it be carefully kept
in mind is likely to do injustice to the full, complex content of the
field of inquiry.

By a "psychological tendency" we mean the natural temptation
to identify one's profession and intellectual position with public
prestige and/or inner security. Thus there are religionists who
affirm that to be saved all the world needs is to return to religion.
Within the field of religion, furthermore, they affirm that the world
to be saved has to come to their particular way of salvation. If
the world can be saved only in this way these religionists must be
important people and their understanding of religion must be of
utmost significance. That gives them a good feeling. As a matter
of fact their own attempts at security may need to be bolstered by
the power of their convictions to compel others. They are convinced in their minds and hearts that men need truth and that to
find truth they must come around to their way of thinking or
acting! Similarly scientists often know that science must save the
world; after all, science seeks truth, and only truth can save!
Able philosophers are caught writing that there is no escape for a
confused world except by a return to philosophic calm and reason.
What the world must have is training and philosophic reason! A
professor of art shows how art alone makes us want to share our
experience in a non-possessive way and that therefore wars and
strife can be abolished when art is made a central experience! Educators are certain in large numbers that they form the minds of
the young, and "as goes education so goes the future of the
world!"

Now, who can honestly say that any one group is wrong? Are
they not all speaking truth? But then, no one can be exclusively
right. The trouble is that we contract the full perspective of the
whole field of knowledge into our own necessary part of it. Because
our field interpenetrates with the others does not mean that it can

take the place of them. Because our own grasp of our own field touches on all the problems within it does not mean that our own perspective or power of insight can take the place of those who have spent much time looking patiently at the same problems from a close-up view where we simply had to connect and adjust our thoughts in a less thorough fashion. The problems of knowing seem endless, and yet there are actually resentments at other people's success in looking at truth lest there be nothing left for the rest to declare. Psychological tendencies are invidious distortions of truth; or they are blinders on our eyes lest we become frightened and insecure, mentally dizzy, by looking at all that we otherwise could see and by so looking arrive at the impossibility of self-security. Mental security comes only by faith and co-operation by faith in truth in all it is and means and in our willingness to find it more and more as well as peace, power, and creative zest through a fellowship of inquiry which the self can never find till he be willing to abandon his isolation and attempts at self-security. Our biggest problem is not the main fixing of methods. Our biggest problems are rather the logical and psychological tendencies tempting all investigators in all fields. In one sense it is deeply true that the method is never bigger than the men who use it. Only when we are aware of our own littleness of heart as well as of mind can we safely proceed to analyze any method. The investigator of a method not primarily his own must be doubly aware of his littleness.

1. The first temptation to abuse the scientific method lies in its use of tentativeness. This aspect of science is also necessary to life, but the logical tendency in science to complete skepticism until full proof is established, while it constitutes practically no problem within its own field of inquiry, nevertheless becomes a major problem as soon as it is carried beyond science to the quest of what is most important and what is most real. We must ever keep in mind that what we are seeking is the right interpretation of right whole-response. What we really are asking now is not: will scientific method do for science? or, can scientific method find truth? It is rather, can this kind of scientific method serve as the

only road to the full truth? Can right science be the same as right religion? Or can the content of science constitute the content of that which is ultimately most important and most real?

Science is built on patient, non-committed waiting until all the evidence is in, thoroughly interpreted and tested. The facts must decide. If the facts are not in, or not clear, the scientist must take no definite decision till he find what they are. This admirable attitude of open-mindedness, this humility before truth, is one of the great virtues of science and of the ideal scientist. This is the way it should be in science, for the regularity and impartiality of both physical and formal truth permit such indecision. This is also, as far as it is at all possible, the way it should be in life. Often life and science are falsely contrasted, science requiring tentativeness and life, decision. Yet life to be lived as worthily as possible must be examined as fully as possible. Action needs direction by thought. Whole-response involves whole-reason. Hocking and Bixler have done much to have us understand the principle of alternation whereby worship and work, or contemplation and action, are made to serve one another and the whole of life.[16] There is altogether too much arbitrary living and believing which needs the check and challenge of a careful study of all the facts involved for us to slight in any way this basic aspect which must be a part of all ways of finding truth. Faith itself must not be forced, and no one should accept his faith, anyway, without much pondering and searching of heart lest in the light of better knowledge and more careful weighing there be a better one.

Life, however, is different from science. If it were only a matter of making up our minds at what point we could believe or act! If we could only give ourselves so and so much time to examine the evidence! The fact is that we are always believing, always acting, always deciding. Every moment of active life, we are making whole-responses; whenever we do anything worthwhile at

[16] Hocking, *The Meaning of God in Human Experience,* Chapter XXVIII, "The Principle of Alternation." Bixler, *Religion for Free Minds;* cf. Chapter XII for an illuminating study of the more comprehensive dualism and rhythm in the religious process.

all we are deciding on what is most real and most important. As a matter of fact when we are doing the trivial things of life we are also making a decision which hangs together with our characteristic whole-responses. The practical decisions of life go on all the time and include reason's continual illumination of them. Tentativeness as to the important issues simply means a paralyzing of creative life and a choosing by default to act on lower levels of good. To refuse to act on the good until it can be proved true means to act in actual trust on what is less good even though that is all the while not proved to be true. Life cannot be conclusively proved. Tentativeness must be a methodological lead in life. We need contemplation, examination, inspection. Yet even that is an escape unless it be focused directly on positive action along the line of the highest whole-response possible.

Action without reason means undirected whole-response, a drifting to and fro according to impulse and inclination. We need the fullest possible measure of methodological tentativeness within whole-living. Yet that very wholesome tentativeness constitutes a great temptation and danger both to individual life and to civilization. The logical tendency may be carried over from science without change of pace or attitude to accord with the vital difference of whole-response. A person may simply not realize that scientific method cannot be thus applied and may even pride himself on open-mindedness and tolerance while all the time his own life is parasitical on the lives of those who care for and who commit themselves to the common good according to our highest needs and faith. Agnosticism is not open-mindedness; it is culpable inaction. Tentativeness in morals and religion, except in terms of a humble and teachable positiveness, is not a matter of humility and fair play; it is a matter of stabbing the good in the back by treachery; it is an insidious alliance with evil. Ignorance and thoughtlessness about this subject, though understandable because of our bringing-up, education, and general attitude, are yet guilty; for both are to some extent lack of concern for the truth of the common good. Even the paralysis of mind and heart which comes from despair at not finding the full truth and therefore not being able to act confidently is a guilty state of mind. Such lack of hold on any compelling reality comes greatly from "the scepticism and unreality that too much grubbing in the abstract roots of things will breed."[17] Responsible action for the good not only replenishes emotions but clears the mind for more actual, significant thinking. *Adequate thinking is through whole-response.* When the whole man thinks he feels and acts in relation to his search for whole-truth. Agnosticism is a depth decision. We can at least believe in as much good as we see possible and keep having a positive attitude. That much we can know. And this right attitude, many have found, opens their minds to new insights and significant assurance. "Where attainable knowledge could have changed the issue, ignorance has the guilt of vice."[18]

That is why the logical tendency is mostly an occasion for the psychological. And that is how one shades into the other. The prestige of science and the general need to carry tentativeness as far as possible in whole-living give ground in logical tendency for the psychological; no one is wholly guilty. Yet in our extreme individualism we tend to make the truth go further than it will and thus make it into a lie. The worst lies are dangerous half-truths or plausible distortions of truth. If we do not want to put the truth of the common good first in our lives; if we do not want to live up to the highest morality and faith of fellowship, for fellowship of some kind is a fact, we simply hide behind the truth that this faith cannot be conclusively proved. We thus make excuses, live in faiths which divide men, live in faiths based on competition, social superiority, pride in individual achievement, possession, or position. All the while we live in insecurity, complaint, fear, and lack of the peace and power of true fellowship. Decide we must, and decide we do. We extend the logical tendency beyond the limits of its proper use and then color it with our defensive emotions. The writer has been startled by the tense emotional resistance on the part of mature people, seemingly, to the very ob-

[17] William James, "Is Life Worth Living?" in *The Will to Believe and Other Essays,* p. 39.

[18] Whitehead, *The Aims of Education,* p. 23.

vious fact that all of us have to make responsible decisions one way or another. He has become thoroughly convinced that the question of tentativeness in the search for the most high and the most good is often less a matter of reverence for truth than it is a desire to avoid responsible decision, particularly the decision that will be costly to the isolated self, even though such decisions lead to positive living and to the joyous zest of freedom in fellowship. Whole-reaction must be positive, forthright, decisive, daring, creative, full of living faith. Tentativeness must have a primary place in science; in life it must be subordinated. In this realm scientific method and attitude can render life great service; but it cannot serve as a substitute for life or set itself up as the mistress of truth.

One of the most tragic aspects of this problem is connected with the problem of indoctrination. We have felt that children should be left open-minded about moral and religious questions. That has had at least two unfortunate results. Children have grown up not only illiterate in the fields of whole-responses to the most high and the most good but with a general confusion which has characterized much of their living. It is better to teach children something constructive, though inadequately, than to teach them nothing. Nor is there any reason that, when whole-living requires humility and inquiry, indoctrination should be doctrinaire. The open mind must surely be one aspect of indoctrination. The other result is due to the fact that evil is never slow to indoctrinate. While the European liberals hestitated to indoctrinate, liberalism was swept out by fanatical, indoctrinating men with partial, divisive dogmas. All knowledge is a social act. Our best moral and religious knowledge is a precious heritage. If that is not taught under the proper circumstances in some way we openly declare it unimportant and declare, although unwittingly, for worse morals and religions. If we cannot teach democracy, for instance (as many of us heard all the way through our education), as better than other forms of government that we know, we have no right to be surprised when democracy is scorned. The teaching of democracy is not by itself the approval of the *status quo;* for the teaching of it should be the teaching of the ideal democracy and the constant study of how it can be actually improved. To say that science has simply paralyzed our capacity to act and to believe is again, besides being unfair to science, at least partly an excuse, to cover up our failure to make intelligent and responsible whole-responses as to what is most important and most real. Tentativeness is part of scientific method; science is in the service of man; man must act; his full truth must be the whole man thinking as he keeps deciding the ultimate issues of life. Science can serve but cannot substitute for life in its quest for whole-truth through whole-response.

Yet are we not, after all, confusing two different things? Are we not simply saying that truth is whatever works toward personal and social adequacy? Are we not reasoning straight from the needs of whole-response to the presence out there, the way things truly are the way they really work, of realities which adequately correspond to the facts? Then have we not simply turned back and accused those who do not share our faith of lack of responsible decision and whole-thinking? Professor Arthur E. Murphy in a personal letter (March 31, 1945) stressed that "the fact that the belief would be helpful if it were reasonably justified does not constitute a reason for believing it thus justified in fact." This we grant. We would agree that all men of good will must work and feel for the good if they would live right. Our analysis of knowing has shown that this is also necessary if they are to think right. Whole-response and whole-thinking are under strong pressure to be harmonized by an organic self.

But besides, organic needs do reflect thus far on the truth out there. Need is a dynamic relation involving intrinsically the self and his world. Herrmann rightly writes: "When one confesses to oneself that one cannot walk without crutches, one does not thereby prove that he *has* crutches but only that one is lame."[19] Yet this is only partially right, for there is not merely empty need and no response. That is an abstraction. We see partially met needs. What is important is to some extent real, at least to whatever extent it has been realized. Realization involves the world as to both the development of the need and the partial meeting of it. If we can

[19] Herrmann, in Baillie, *The Interpretation of Religion*, p. 293.

find what the ideal realization would be, then we can assess the relation between realizability and realization. Even so the argument can never go beyond present realization except in terms of potentiality, unless there are other solid reasons for understanding that the present relation between need and its realization is not the primary consideration in the problem of to what extent the most important and the most real go together. If the false extension of scientific method to values makes for a tentativeness there which not only prevents further realization but actually destroys present attainment, we can at least say that this vital line to truth is spoiled by false science, science used falsely, or science so-called. Science as science is not to blame but men who have failed to understand and heed the temptations of logical and psychological tendencies connected with the scientific use of tentativeness.

2. In the second place science is better fitted to describe than to prescribe. Those who want a strict use of the term insist that it cannot prescribe at all. If because of its own distinctive nature science can tell only what things are and how they function, but cannot tell what, how, and why things ought to be different in order to exemplify the most important and the most real, science is naturally ruled out entirely from adequate prescription. Then science obviously cannot give us whole-truth through whole-response. We want to be careful, on the one hand, to use science as far as possible, but, on the other, we definitely do not want to bolster belief in the sacred, for instance, by relying upon the popularity and prestige of science. We are neither for nor against science, but for the truth. Science cannot prove religion. Nor can religion as whole-truth do without it. If we could acquiesce in the common notion that science describes while religion prescribes and that therefore they have completely independent fields and functions our problem would be much easier than it actually is.

Yet adequate prescription is based to a great extent on description. In the physical world prescription is a matter of description. An engineer must do such and such if his bridge is going to be so and so, and bear so and so much traffic. Prescription here is merely conditional description. The prescriptive operation is merely predictive description. But as soon as we leave this realm of fact we meet other problems. In a broad sense, for instance, medicine may be called a science. Sidney Hook has shown how health is a universal based on ideal description rather than upon average, or general, function.[20] Here prescription is more than mere description. It is selective prescription. Yet this is primarily true to the extent that man is merely a natural creature. There are approximate laws of organic chemistry, for instance, that apply rather dependably. But there are also laws of the mind and spirit which have a general bearing upon the diagnosis of the patient and upon the proper prescription. Yet the more physical the trouble is the better the result of the prescription can be predicted. The more it is a matter of mind and/or spirit the less certain is the prescription. Now, some theoreticians reduce all medicine to physical structure and functions. Others go all out for attributing health conditions, even what seems of a purely physical nature, mostly to the conditions of the deeper *psyche*. Endocrinology, for example has held either that glands, a physical function, vitally influence the patient's outlook on life; or else, all the way to the other position, that the *psyche* disturbs the body because of its deep fears and poisons the system *via* the secretions from the endocrines. Aphasia, again, has been held to be a matter of localized physical functions, or else a matter of the whole organism where to treat the lesions correctly the whole person as a person must be treated. The fact seems rather to be that neither just localism nor wholism is true by itself but that man is an interaction of body and spirit, of physical function and mental attitude, of local function and total function. On the physical side prescription is easier, but even on the mental and spiritual side prescription depends largely upon previous observation, that is, upon intelligent description. Here, however, the problem of the patient's freedom enters the picture, and those who have practiced medicine long often feel that the personal relation is as important as, and more important than, the physical prescription. Prescription now varies with the personal

[20] Hook, *Reason, Social Myth, and Democracy*, p. 285.

equation, and with every whole-response, and cannot be reduced to mere descriptive prediction.

As a matter of fact the physician who has true concern for the patient and who can make the patient believe in himself and in the universe has often more to give than medicine. Dr. Loring T. Swaim in an address to the American Rheumatism Association has pointed out how the physician needs to treat spirit, mind, and body in order to help him as fully as possible.[21] If the spirit is low, if the mind is without positive work and interest, or if the physical part of man is neglected—in short, if any part is wrong the patient will be less than well. These aspects go together more than we think because man lives as a whole. Yet any of the three may constitute the basic problem. If, however, love and trust are needed for men to be made fully whole we are beyond prescription based on either average description or typical function. Health, as used by Sidney Hook, is supposed to be an analogy which bridges the gap between fact and value because the self exemplifies both the physical and the mental aspects of experience. Yet the analogy holds good only as it is pressed toward the physical side, and even then, in medicine, it is forced. Medicine can take for granted the value judgment that life is better than death even as science takes for granted that truth is better than error. Yet the ends of life, what to live for, what kind of faith is best, questions involved in whole-health, these things, science, in the strict sense, cannot prescribe. They follow from no description that does not involve a value judgment and a faith judgment. Even though these value judgments and faith judgments are not arbitrary, but must rather be founded as far as possible both in fact and in accurate reasoning, nevertheless to include them within the method of science is impossible. This we say for two reasons. The first is that the scientists have a well-defined theory, and if they even object to Whitehead and Eddington as being "unscientific," how we wrong them if we extend the method of science proper to cover ends of life which cannot be proved at all conclusively by any

[21] Presidential address to the ninth annual meeting.

merely descriptive method. Science then loses its real meaning and function. In the second place, science wants to operate as far as possible without any personal equation and without such emotional factors as trust and love. As a matter of fact in science we ought to be as skeptical as possible of every method and result. To call prescription for whole-responses scientific is therefore simply a travesty both on the name and on the reality of the method.

We want to use science as far as possible. We have, consequently, not made a quick distinction between science as description and religion as prescription. The truth is not that simple. Yet methodologically we must say that science is generally limited to description, and that whole-searching for truth cannot stop with description. To know the truth through whole-response, we must do it; and to do it, we must prescribe beyond the actual; for the actual is definitely not the highest truth that we know to be possible. Truth includes at least possibles for human welfare that are not now actual. These possibles are not operational, descriptive prediction, in any limited sense. In later chapters we shall have to deal with the question of how then we can *know* what to prescribe. All that we can see now is that we cannot stop with science if we are to know and to do, and to do and to know, more and more of the truth, beyond the possible which is based simply in the actual, of what is most important and what is most real. At the present stage we have no right, however, to say more than that truth includes possibles for good not yet actual, and that these possibles are candidates for examination whether they are also real in fact out there in some vital sense since they refer back to a relation of balance between the organism and the world that supports it. To love truth and mankind we must, however, be on our guard against the turning of a limited method into metaphysical fact, or into a status of permanent ignorance. Because science is methodologically limited to exact description mostly of physical fact, we may not conclude on the peril of truth, life, and civilization that the truth out there is thus limited, or that our knowledge of what is out there is thus limited. *That* is to "transform what is merely an artifice of method into a doctrine of reality."[22] *That* is falling prey to the logical and psychological tendencies which constitute the most insidious dangers to adequate thinking. Because science says that it cannot handle a certain aspect of life, scientists or onlookers have no right to say that therefore it does not exist. *That* is either confused thinking or willful blindness, and the fault is not that of true science, but of science so-called.

3. The third possible obstacle to truth which comes from the abuse of scientific method in line with its logical and psychological tendencies is the denial of freedom. Whole-response is our primary experience. It is an irreducible aspect of the given. Such response is selective. It is "taken rather than given,"[23] and comes "in the making and because of the making."[24] Science deals with regularity and prediction. Freedom is not subject to science. Freedom is part and parcel of spirit, of our inner selves. Only by freely recognizing this truth and by doing something significant with it can we be free in the truth. As a matter of fact we take it for granted in our own lives. Else why shame, why satisfaction, why guilt, why responsibility? Surely every day society and family life are built on this basic fact. Freedom is a fact of primary experience. Be it said, however, that obviously freedom is neither infinite in a world like ours, nor unweighted by our own past and the unequal stimuli from the world outside. Freedom is within the conditions of our situation and according to the stature of each self. We have certain choices within certain limits, certain reactions in terms of the degree of organic unity, of character and purpose, within a certain self, and certain powers with which to act, or to refrain from acting, and to act in this way or that in relation to certain varying and unequal possibilities. This kind of actual freedom within limits and conditions is a fact. And this freedom, furthermore, is itself creative of new facts, particularly the fact of

[22] Allport, *Personality, a Psychological Interpretation*, p. 19.

[23] B. Russell, "Dewey's New *Logic*" in *The Philosophy of John Dewey*, edited by Schilpp, p. 139. The phrases in the context deal with the denial of "passive receptivity."

[24] Whitehead, *Principles of Natural Knowledge*, p. 14.

new self-determination or self-formation. Much discussion between freedom and determinism is lost because of an all-or-none attitude by men falling prey to logical and psychological tendencies.

The logical tendency to deny freedom in the name of science is easy to understand. Physical science deals a good deal with abstractions. Its greatest competence is within the areas of complete predictability. It depends upon controllable conditions. It works in areas where law, or uninterrupted regularity of occurrence, is of the very nature of things to the point of being assumed as an ideal and actual condition—if only the actual were completely known. Mechanism is not a necessary assumption of science, but it is a logical tendency, an ideal working presupposition. Any deviation from complete predictability is treated as a "recalcitrant fact," as a stubborn datum to be more fully analyzed and explained. And this is as it should be. It is entirely natural that physicists and other scientists should be loath to accept Heisenberg's "principle of uncertainty" as indicating freedom inasmuch as it merely declares that the actions of atoms with regard to any individual atom are unpredictable. Scholars like Russell, for instance, insist that we should say "the Principle of Limited Measurability."[25] An astronomer working with well-nigh perfect predictability of the actions of the heavenly bodies is naturally offended by this sign of weakness (on the part of men of strict science) even though in another field. In physics and astronomy the question of freedom, however, has little relevance to life. We are not dealing directly with the field of freedom. Whether or not Sarton is right that "on account of the infinite complexity of causes and of the dissipation of energy, physical events never repeat themselves exactly. The planets do not follow twice the same trajectories,"[26] is of small importance to our problem. That just means that we are not omniscient and that even the scientist if he tries to be must falter and fail.

When we move up to the field of life, and particularly to the

[25] Henry Norris Russell, "Determinism and Responsibility," in *Science, Philosophy and Religion,* Third Symposium, citing Max Born.
[26] Sarton, *op. cit.,* p. 9.

field of human freedom, the question is crucially different. The logical tendency is toward mechanism. For purposes of explanation it makes a real difference, however, whether animals are Cartesian machines or whether they are partly motivated by purpose. Whitehead in *Nature and Life* has pounced with depth of conviction and piercing insight on the combination of the philosophies of Newton and Hume in the study of nature.

> The universe, as construed solely in terms of the efficient causation of purely physical interconnections, presents a sheer, insoluble contradiction.[27]

> Two conclusions are now abundantly clear. One is that sense-perception omits any discrimination of the fundamental activities within Nature. . . . The second conclusion is the failure especially of science to endow its formulae for activity with any meaning. Science conceived as resting on mere sense-perception, with no other source of observation, is bankrupt, so far as concerns its claim to self-sufficiency. Science can find no individual enjoyment in nature: Science can find no aim in nature: Science can find no creativity in nature; it finds mere rules of succession. These negations are true of Natural Science. They are inherent in its methodology. . . . Such Science only deals with half the evidence.[28]

These observations, of course, have especially heavy bearing on biology, as Needham has seen in the chapter referred to above. Yet even in this field we have not reached the crucial point.

We approach this point in psychology. To omit individual freedom here is disastrous to adequate interpretation of the field. Yet of

> . . . the several sciences devoted to the study of life-processes, none, peculiarly enough, recognizes as its central fact that life-processes actually occur only in unified, complex, individual forms. Sciences find the very existence of the individual somewhat of an embarrassment and are disturbed by his intrusion into their domains. . . . Why is it that science and common sense part company over the fact of human individuality? The answer is that science is an arbitrary creed. . . . The *person* who is a unique and never-

[27] Whitehead, *Function of Reason*, p. 20.
[28] Whitehead, *Modes of Thought*, pp. 210–211.

repeated phenomenon evades the traditional scientific approach at every step. . . . The generalized human mind is entirely mythical. . . . Each person in the course of his life modifies his common hereditary equipment of impulses in ways that are peculiar to himself; he likewise develops new and autonomous interests. . . . Definitions are always arbitrary, even those in science. Therefore anyone who wishes to restrict the meaning of the sacred phrase "the scientific method" to the three-fold process of analysis, abstraction, and generalization is at liberty to do so. If the psychologist wishes to accept the narrow definition, he too is free. But in so doing he must not [we repeat] transform what is merely an artifice of method into a doctrine of reality.[29]

The last sentence is exactly what we mean by the temptation of the logical tendency to scientific method. The logical tendency is to accept the ideal, or narrow, definition and then force all reality to conform to it, thus either ignoring or distorting it, perhaps at the most vital places. Psychology is free to exclude, not to deny, human freedom. Method exists to make truth available, not impossible.

When we come, moreover, to the problems of inwardness, of decision, of moral freedom, of the spirit, our fact of freedom is at the height of common importance. To handle these questions of inner motivation and ultimate purposes with regard to what is most important and what is most real we need either to go far beyond psychology or else to expand psychology into a metaphysical or religious investigation, which can be done only from within the willing and completely surrendered spirit. It is much better, however, to keep psychology as much of a science as possible and let it handle in that way all the data it possibly can. The more material it can handle well the better it is for knowledge as a whole. What is needed is to see the difference betwen physiological psychology, personal psychology, and the utmost reaches of the spirit in its ultimate ends and quests. What we need is more inquiry, more careful investigation by every possible method. We must watch therefore lest we fall prey, unaware, to the logical

[29] Allport, *op. cit.*, pp. 3, 5, 18, 19.

tendency of the scientific method to eliminate the individual, not merely as the uniqueness of each leaf is ignored by botany, but to eliminate the primary fact of human freedom itself, one of the cornerstones of individual and social adequacy.

How the logical tendency turns into the psychological is equally easy to see. The psychological tendency of our natural selves is to think defensively in areas where our direct security or responsibility is involved. We all long for security of some kind and try for it in some way. Yet ultimate security must walk through the path of responsibility. We want to find security in ourselves. To make this possible we limit our problems to ourselves, shutting out those of society which we know to be beyond our control. We also ignore our cosmic connections. Attempted self-security builds on self-centeredness only to fail because it has ignored the real world of which it is inseparably a part. Cosmic responsibility, however, points to cosmic security, and to rest for the weary self beyond its own strength and competence. The natural person wants security without responsibility and can never find it. Freedom entails responsibility. Freedom to choose in terms of cosmic relations involves cosmic responsibility, but also resources of cosmic strength and security. When this responsibility takes on its full scope without cosmic help freedom becomes a burden and increases the sense of guilt, failure, and frustration. Thus the natural self tends to deny freedom in order to avoid responsibility. Seeking for security without the willingness to pay the cost for it through responsibility within the structure of the world, the self finds neither freedom nor security. Rather he finds anxiety and the enervated will. Only through trust in what is most important and most real out there the way it really works can the self find security and freedom. Yet such trust involves the giving up of the false freedom, freedom without the eternal law and without the cosmic order, to find freedom within the eternal law and within the cosmic order of what is most important and most real.[30]

[30] Our analysis here takes for granted that what is truly needed *is truly real* in an experiential sense. We shall show later on how, why, and in what sense this is so in the full sense of truth.

The natural thing to do when things go wrong is to blame others, or circumstance. Those who have dealt much and long with people know how exasperatingly true this is. In some individuals the tendency goes to the point of neurotic isolation and pathology. But the tendency is in all men, with the exception of the saints, and they, too, have known days when they knew this experience to be true. To blame others or circumstance is to defend the self in his castle of attempted self-security. Only those who need no such castle can look fearlessly and critically at their own selves. Others may think that they can, but objective observers find the self-righteous most blind to their worst faults, and "none is so blind as he who will not see." Before God, however, all are naked and for this reason, above all, man wants to deny freedom. Deep down in all normal hearts there is the sense of responsibility, the sense of the larger relations of life, but as long as men do not want to give themselves completely up to this responsibility of freedom, if they deal with the problem at all, the tendency is to explain away freedom as man's feeling of nature's adjusting itself within him to which he falsely attributes the idea of freedom, and consequently feels unnecessary responsibility and guilt. Or, actual freedom is rationalized by the stressing of the individual as supreme without any standards or sanctions save the human will alone in relation to some possible or ideal course of conduct which would be good if realized. Freedom, involving the far reaches of responsibility within actual relations and within a cosmic structure, is a direct part of whole-experience, and a key to individual and social salvation. As far as science can deal with any aspect of it, the more, the better. Because of either the logical tendency of science or the psychological tendency to avoid responsibility tempting us all, we must not, however, twine the two tendencies together into a wholesale belittling or denial of this primary region of the human spirit. As individuals and society we shall have forfeited our birthright when we have sold out for any reason at all the primary fact of human freedom.

4. The fourth limitation on the part of the scientific method, in the strict sense, is its incapacity to deal with motivation. We know

pretty much what ought to be done. We talk about it in general terms and want others to act according to what we know ought to be. Yet we may all tend, more or less, to make ourselves the exception to the rule. We like the benefits of a desirable moral and social order, but we fail to live up to it ourselves. This failure, however, is not entirely one of bad faith. Nor is it merely a confusing of our actual self, which we seldom see truly, with our idea of what we actually are, which is a much idealized version of ourselves. Actually we often long to be far better than we are; but mere trying seems to fail basically to change us. To many people moral struggle seems useless. In spite of trying they fail, and then fail again exactly at the points where they know their own weakness. What they need besides the will to do is the power to do. Beyond the intent they need the deed. And concrete direction and the will power to do go hand in hand. Augustine found that the philosophers saw the promised land but could not find their way there.[31] That was why he finally chose Christ as the light and the power to walk in the way.

We have seen that prescription involves ends. Ends involve purpose. "We are *directly* conscious of our purposes as *directive* of our actions."[32] This power to direct action within set conditions is freedom. Yet freedom merely in metaphysical terms, the ability to choose one thing or another, cannot solve the problems either of individuals or of society. We need also ethical freedom, and the living spontaneously according to the inner demands of the right spirit. Metaphysical freedom exists, we shall find later on, in order that we may find ethical freedom. Yet such freedom can be had only when the self finds the power to live up to his ideal, the ideal that he conforms to out there as things truly and importantly are. How to get that power is the problem of motivation with which science as science cannot deal. We are forced to work with conclusions not yet arrived at in order to indicate what some of the limitations of science are in the finding of the full range of what is

---

[31] Augustine, "Confessions," in *Nicene and Post-Nicene Fathers,* Vol. I, p. 115.

[32] Whitehead, *Modes of Thought,* p. 213.

both important and true. The problem of motivation is one of the deepest of our age and to it we must devote much careful work later on. At present it is necessary to see only that it is a matter of whole-prescription for whole-response which is beyond the limit of the proper efficacy of the scientific method. This is no fault of science. The only fault there is, is on the part of those who stretch scientific method so thin that it never comes to vital grips with the problem, and thus can be helpful neither to the scientists nor to the helpers of humanity. The central areas of life cannot be sacrificed on the altar of any method. Those fail science who treat it as an idol to be worshiped, instead of a servant to be used. We must have more and better science, but we must constantly guard against false science, science falsely used, and science so-called. Science has not failed man, but man keeps failing science. George Sarton has rightly said:

Any remedy for a social evil is always at bottom a moral remedy. To be sure, the evils must be investigated as thoroughly as possible by the use of scientific methods, and their correction will involve the application of similar methods, but the wish and strength to cure the evil are moral factors, and without them there can be no improvement. . . . Science has never been more necessary than today, nor less sufficient; in the future it will become more and more necessary, and more and more insufficient.[33]

This is indeed an excellent summary of a truth applicable to this fourth limitation on the part of the scientific method.

5. Science is also limited in the proper efficacy of its method because it is objective. In the strict sense of science this is, indeed, one of its greatest virtues and one of the reasons that it has won such great respect among people in general. Yet the most vital part of life is always the subject, the person investigating the object. What shall it profit us if we know all about the inorganic world, the world open for public inspection, and fail to understand our own hearts? Calvin well expands the old Socratic adage that

[33] Cited by Hutchins, "Education for Freedom," in *The Christian Century*, Nov. 15, 1944.

"to be curious about that which is not my concern, while I am still in ignorance of my own self, would be ridiculous":[34] "There is much reason in the old adage, which so strongly recommends to man the knowledge of himself. For if it be thought disgraceful to be ignorant of whatever relates to the conduct of human life, ignorance of ourselves is much more shameful, which causes us, in deliberating on subjects of importance, to grope our way in miserable obscurity, or even in total darkness."[35] Yet full self-knowledge, or knowledge of the full self, is always subjective, introspective, and must be had through inner meditation and searching of heart. "For what man knoweth the things of a man, save the spirit of man which is in him."[36] Can we even understand the pain of a toothache objectively? How much less can we know the yearnings of the spirit? There are sections of life which can never be shared, not only the way we can never experience the qualitative givenness of any sensation or situation of anyone else, but in the further sense that there is no public object for others to see. A few know us fairly well, but only as we keep revealing intimately our deeper selves, whether in the depth of temptation or in the higher reaches of spiritual attainment. Yet they know only as we tell, and our telling is a continuous frustration.

"In ordinary language, a problem must be felt before it can be stated."[37] But the knowledge of ourselves can be felt only by ourselves. Others must know us as we tell of the "situation" which is "*had* immediately." Whatever the truth about the most important and the most real is, it must include organically the deeper reaches and perspectives of the self. Such a knowledge can be had only from within, and the depth of it will depend on the depth of the knower. He can then suggest his knowledge of himself and compare his findings with close friends, but the wealth of his findings

---

[34] From "Phaedrus," in *The Dialogues of Plato* (Jowett, trans.), Vol. I., p. 434. Professor Outler points out, however, that γνῶθι σεαυτόν was a gnomic proverb in Greece.

[35] Calvin, *Institutes of the Christian Religion* (Allen, trans.), first American ed. (1816), II, i, p. 257.

[36] I Corinthians 2:11.

[37] Dewey, *op. cit.*, p. 70.

whether of himself or others depends upon the self making itself known. This can never be a mere matter of objective measurement and laboratory technique. The self is sovereign in the knowing of itself and can be treated only as a subject. There are some, today, who are making much of the contrast of "thou" and "it" knowledge, writers like Martin Buber and Karl Heim, but already a hundred years ago Sören Kierkegaard challenged the very foundation of scientific knowledge as ultimate by his insistence that what is most important and genuine is the knowledge of the individual as a subject: "Subjectivity is the truth."[38] Berdyaev today sounds the same note: "The mystery of reality is not solved by concentrating on the object, but by reflecting on the action of the subject."[39] We dare by no means follow too far along this trend. Adequate knowledge must always be a careful blend and balance of subjective and objective knowledge. The knowledge of spirit itself cannot be apart from natural, cultural, and historical factors, and all these intertwine and interact. Yet this much we can say with complete confidence: Any interpretation of what is most important and most real that leaves out the subject as known the only way it can be adequately known at all is partial knowledge. Strict science is objective knowledge and this fact marks one limit of the proper efficacy of its method.

6. Strict science has often become a handicap to the social sciences by becoming a false ideal. The logical tendency toward the kind of clarity and demonstrability possessed by the natural sciences has constituted a strong temptation to oversimplification in the field of the social sciences. The attractiveness of the general principle, so effective in natural science, that "in attempting to explain phenomena, it is necessary to adopt the simplest hypothesis that will coördinate the facts"[40] pulled the social sciences toward the tangible side of social problems at the expense of the deeper and less tangible problems of ends. The pluralistic method of science (which we have not yet discussed) helped to produce a theory of

---

[38] Kierkegaard, *Concluding Unscientific Postscript*, p. 187.

[39] Berdyaev, *Spirit and Reality*, p. 4.

[40] Dampier-Whetham, *op. cit.*, p. 53.

cultural pluralism which tended to become its own end and standard. It is well to be clear at this point. The more strict science can adequately handle the problems of society the better. The more the social sciences can profitably imitate strict science the better. These sciences can describe certain aspects of social life, and by being as strict as possible and by excluding all content except that which they can handle, they render a most important aid to significant social decision.

When these social sciences, however, model themselves upon the natural sciences in method and standard, consequently refusing to handle the more important questions of social decision, and when they then go on to deny that there are problems beyond their sphere of competence or to deny that they can be handled importantly and in truth by any method whatever, then the logical tendency of a method good in its proper place has indeed become evil and damaging to what is both useful and true. Or when they accept responsibility for the whole field of social problems and then select only such material as can be conveniently analyzed and generalized in the fashion of physical science, they deceive, destroy, and thwart society by their dogmatic *a priori* handling of the facts. Then their method becomes a blinder. Those who accept the claims of a false social science are accordingly left without guidance from either philosophy or religion, in any respected and compelling sense, in the very spheres of their crying needs. Therefore the storm of confusion, divisiveness, and destruction overtakes society.

When defensive emotions, whether personal or professional, are also added to this logical tendency we are up against the stubborn fact of psychological tendencies. "None is so blind as he who will not see." All thinking is emotional, and if the social scientists put themselves or their profession first, actually, regardless of their statement of intent, then as night follows the day these same social scientists will deny or ridicule all adequate efforts to salvage the highest human hopes and truths, and will take a too limited and a not fully responsible attitude toward society. They will not be content to recognize the limit of the proper efficacy of their method and to serve the common good by their patient descriptions. They will love their books and ideas more than the people in their deep distress. They will, nevertheless, lay claim to knowing and speaking the full truth, or all possible truth, on the subject. There precisely lies the heart of the mischief.

No human being is able to separate the psychological from the logical perversions of method. Only God can do that. Even for the interpreter himself to see the combination in his own life with any degree of clarity, he must live a deep life of continual surrender to the full demands of truth, being cleansed as with constant fire in the inward parts. This matter of "the eyes of your understanding being enlightened," or literally "the eyes of the heart," is no easy matter.[41] Who, then, can say to what extent a social scientist who will deny the most obvious facts of life, for instance the relevance of religion to concrete social acts, is under the blinding spell of the method and mentality of strict science, and/or is fighting religion in his own life, whether in his past or his present life, and/or to what extent he is laboring with misunderstandings and false associations in both fields plus problems, known or unknown, in his own life? The truth of the situation is very likely not less but far more complex in all the interactions of a lifelong struggle among, as well as co-operation of, mind, heart, and will.

There has been much confusion, much loss of power and of co-operation, and much paralysis of enlightened social decision which has resulted from unclear trumpets and from trumpets sounding to action from scattered and incompatible positions. Critical social science is a deep need of this complex hour. We need much more of it. But critical social science must not stand in the way of, but rather help all it can, the creative social decisions which must be rendered through whole-vision and whole-response. These, as we shall see, are not leaps in the dark, but intelligent and founded decisions not only for the general welfare but in line with the highest known truth. Strict science has a limited function within the inquiry dealing with social problems and decisions.

7. In the seventh place science cannot deal with the question

[41] Ephesians 1:18.

"why?" It can tell us the what and the how of things. It can describe the nature and the function of its objects. The only whys it can answer are those of the whats and the hows. For the classical tradition to explain was to relate to a purpose. For the modern mentality to explain has been to relate to a cause. For the human mind to rest in depth-response and depth-understanding is to be stayed in meanings. The whole structure of human thought and action is intentional. This craving is our deep need of the like for the like, of the organic for the Organic, of purpose for Purpose. If this need is false, if it meets no reality out there the way things really work, if it finds no response in critical truth, then we had better simply recognize that fact. But the fact that a certain method cannot deal with the problem is not reason enough to ignore it. That is the false use of science. That is to do violence to the true intent and real sincerity of science in its bowing to facts the way they really are. That is a sin against the true scientific attitude of open-mindedness. That is the substitution of logical and psychological tendencies accompanying scientific method for the method itself. Later we shall show at length that there are consistent, careful ways of talking about purpose, telling it to others, and of testing the relevancy and the organic relation of the facts and meanings that are involved in the fact of purpose.

The fact is that we are *"directly* conscious of our purposes as *directive* of our actions."[42] Purpose is as much a matter of primary experience as freedom. The scientist may not recognize purpose in method; he has excluded it; and that is well *for his purposes.* The scientist as a man is well acquainted with purposes and the purposes of others. He knows that there are purposes until he begins to talk professionally and defensively to sin against truth. Purpose is a fact of experience. Not only, moreover, is it a fact of experience but it may be seen even out there the way things work beyond human agency. Science does not deal with it. "Science is not discussing the causes of knowledge, but the coherence of knowledge."[43] "It seeks for the cause of the knowledge of the thing

[42] Whitehead, *Modes of Thought,* p. 213.
[43] Whitehead, *Concept of Nature,* p. 41.

known instead of seeking for the character of the thing known."[44] But when we go beyond that limited method of science, "the universe construed solely in terms of efficient causation of purely physical interconnections, presents a sheer, insoluble contradiction. . . . It is well to be quite clear on the point that Reason is inexplicable if purpose be ineffective."[45] Lawrence Henderson, in *The Fitness of the Environment* and *The Order of Nature,* points out that the complexity, regulation, and metabolism characteristic of life are too intricate processes in the reciprocal adaptability to be accidental. "For, however present order may have been developed out of past confusion, the organism and the environment each fits and is fitted by the other."[46] Henderson's summary at this point is well worth pondering: "We may progressively lay bare the order of nature and define it with the aid of the exact sciences. Thus we may recognize it for what it is, and now at length we see clearly that it is teleological. But we shall never find the explanation of the riddle, for it concerns the origin of things."[47]

It will be exactly at this point that we shall deal with the riddle as best we can in our chapter on religion. The universe shows us both mechanism and teleology and only a clear understanding of their meaningful relation can give us truth. We shall then show that the crucial questions for interpreting the full truth are not immediate teleology, as Henderson saw, but the question of history, of origins, of actualization, of the organic assimilation of the new, and of "the tendency" whereby what is continuous in the past somehow fits together with discontinuous ingressions of historic novelty in terms of a new perspective and a new organization of both content and interpretation. We shall then see how clearly existence reveals at least partial purposiveness. This whole question, however, is beyond the scope and function of science in the strict sense which describes the processes of existence and does not go into the whys beyond the hows and the whats. Practically, of

[44] *Ibid.,* p. 39.

[45] Whitehead, *The Function of Reason,* pp. 20, 21.

[46] *The Order of Nature,* p. 3.

[47] *Ibid.,* pp. 208–209. Henderson's use of teleology is not on as high a level as Whitehead's use of purpose.

course, the direction of individual and social purpose is more important than the question of origin and reality. We simply cannot ignore the presence of purpose and the question of worthy ends. But with regard to truth the question of the origin of purpose in history is going to be of even more importance than the practical problem of the direction of personal and social purpose. Thus both practically and theoretically we are at the heart of a need and a truth which science, strictly speaking, cannot handle.

8. Scientific method cannot, obviously, deal with the ultimate. That is a philosophic, metaphysical, and religious problem. The writer once had a conversation with a thoughtful social scientist who wanted to include under science every question of what is needful and true. When the question of what is ultimate came up, he frankly admitted, however, that such questions did not come within the working compass of scientific method. Yet one of the deepest problems of life, for instance, as clergymen and psychiatrists soon come to know, is the fact of death for every life. We know that we are going to die and the fear of death is a constant accompaniment in the depth-conscious of the will to live. There is, besides, the secondary problem of lives so frustrated that the will to death either robs life of significant action or leads outright to a hoped-for escape into death. Dean Willard Sperry once remarked in connection with a funeral at the Harvard Chapel of one of its greatest scholars that the academic mind resented being reminded of the fact of death. Somehow that kind of thing did not belong in the real life of inquiry. Academic life, however, is that far the artificial life. Teachers live vicariously with the young and are often tempted to escape into the fountain of this perpetual youth of the campus. Man transcends time and knows that death always stares him in the face, mayhap today; if not, tomorrow. Death rushes at each one of us with lightning speed. A lifetime is but a moment and it is gone. Existence may be ultimately meaningless or it may be through and through meaningful and responsible. Like a spoiled child natural man wants the universe to be both meaningful and comfortingly protective. He would like it to have meaning, and yet to let him live the way he wants to live

without its making demands upon him. He therefore hesitates in his interpretation of whole-response, except as his interpreting be based on patient study of the truth and surrender to it; sometimes he imagines that there is a benevolent purpose which will somehow take care of him and his destiny, rearing him gently; sometimes he prefers his own irresponsibility and simply concludes that there is no ultimate meaning, at least that can be known; and sometimes he hides himself in work and in things, in position and in possession, and tries whatever may be his exact part-thinking or conventional profession of belief, not to think seriously and decisively about the problem of the ultimate at all. Yet no life can be full and free that has not faced for itself the most basic of all problems, the question of the final meaning of its own life. This crucial area is outside the scope of scientific method.

Science may, moreover, be the occasion of two kinds of ultimates that do not follow from the method of science itself. Since science deals with what is here and now actual, particularly along rigid descriptive lines, the logical tendency of thought has made it easy to assume that this area equals the whole area of truth. The description of what is here and now actual, particularly what can be described in terms of scientific method, has consequently in large circles been taken for granted as the nature of final truth. If such description is the most careful, critical, and adequate account of what is really there the way it truly works, we shall naturally accept it as such and make the best of it. Illusions will not help us. Even if we keep saying them to ourselves in order to comfort ourselves in a heartless world, such dishonesty merely raises havoc in the depths of our lives. Either we find by the open method of truth that the ultimate has meaning, and a meaning for us, or else we must admit that it has not and follow the ancient saying to "do what men may and bear what men must."

But the false use of science has led to a naturalism which has simply for the most part been taken for granted as demanded by the method of science. Truth to tell, of course, society has had little choice other than either the careful method of science or some arbitrary, external revelation. We await a spacious synthesis of knowledge that will give us a creative vision of the ultimate that can stand up under the hardest critical tests. In all parts of the world "the acids of modernity"[48] have eaten away the older interpretations of the ultimate. The interpreters of both philosophy and religion have all too often failed to dig deeply enough to offer the thoughtful any decisive truth about the ultimate that could stand up under close scrutiny. Knowledge has come into history so fast, and then seemingly faster, until the interpreters of thought have been bewildered and perplexed. They have been overwhelmed as by a flood. The philosophies of life and the theologies of religion have not robustly enough challenged the deeper logical and psychological tendencies which made naturalism such an obvious ultimate of our time-spirit.

But strict science as a method does not deal with the question of the ultimate at all. Naturalism is but a barnacle on the scientific ship of truth. Naturalism must pass our muster in the proper connection. Here it is enough to point out how the logical tendency of the scienctific method helps those who want to escape from the responsibility of the ultimate in that they may easily avail themselves of the idea that naturalism is the scientific view of reality in order to hide themselves from a surrender to truth and responsibility which they are not prepared to make. The logical tendency is thus fed on by the psychological. Recently the writer spent an afternoon with some students at their request on this question, and found that their problem was less intellectual than emotional. They offered every shred of evidence and every farfetched argument to prove that what science tells about the ultimate is the only truth that we can know even though science professedly does not face this metaphysical question. Their intellectual and emotional difficulties were all mixed together. "Science" can be made into a religion, and is one to numberless people, and they will be far more emotional about it in a defensive fashion than their religion allows them to be. If science is made an idol, however, open neither to careful inspection nor to the drawing of the limitations inherent within its own nature, this is in no way the fault of

[48] Walter Lippmann, *A Preface to Morals*, p. 8.

science or of the true scientist. This is science falsely used, false science, and science so-called.

The second effect on society of the fact that science cannot deal with the ultimate, and that therefore a naturalistic metaphysics has often been assumed, we find most difficult to analyze correctly. We may call it "materialism" in a rough sense. Materialism as a theory of ultimate reality is seldom held. Modern physics, for that matter, has helped to prevent such a crass philosophy from taking root. Matter is a form of energy and not an ultimate category. Yet a practical materialism has been furthered by "scientific" philosophy. We have a kind of philosophy which either denies that God, values, and even mind as mind can be dependably known and a kind of philosophy which denies their existence outright. These philosophies rooting largely in "scientific" method have helped to increase a practical materialism. Even the mind is denied as being anything but a biological operation. Mind is but an instrument, and its ideas have no reality of importance except as possible modes of operation in adjusting the organism to an environment which is not significantly of the nature of mind, ideals, or personal life. As soon as the full facts of experience are appealed to including mind and personal life the appealer is accused of sticking in an outmoded dualism. These kinds of naturalism have led to a materialism which cannot be laid directly to the charge of scientific method but rather to the logical and psychological tendencies that have largely helped to foster this mentality and mood. This earth-bound philosophy is itself, of course, to some extent a reflection of our spiritual poverty, of our uncertainty at this juncture of interpretation, of our sense of homelessness during an age of adjustment, but it is a boundedness of spirit which, we shall see, is not warranted either by the facts or by strict thinking. It is very likely more the outgrowth of our concern with the material and the effect of our success in the realm of the physical sciences. The reality and importance of the spiritual side of life have to a large extent been choked out and become unreal in whole-decision by too avid concern with the material side of life.

Our religion of physical progress, which is both a cause and an effect of this naturalism, has helped to create the pitiful hope that "control of nature" will solve our human problems. The radios blare at people that every day will be a honeymoon when contrivances make comfort complete and give ample time for leisure. People are all too ready anyway not to blame themselves for their failures and frustrations and to sleep away even more deeply into the narcotic dream that external changes will bring in the kingdom of happiness. By taking away, on the one side, ultimate faith and hope, and on the other, ultimate responsibility, a false science has made it natural for people to disregard the deeper call of the spirit and to heed carelessly the cravings of the natural man. Mere material progress we know, without worthy ends and lives, leads to wasted physical resources, to unbalanced and sick minds, and to weary and frustrated spirits. The success of science in the material realm is all to the good. But it must not lead us to suppose that the control of physical processes will by itself free us from the problems of mind and spirit. Science can be and is being made into an escapist philosophy—into a dodge of moral disciplines and spiritual responsibilities without which no life can be full and satisfactory and without which society is bound to meet ever new disasters.

Whether or not we can deal with the question of the ultimate from the point of view of truth is a later problem. One thing is certain: If we cannot, we have lost our deepest source of direction and strength. The only authority big enough and the only motivation vital enough to bind us all together in a free creative fellowship, in a completely faithful common concern, are those which go beyond the arbitrariness of human convention, the fickleness of human desire, the divisiveness of human pride and ambition, the confusion of historic and social standards, and the divided evidence of our natural environment. Our hope lies in the possibility that men can be big enough to see their own smallness and weakness in the light of some steady perspective which lifts their vision far above and beyond themselves and gives them the will and the power to live above their usual wants. A new world can come if men can find out that fully to live is to be lived by a power not their own and within a fellowship in that power which gives new meaning, zest, and joy to life. If a pattern and a power of ultimacy can be found that speaks to us, once we see it and want to conform to it, with a voice that is not our own and with a truth that we dare not hide, and much less hide from, except at the peril of our lives and our civilization, then our common wants and human failings may be transformed and reformed by the participation in that pattern and power which comes, even in its breaking of our former wants, not to destroy but to fulfill. Science cannot, in any case, tell us what the nature of ultimate reality is; and the stuff with which it deals cannot save. What is here and now actual cannot cure itself. If we are to have an authority that is neither arbitrary nor artificial yet adequate to provide both unity and freedom, both responsibility and creative zest, we must have something that is anchored in the ultimate nature of things. To those who feel deep compassion for mankind in its confusions and struggles, and to all who experience failure and frustration, the problem of anchoring authority in the ultimate is of first-line importance.

9. Modern scientific theory has also done much to increase our tendency to think in relative terms. Relativism is not new. How clearly it is stated, for instance, in Sophism and in most skeptical literature of the ages. The stress on relativity in modern physics and history have, however, aided a natural tendency of the mind to relativism when it is confronted with overpowering complexity, and has given this tendency, so to speak, "scientific standing." The relativism of physics asserts, at least as an amateur understands it, that no absolute perspective is available to human observation, "that a combination of exact position with exact velocity is not observable."[49] The general principle has been put thus: "that we observe only *relations* between physical entities."[50] We know no absolute space-time, but only concrete observations from special positions under special conditions by concrete observers at particular times. All physical measurements are subject to a system of

[49] Eddington, *The Philosophy of Physical Science,* p. 35.
[50] *Ibid.,* p. 31.

references or a frame of reference. "The terms 'at rest,' " for instance, "and 'in uniform motion' have no absolute meaning. The principle that all inertial systems are equivalent for the description of nature is called the *principle of relativity*."[51] We cannot experimentally define a universal time inasmuch as experimentally simultaneity has no fixed meaning independent of a frame of reference. "Two events which are simultaneous with respect to one frame of reference are in general not simultaneous with respect to another frame."[52] "Our definition of simultaneity is, of course, to a certain degree arbitrary. However, it is impossible to devise an experiment by means of which simultaneity could be defined independently of a frame of reference."[53] We shall not discuss the field of modern physics, where we are outsiders, beyond suggesting that the principle of relativity refers to experimental problems of measurement, particularly with the finding of an all-inclusive frame of reference connected with the "ether." We frankly and by necessity stand apart from the different problems and contentions among the relativity physicists, the quantum physicists, and the experimental physicists. Bergman is clear that the theory of relativity has not "succeeded in establishing a conceptual relationship between" the electromagnetic and the gravitational field; has failed to "furnish us with a satisfactory theory of matter"; and the "quantum phenomena are completely outside the scope of the general theory of relativity."[54] Nor can we experimentally confirm or reject Eddington's radical thesis that "all the laws of nature that are usually classed as fundamental can be foreseen wholly from epistemological considerations. They correspond to *a priori* knowledge and are therefore *wholly subjective*."[55] Obviously physics is itself in a most creative and expanding stage.

What we can say, however, is that the fact that no absolute reference is available to experimental physics, for instance, or that quantum physics deals only with probabilities, in no way under-

[51] Bergman, *An Introduction to the Theory of Relativity*, p. xv.
[52] *Ibid.*, p. 32.
[53] *Ibid.*, p. 32, note.
[54] *Ibid.*, pp. 241–242.
[55] Eddington, *op. cit.*, p. 57.

mines on the level of our lives and thought either public time or public knowledge. We obviously lay no claim to any idea that our point of view is absolute or that we are omniscient. C. I. Lewis well observes: "Probable knowledge is always relative to him who has it."[56] "True knowledge is absolute because it conveys an absolute truth, though it can convey such truth only in relative terms."[57] For our part, we should prefer to say that all real knowledge refers in the end directly or indirectly to the ultimate principle of explanation. There would be no proximations to truth if there were no truth. Newtonian physics constructed an absolute of space and time, but this is not to be equated with the true absolute beyond all human observation. The Newtonian system contains its truth within its proper perspective and Einsteinian physics is merely another approximation to the truth which gives meaning and operability to both within their scope of truth. We must not absolutize either our relativity or our probability; we must not absolutize any of our limitations. The fact that we cannot experimentally control public time in physics does not do away with the fact that public predictions in astronomy, for instance, do come true. There is a genuine, practical public time and public knowledge which we use every day. The business of the world is well transacted, as far as it depends on measurable time, on the acceptance of public time, adjusted as needs be to the different regions of the world. Whatever problems are connected with the experimental definition of simultaneity and the problems of absolute frame of reference for physical measurements, Plato's conception of time as measurable regularity and "the moving image of eternity"[58] still has its truth to contribute.

After all, as Edwyn Bevan has observed, no one can observe an event before it has occurred.[59] Whitehead writes that "it is usually

---

[56] Lewis, *op. cit.*, p. 326.

[57] *Ibid.*, p. 167.

[58] Plato, "Timaeus," in *op. cit.*, Vol. III, pp. 456 ff.

[59] *Symbolism and Belief*, p. 107: "It is to be noted that however widely the order of perception may differ for different observers after the event has happened, no exponent of the theory of Relativity has shown that any event can be perceived before it has happened. The actual moment of

assumed that relative space implies that there is no absolute position. This is, according to my creed, a mistake."[60] Whether we talk about time or space or time-space, there is a definite stable content for rational discourse and action which is dependably meaningful to us. Poincaré and Bertrand Russell may argue whether alternate metrical geometrics are merely conventional or not, whether it can be proved within the categories of natural knowledge that the earth is larger than a billiard ball,[61] but for our purposes, for the purposes of common rational discouse, we have a knowledge of time-space that will keep serving humanity even all the while the technical experts keep changing and improving the statements of its relations. Naturally when we come to discuss time and nature we shall have to probe more deeply into these problems, but even here we can say that all the life of knowledge including science has to take for granted the main perspective of public time and rational discourse. Else public life, including the academic, would become anarchic. To make relativity central rather than the absolute is to fail in our thinking exactly at the same point as those who make the problem of error more basic to a theory of knowledge than the primary fact that we do know at all. Socrates' basic teachings still stand: that there is an absolute and that it can be known. Naturally it can be known to us only in relative terms else we were omniscient. But reality cannot *be* all relations; and mere flux, moreover, cannot be *known* apart from some fixity of form. Knowledge depends upon some regularity and dependability of occurrence. Relativity is a phase of knowledge, not its essence.

History is not a science in the strict sense; yet it includes all possible accuracy and objectivity as standards, as does all true knowledge. Some have patterned the study of history, like Langlois and Seignobos, pretty much after the ideal of science, and for this reason we are not out of place in mentioning historical relativism

happening in objective public Time sets a limit behind which variation in perception cannot go."

[60] *Concept of Nature*, p. 105.
[61] *Ibid.*, pp. 121–124.

as a widening of the problem of relativity in physics. When this writer entered college he asked the head of the history department, Warren O. Ault, what he considered of primary importance in the field of knowledge. The reply was to the effect that relativity would be our most important word during the next fifty years. Richard Niebuhr in a personal conversation stressed that historical relativism had more importance to his whole way of thinking than the scientific variety. According to this historical relativism,

> "Our reason is not only in time-space, but . . . time-space is in our reason. . . . Man, it points out, is not only in time but time in man. Moreover, and more significantly, the time that is in man is not abstract but particular and concrete; it is not a general category of time but rather the time of a definite society with distinct language, economic and political relations, religious faith and social organization.[62]

Historical relativism claims that there are no universal areas of intellectual interpretation and conclusions. In religion there are no doctrines that can be universally compared. Each culture is to be understood solely from within its own organic development and presuppositions. To compare one part of a religion or a culture with parts of other religions and cultures is to compare dead organs which have no vital meaning except in relation to their own wholes of which they are inseparably aspects. Richard Niebuhr has guarded himself from the more destructive claims of historical relativism by means of an external history; yet the main trend of his thought, taken illustratively, tends to make most important by far the relative aspect of knowledge.

We need this stress. It ought to prevent dogmatic arbitrariness and theoretical finality. Yet the historical relativists are temporarily drunk with the wine of the wholeness of particular strands of history and are often too tipsy to see the organic whole of humankind. There is a common human nature within a common cosmic environment making universal exchange of both goods and thought possible. Mathematics and chemistry, hygiene and biology,

[62] *The Meaning of Revelation*, pp. 10, 13.

economics and psychology have application in China as well as in America. There are no absolute boundaries between cultures. Nor are there such abrupt boundaries between human beings anywhere. Later on we shall devote separate sections to show how all religions depend upon common traits in human nature, common problems of life, of death, and of fellowship, and face a common mysterious universe which gives a common bond to all human thinking. We are, however, deeply indebted to those who stress relativity for the sake of delivering us from a false narrowness and finality. We need to remember that history has always a relative element, is not subject to rational prediction or abstraction in terms of physical science, and must be studied with a fine eye, on the one hand, to what is individual and, on the other, to what belongs to our common humanity. Within the common needs and nature of man history exemplifies creative diversity. Its separate strands, enriching the whole, are not to be reduced to any one static standard capable of inclusive generalization. Yet this diversity must never deny the truth of human community in nature, need, or intellectual content. Albeit the two are far from congruent, there is a community both of seeking and of finding.

Relativity in science and history has engendered definite logical and psychological tendencies to exaggerations and distortions outside these domains. Disintegrative sophism still raises its devouring head selling half-truths for whole-truth and leading many astray. The demonic aspect of thought is that unless it be in right perspectives and proportions it becomes destructive and doubly dangerous because of the very truth it contains. Truth it is that works even in the distorted forms of thought; but distorted truth is dangerous to life. Both the errors of mind and the craftiness of the heart fasten on the truth in false thought and shield themselves, consciously or unconsciously, and admittedly or unadmittedly, even to the thinkers themselves. The corrosive acids of modernity have found few acids more capable of dissolving, not only false certainty and guilty dogmatism, but also the inner fabrics of creative faith and moral integrity than just this very acid of relativism. Those who seek truth unafraid, in a faith beyond their littleness, must be particularly on their guard against the insidious attacks of this acid. As we proceed throughout the book to discuss philosophy and religion we must ever be on the watch to fix the right relationship between identity and variety, the fixed and the fluctuating, the ultimate and the relative.

10. Another general tendency which has been aided by the scientific method is the stress on analysis and criticism in education to the sacrifice of sufficient stress on the appreciative and the creative. We have to be especially cautious on this point for the natural inertia of the human mind and the defensive nature of the human spirit make analysis and criticism easier and more congenial at any time than appreciation and creative vision. Yet there can be little question that the scientific ideal and mentality of our civilization has furthered the former and thwarted the latter. This is not the fault of science or of the scientist, except for their being eminently successful in their method! The trouble comes when the method is made a general rule for thought and life. The logical and the psychological tendencies which make this an easy thing to do are too mixed up to isolate. When educators make children learn to count on their fingers in order not to learn abstractions, they simply reveal a lack of understanding of knowledge as a social act. All important knowledge operates with the accumulated wisdom of the race, with knowledge that can be used deductively, though open to constant test as to its relevance for experience. This mistake (which has actually handicapped children who have not been allowed to learn the multiplication tables outright and definitely as proved facts from the beginning) is due to the educators' falling prey to the logical tendency. When men who lack creative ability, however, reduce scholarship even in the creative fields to the safe territories of learning facts, the psychological tendency of defensive thinking, and perhaps even of envy, has entered. Be that as it may, practically any sophomore can pick Shakespeare apart with much self-assurance, but who can write as he did? In some circles any sign of enthusiasm even for the great masters, let alone present leaders, shows poor taste and a lack of critical acumen. Historians can dig away at concrete facts, but

how many can make history live as a flaming torch illuminating the present? How many have been able to see the deeper unities and synoptic relations? There has been a swing of late toward synthesis as an ideal, but how far will it go in depth and power? The fact is that the historian must, of course, master science as a method and attitude, but to become fully competent he must go on to philosophy and theology, to the problems of ideas, human nature, and ends, perhaps even to the meaning of history itself in the light of our ultimate perspectives and concerns.[63]

In all of life, like history, literature, ethics, and education we must turn more and more to appreciation and creative synthesis. The masters are there to understand, admire, and emulate. When the greater genius comes along, let him go beyond them. But genius is rare. The masters have too often been analyzed and criticized in terms of abstract, ideal categories which belittle neither the commonplace instructor nor the callow student. The masters should be the ideals until greater masters make concrete higher ideals. Only those who are big enough to know their own smallness, honest enough to recognize what is better than their own, humble enough to appreciate it, and good enough to enjoy it, can find the contagious satisfaction that helps rather than hinders the human spirit. We have developed skill at the expense of vision. We have worshiped the finding of fact and suppressed our need for spontaneous enthusiasm. We have generally been frustrated, rather than free souls. We need criticism. Brand Blanshard is right in saying that if criticism spoils enjoyment, if analysis thwarts synthesis, if close inspection prevents vision, our intellectual muscles and the fiber of our spirits are too flabby.[64] We need the influence of science; we need criticism without mercy to false presupposi-

[63] Cf. Cochrane, *Christianity and Classical Culture,* Preface: "However difficult the religious and philosophic issues to be encountered, they cannot be neglected by the historian except at the cost of missing what is central to the events of the age."

[64] *The Nature of Thought,* Vol. I, p. 239: "A mind with muscles so flabby that it sickens under a little gymnastics is one whose creations we can afford to lose. And the fact seems to be that analysis, if not indulged to excess, is an aid, not a hindrance, to appreciation."

tions or sentimentalisms. But when the analysis and the critical attitude of science become the primary stress in life as a whole, facts obscure vision, validity thwarts adequacy, knowledge prevents understanding, and skill chokes creativity. Science is discipline for life. It must be in the service of life. We must have the fullest use and the least abuse of science. The true genius of science is revealed when we know and heed its limitations. "Only the believing ages are the fruitful ages."[65] True greatness has the capacity for rigorous criticism, but beyond that the capacity for simple and genuine appreciation, and if not for actual creation, at least for inner creative understanding and insight.

11. Another limit to the proper efficacy of science is that it is pluralistic. There is no science that combines the result of all the sciences; no method that subsumes and relates in terms of fact and meaning all the branches of science. The philosophy of science must use the speculative rather than the experimental method. In that sense it is not strict science. There is one method for chemistry and one for physics; one for biology and one for astronomy. Each science has its special field and tools within the logico-empirical field of knowledge. That field of knowledge is but a segment of all we experience. The whole province of values is entirely left out besides all those we have already discussed. Except for the common field to which they refer, it is more correct to speak of the sciences than of science. We cannot take any specific method of science that is actually used, to interpret whole-response. Each science must rather do its best work and contribute its own say to the full truth. That which deals with the whole must be a synoptic method and that which deals with living meaningfulness must itself have the capacity for living truth—up to the highest superorganic point of personal purpose. If we could stop the loose talk about "science says," and substitute the exact language as far as possible of each science, we should have gained considerably toward combating a popular use of the term which is often defensive and destructive. If science is used in the sense of disciplined intelligence, we cannot stop with the logico-empirical realm and the

[65] Goethe, in G. A. Gordon, *Immortality and the New Theodicy*, p. 56.

descriptive approach; if science is used strictly, we must keep in mind its pluralistic nature. "The spirit," for instance, cannot be studied by "science"; if such a concept has any meaning at all within the logico-empirical realm it must be studied by chemistry, physics, biology, experimental psychology, etc. It can then be determined more exactly whether the particular method is adapted to deal with the particular question or whether it falls outside the limits of its proper efficacy. Science is pluralistic in nature and not synoptic to deal as "science" with the interpretation of whole-response.

12. The general tendency of scientific method, moreover, is to reduce the content of truth to fit the method. The whole tendency of the method, as we have seen, is, furthermore, toward what can be proved in the laboratory or by exact mathematical calculation. Consequently the spiritual tends to be reduced to the psychological; the psychological tends to be reduced to the biological; the biological tends to be reduced to the chemical; the chemical tends to be reduced to physics; physics, many say, tends toward the mathematical; and then in some instances the whole tends to evaporate into some vague mysticism. Or put our reduction above this way: Spirit is nothing but mind; mind is nothing but capacity for organic adjustment; the organic is not vital in itself but the outcome of combinations of chemical compounds; chemical compounds are forms of energy; energy can be treated best as form of flux or pattern of force; and sometimes the interest goes over into the problems of pattern. Thus quality is even under pressure to be translated by means of dynamic terms into certain functions of quantity. Right now we may be emerging from the heyday of this reductionistic period, but many will recall rather recent attacks on morals as conventional and on spirit as imaginary simply because they could not *as such* be reduced to any point where they could be treated with the exactitude of science. The requirements of method have been confused with a doctrine of reality not only by the popular mind but all too often also by the academic mind. This confusion has caused untold anguish of spirit and starved the moral convictions of untold numbers into moral collapse. When

we come to discuss the problems of the ultimate we may find that a clear seeing of certain truths will remove road-blocks on the way to adequate seeing and believing; the reason for our poverty is mostly methodological and psychological, although here, as ever, only perfect wisdom can untangle the strands of our not seeing because we have not the opportunity to see or of not seeing because we want not to see.

13. The tendency of the scientific method has also been to split value from existence. The natural world can be tested; it is uniform dependably enough to lend itself to scientific investigation. The method of science has, in fact, been developed in connection with the concrete investigation of nature. The world of value, on the other hand, with its unaccountable choices, its personal preferences, its changing intensities varies from person to person and from time to time. Naturally this world of value seemed to lack truth and reality since it could not be dealt with successfully with the most successful road to truth that modern man knew. It was altogether understandable that many should begin to think in terms of a world of existence, the truth of which can be tested and confirmed, over against a world of value grasped only arbitrarily by our emotions and by our emotional thinking. The less thinking was colored by emotions the more true it was supposed to be; external and part-thinking thus came to take the place of whole-thinking.

Because we cannot put a thermometer into our mouths and expertly measure goodness the question of goodness became a matter of embarrassment to method and in numerous instances, especially in academic circles, was either ignored or ridiculed. Professors who were asked to speak about situations which bothered students or to declare themselves on moral and spiritual issues often took a patronizing attitude saying that they spoke only on topics that they could know something about. The tendency to ignore this primary field of the human spirit was both logical and psychological. With respect to the logical tendency, the mind's drive for clarity and exactness was thwarted, while with respect to the psychological tendency, the spirit was uncomfortably reminded that there are crucial realms of life which cannot be controlled merely in terms of external manipulation. For these reasons the modern mind generally looked both skeptically and wistfully at any and all efforts to establish the truth about values. Science could not help us to settle either what was needful or what was true. False science could say that this question was unimportant or beyond all knowledge. True science had to stick to its task. In the meantime both individuals and society groped for light in the field of value; and in the world of half-truth where value was ignored, false cosmologies sapped initiative and energy. Whitehead has rightly written that "the separations of perceptual fact from emotional fact; and of causal fact from emotional fact; and of perceptual fact, emotional fact, and causal fact, from purposive fact; have constituted a complex of bifurcations, fatal to a satisfactory cosmology."[66] This piercing observation ties up this last point with some of the preceding questions as well.

Kant's splitting away the world known through science and mathematics from the world known through moral judgments, for instance, was mostly the result of the problems posed by the development of the scientific method. Often we read that this regrettable split in the modern world between value and existence was caused by his philosophy. His philosophy no doubt aggravated it. The very split in his philosophy, however, was mostly caused by the limitations inherent in the scientific method to deal adequately with the most high and the most real. His methodological split had the effect of further splitting modern thinking, since a great number of thinkers instead of seeing Kant as a whole made one or another of his approaches the only or chief road to truth. Thus some followed the first critique; some, the second; some, the third; but some fortunately also stayed in the full light of the proper proportion of all three as the only full orbit of insight. The split even went into theology. Ritschl distinguished sharply between theoretical and value judgments and to make more sure of the separation

[66] *Process and Reality*, p. 444.

he then distinguished between concomitant and independent value judgments.[67] The former accompanied all theoretical judgments while the others were distinctly religious judgments. Modern theology has since then seen a good many variations of this theme where science in some way or other dealt with existence while religion dealt with value. Whether the most high is also the most real has sometimes and in some circles been a problem to be definitely ignored or soft-pedaled. Some simply deny the relation outright. Religion "works" in experience; it satisfies our emotional cravings; religion helps to change society—such statements have often taken the place of the real claim of religion that it must do its work "by way of its truth."[68]

What is of utmost significance, practically, is that this split tended to put the study of value into a decidedly inferior place in education. And with regard to that intangible *status quo* in general which most deeply influences people, men's thoughts were decisively swayed from their earliest schooling into a conviction that what went on in the laboratories was of utmost importance while what went on in the class of philosophy or in the halls of worship was both less important and less real. This feeling was spread in literature, in newspapers, from lecture platform, over the radio, in business mart, in college forum—and in all the subtly indirect as well as direct ways by which men's minds are molded—until this attitude became typical of our times. This generation knows, however, that the ways of science without the vision of inclusive purpose can mean dark death and the setting back of the clocks of time. The laboratory without responsible whole-response to the common good may mean the burying of our hopes instead of the proud nursing of our wonder child of progress. Scientific control by the wrong people can turn the world quickly into a place where

[67] Cf. Ritschl, *Justification and Reconciliation,* pp. 204–205: "We have therefore to distinguish between *concomitant* and *independent* value-judgments. The former are operative and necessary in all theoretical cognition. . . . But all perception of moral ends or moral hindrances are independent value-judgments."

[68] Hocking, *The Meaning of God in Human Experience,* p. 139: "Religion does its work by way of its truth."

science itself must suffer because objectivity is not allowed where it is needed and freedom is banished where it is the very bread of life. If we are to find what is most important and most real, we must at least not be blinded by the logical and the psychological temptations of method which when properly resisted lead to truth and healing but when out of control blur our perspectives and bring on violence. We cannot long live with ingenious means without great ends. Ends, however, are in the realm of value and must neither be split from the question of truth nor be made secondary to the laboratory technique.

We have called this chapter the circle of science because the reader may draw a circle around that field which properly belongs under the scientific method. Take any two poles and draw a circle through them. One pole will be that of the strictest possible laboratory verification; the other will be that of pure logic. At either of these poles validity will be at its maximum whereas adequacy will be at its minimum. That means that where the field of knowledge can best be tested in public terms there is also the least of complete explanation of all the factors involved including the total background of relationships without which that bit of knowledge would lose its significance. All live knowledge is a combination of actual and formal knowledge and the fuller and more significant the area for meaningful living the less it can be reduced to mere form or to mere fact. On the other hand, the more adequate the knowledge is the less valid it is in this sense of public testing. The whole circle, even of the field of science, cannot be reduced to one of the sciences, and all the more, cannot be reduced to one syllogism or to one laboratory experiment. This is a fact generally characteristic of knowledge. Yet the prestige and popularity of science in the modern world has shifted the emphasis far too much toward validity and has therefore undermined the vigorous and fully supported investigation, and acceptance, of the fields that must deal with adequacy as a primary standard.

Neither validity nor adequacy is to be equated with truth. Truth cannot be had without the fullest combination of both. In later chapters the reader can draw similar circles for philosophy and for religion. When all the circles are put together, for the mid-point of all must be the same, they will be seen to handle overlapping fields, but science will have its chief function in relation of physical nature and to the purely formal realms of logic and mathematics; whereas philosophy and religion, although both deal with the whole of experience, will be seen to have additional areas and differing chief functions. Yet all must have access to the whole field of human knowledge and compare notes co-operatively with those dedicated to, and trained in, each special field. Each circle will have peculiar problems, peculiar approaches, peculiar tendencies, and peculiar temptations.

Let it be said, and let it be said again and again, that all fields cover as far as possible all aspects of knowledge; they deal with the whole gamut of knowledge. We live in a universe and all knowledge is related to the whole truth. There must be no invidious barriers, no attempt to keep any field above public inspection either as to method or as to conclusion. All knowledge must be put as far as possible within the common grasp. Terms must have no hidden meanings. They must be defined as accurately as the thinker, or group of thinkers, can define them. We may well rejoice in killing all our "sacred cows." Truth, as far as we can reach it, is that which cannot be knocked down by those who are both fully honest and truly competent. Our sole concern is to find the best way that each method can co-operate. The more science can explain, the better. We cannot long live on illusions or on appeals to ignorance. We must live by knowledge, not by the lack of it. Much talk of religion, for instance, as dealing with the unknown is defensive on the part of the religious; and offensive by those who do not believe in religion. Those of us who are in the field of religion by special vocation must welcome all truth wholeheartedly: from science both within its own proper sphere, and as far as possible beyond. The only barrier to method must be intrinsic. It must be the unfitness of that particular approach to deal with this particular problem from this particular point of view.

The field of knowledge is like a field in which oats, rye, and wheat are to be harvested. Suppose that each one requires a certain kind of screen for threshing. Because oats require one kind of screen, and because this screen can thresh the cleanest, should we not be foolish not to thresh the rye and the wheat, even though we needed them for full diet, simply because we could not use the same screens as for oats and could not thresh as cleanly? All threshing ought to be done as thoroughly as can be done according to the nature of the grain, and then all the food ought to be eaten and enjoyed for the fullest health and well-being. There are basic problems which science cannot handle and yet we must deal with them as thoroughly as we can in order to obtain satisfactory life, personally and socially. The problems of adequate authority for faith and life, of adequate motivation for the right use of personal freedom and for social living, and the general unitive factors both for academic life and for civilization are of special importance. They have especially heavy bearing on what is most important and most real, on what is needful and what is true. We must, therefore, turn to the next circle, that of philosophy, to examine to what extent it can deal most adequately with questions like these and what, in turn, are its peculiar problems and limitations.

CHAPTER III

The Circle of Philosophy

Our attitude toward the field and task of philosophy is the same as toward those of science. Every field of knowledge shares an interest in, a responsibility for, and a relation to the whole field of human knowledge. It should be encouraged to do as much work and to cover as much territory as it profitably can. By being vigorously self-critical each field can discover its own natural approach including both its inherent strength and its inherent weakness. There must be no external limitations arbitrarily imposed; neither must there be, oppositely, any attempt from within any field to fence off certain areas of knowledge as private domains for investigation. There should be no hanging for intellectual poaching. All of us must be willing to see the truth together for the common good. We must all be thankful whenever we are shown that we are harvesting diminishing returns because we have overextended our area of cultivation beyond the point of greatest yield for our special kind of crop. We have to be on our watch against the natural temptation to make our own approach the most important, or even the only one, and to identify our own sense of security and emotional stability with the exclusive competence of our own method. There is such a thing as a *blinding* self-seriousness.

Modern philosophy, in great areas, is on the defensive. It is under constant and heavy attack from several directions. Scientists, in the first place, are attacking philosophy. An outstanding scholar at one of the world's great universities, for instance, recently made much sport of its chief philosopher, a man of exceptional profundity and learning. This critic of philosophy "worshipped at the holy altar of fact" and fairly spat at people who descended to spin out theories of pure speculation for public admiration, dignifying the mockery by the sacred name of scholarship! The charge that science deals with fact while philosophy deals with speculation, with vague, unsubstantiated generalities, is too common to be elaborated. Only the term "contempt" can do justice to the tone with which certain colleagues are dismissed by scientists as "philosophers." To many scientists the idea is preposterous that science can from now on advance most markedly and most importantly only if leading scientists acquire philosophic competence or if great philosophic minds contribute importantly to the method of science. Many scientists feel strongly, particularly when they become informal and intimate, that philosophy has no important function or field whatever within the whole field of human knowledge. Fortunately not all scientists have this point of view. Many are most humble and open-minded. These refuse to be arbitrary and destructively defensive even though they cannot always follow, either in thought or in interest, philosophic explorations. Some, however, have transcended their own method and have gone over into philosophy to find the fuller answers to their questions. But generally speaking, at least until most recently, the great tradition of philosophy as the rationally competent interpretation of reality as a whole has been basically questioned by the rank and file of scientists.

The idea of scientific positivism, the theory that science is pure description without any theory of reality, moreover, has had mixed results. A good number of scientists have now seen science for what it is, an operational method of limited scope, and have consequently openly disavowed the connection between science as a method and naturalism as a metaphysics. But of those scientists, some have merely gone over to a general positivism and have landed in a paralyzing skepticism as far as all knowledge is concerned. Others have coupled scientific positivism with some kind of irrational philosophy or with some pre-critical, irrational faith, thus in effect compartmentalizing knowledge, somewhat along the lines of the double reason of the Middle Ages. As a matter of fact, the tendency in modern science and mathematics to establish self-contained systems of knowledge, based on the limited presuppositions, operationally, of a particular field, without sufficient regard to knowledge as a whole, to some universal base or continuum, has aided the disintegration of common knowledge in the modern world. Discontinuity has tended to become plain cacophony, whereas it should constitute merely, at the most, a working atonality within the universal symphony of knowledge.

In the second place, the modern criticism of philosophy, in the full sense of the term, comes also from within its own field. In a way the classical tradition began to disintegrate with the rise of British empiricism and came close to death in Kant. Even if those are right who maintain that Kant himself meant all his *Critiques* to be complementary approaches to knowledge and intended his posthumous work to constitute the fulfilling synthesis, it nevertheless remains true that the power with which he treated each approach has helped a good deal to split up philosophy into self-sufficient strands, though falsely so. After Kant only a part of philosophic inquiry stayed within the classical pattern. There is a cry today for a return to pre-Kantian philosophy. But history moves forward, not backward. The breakup which Kant helped to further of what Lovejoy calls "the great chain of being" was doubtless necessary, for it assumed uncritically the equation of thought and being, and theologically of goodness and being, as though these were intrinsic relations of rational thinking instead of dynamic combinations of faith, reason, and action. The hurricane of philosophic destruction which has been sweeping the earth has cleared the ground of much dead wood. Though new growth is sparse and spindling, the time is at hand for verdant and vigorous creative growth of interpretative thought.

Partly as an outgrowth of Kant's first *Critique,* in line with the growing and shaping influence of reductionist science across the centuries, there sprang up a veritable flowering of positivisms, of evolutionary positivisms, making thought nothing but an instrument of biological adjustment, of scientific positivisms limiting truth to the knowledge obtained by strict science, of historical positivisms, or sociological positivisms, of humanistic positivisms, and now of logical and linguistic positivisms! Away with ethics as a branch of reliable knowledge! Away with the philosophy of religion! Away with all metaphysics! Surely a careful reading of this entire tendency of thought, including all its numerous varieties, would make us see that many have been trying to move the tree of knowledge far from its proper place in the midst of the garden of life and have succeeded far too well in clipping close some of its branches that when rightly used are for the healing of the nations. In classical philosophy experience points beyond itself, generally, to signify what is most important and most real in the larger pattern of reality. In much modern philosophy the basic questions concerning the outside world have been reduced to aspects of experience. The question is crucial, however, to what extent experience merely is or also has significance.

What again of the followers of the second *Critique?* What of all the philosophies which make action more important than thought even as a way of knowing, and often even reduce knowing almost altogether to ways of acting? What of the philosophies of the will to live, the will to power, or the unconscious, of economic determinism, of pragmatism, of the unconscious, of fictionalism, and of vital creativity grasped only intuitively, beyond extensive meaning, within the life-processes themselves? What of the modern stress on existential logic which scorns the tameness and falsity of coherent meaning? And has not the third *Critique,* furthermore, had its influence? Have there not been some who have declared religion, man's very reaction to the ultimate, to be nothing but a realm of beauty to be known principally through imagination, symbol, or empathy? "Beauty is truth, truth beauty";[1] the aesthetic category yields the deepest insight into reality. Surely it is obvious to even the casual observer of the thought of the last hundred years that philosophy as an independent field dealing reliably and competently with reality as a whole has been questioned and even largely repudiated by numerous thinkers even within its own field. If philosophy cannot deal with science, on the one hand, and

[1] Keats, "Ode on a Grecian Urn."

with religion, on the other, the full classic claims of philosophy, in any case, are repudiated.

Philosophy has also been under heavy attack from many religious leaders. Conservatives who cannot, or will not, cope with the problems of modern thought, and emotionally unstable individuals who need to depend upon some inerrant authority of external nature beyond the vexations of mind, have welcomed the modern undermining of philosophy. If philosophy is impotent to deal with the knowledge of ultimate reality and with the absolute imperatives of conduct, though it cannot prove religion to be right neither can it prove it to be false. Some conservatives, therefore, have welcomed its declared demise. Philosophy has, on the whole, moreover, been more hostile than friendly to vital religion in modern times. Not without reason do some who are on the defensive, guarding what means most to them, consider a weak friend not worth having if he is accompanied by a far stronger enemy. Philosophy is scorned as a friend if it is at the same time a bigger hindrance as an enemy. Much modern philosophy, moreover, has also been out of order, wooden, superficial, and falsely destructive of both truth and morals. Many religious leaders who care for humanity in its struggle for right and truth have been justifiably suspicious of vain philosophies.

As so often happens, the religious conservatives have found strong allies in the religious radicals. Much of the time constructive liberals have been uncomfortably squeezed in the middle. But after all it is easier to stand steady in the middle, and safer, with less chance of falling over the sides of the ship of truth! The radicals in rather large numbers do away with philosophy to show that we can study religion phenomenologically, historically, etc., but beyond that, they contend, the philosopher is merely dealing with sweeping generalizations, with theories that cannot be proved, and with claims about reality and conduct which represent ingenious rationalizations. The fideists are generally critical, often heatedly, of any use of reason to vindicate, even in the broad sense, any kind of idealistic or spiritualistic metaphysics. Thus for opposite reasons the conservatives in large numbers and the radicals in perhaps larger proportion welcome the undermining of philosophy as a guide to truth and life in the modern world. With all this criticism of philosophy, on the one hand, which we have not tried to describe but only to suggest, and with the classic claims for it, on the other, still held by many competent thinkers, we must be most careful as we try to open up the basic field and function of philosophy in the whole field of human knowledge.

Before we turn to this basic task we had better point out that this dismissal of philosophy is due not only to intellectual problems but to many of the same logical and psychological tendencies which we traced in the last chapter. It is greatly a part of the general spirit of our times. The disintegration of life and thought which has followed the victory, not of true science, but of an over-inflated, "quack" scientific method and attitude, has touched by its acids of skepticism also the field of philosophy. The reaction against the whole classical tradition is the victory of an atomistic, nominalistic scientism which is the root malady of our age. Today we see reactions toward realism in the classical sense in the modern stress, for instance, on *gestalt,* or whole-pattern, in psychology, on organism in philosophy, and in attempts all along the line to retrieve some of the cohesion, unity, and stability of the classical tradition. Nevertheless the general mentality of our age must change before philosophy can get back its importance in the life of learning and of practical decision. But this in turn can change only as hand in hand with this desire to get back to constructive steadiness we see and acknowledge both our mistakes and the large problems of the past which were not bothering its thinkers. The remedy lies in the correcting of our mistakes and in the finding of the deeper, newer, and more creative unities which alone can make us march together both with clear consciences and with firm steps. An age rent asunder by skepticism and relativism can hardly pick itself up and put itself together again sufficiently to appreciate and believe in inwardly compelling standards for truth and conduct. Inward compulsion is strong enough only when it is the willing whole-response to whole-truth.

In order to have as much clarity as we can command we shall

compare the field and function of philosophy with the fields and
functions of science and religion. After that we shall go on to compare standards of philosophy with the standards of science and
religion. Needless to say, the treatment in all instances will be suggestive rather than exhaustive. Although we shall keep in mind,
moreover, the bulk of historic emphasis on the part of the different
disciplines, our task is not historic analysis but, rather, for the
main part, the establishing of the standards which are inherent in
the subjects and their natural relations among themselves according to their intrinsic position in the whole field of human knowledge.

In general, then, we can say that the field and function of science
are pluralistic while philosophy deals with the whole of reality.
Science particularizes while philosophy generalizes. There is one
method for biology. This cannot be applied directly with full satisfaction, for instance, to astronomy; and the astronomical method,
again, is hardly transferable to psychology. Philosophy, on the
other hand, tries to systematize all that man knows in order that
we may understand relatedly the world in which we live. Philosophy takes the whole field of human knowledge for its object of
inquiry and deals with it primarily in order to interpret it. These
differences are basic intentions, tasks, and directions. They are not
fences separating science from science, science from philosophy, or
vice versa. Astronomy uses chemistry and physics. History must
know psychology in order to interpret rightly significant move-
ments and decisions. Botany and ecology have much in common.
Even though co-operative in function and partly congruent in
fields, each science has nevertheless its distinctive function alongside of, as well as along with, the other sciences. Similarly physics
may use philosophy; and modern philosophies have to pay careful
heed to what the physicists are telling us. Scientists can turn to
philosophy for aid in the general problems of method, finding
there ideas which have decided bearing on their particular science.
Gestalt psychology, for instance, can both learn from and also
teach philosophy by its findings. It can establish that perception

of the whole precedes perception of the parts; but is it not philosophical if it claims that an integrator can be *understood* fully only in terms of his own wholeness? A teacher of *gestalt* psychology remarked that the personal whole can be understood only in terms of the larger whole of the relevant environment. Here science and philosophy surely co-operate to arrive at conclusions. An organismic philosophy would then go on to say that no part of the environment can be understood except in terms of the larger whole of which it is a part. There can obviously be no impenetrable barrier between psychology as a science and the bearing on it of the philosophical and theological problems of psychology. An impatient and premature attitude would falsify the field and the function of each science by a defensive, easy oversimplification of them. Yet the fact remains, when all this has been readily acknowledged, that the intent, function, and basic delimitation of the fields of science are operationally different. There is a division of labor in the whole field of human knowledge which must be observed and respected, even though it is ever subject to the inspection of whole-truth, as well as by other part-truths from their particular angles of approach. In this sense science is pluralistic while philosophy is the systematic interpretation of all that we know.

The *field* of science is the logico-empirical, or that of mathematically measurable sense-data, whereas philosophy deals with the whole field of human knowledge. As we have said in the preceding chapter, science does not deal except *post factum* with large fields of direct experience like value, ideals, freedom, etc. because they are not part of its self-chosen and natural field. True science simply excludes them, not as unreal, that is metaphysically, but as irrelevant, that is methodologically. Philosophy, on the other hand, deals with all experience, striving even to understand and to interpret the furthest flights of spirit, and to relate this and all to the generality of experience. The *function* of science and of philosophy may seem precisely the same: to know. But science is more centered on its task to describe while philosophy has for its chief undertaking to relate. Science describes; philosophy relates. From another angle science analyzes while philosophy explains. Science finds the nature of the object while philosophy concerns itself chiefly with its meaning. Science records the fact and its bearing on the world of fact while philosophy brings to bear on the meaning of the fact the meaning of the world and on the meaning of the world the meaning of that fact.

The "philosophy of science" is a most dangerous term. It can mean at least two different things. It may mean the systematic treatment of all which the sciences have in common. This is, strictly speaking, no philosophy, but a compilation of facts already united by an assumed universe. It can, of course, be considered a miniature philosophy but it had better be called the principles and content of natural knowledge. Abstraction may be made of scientific method by virtue of which the general principles of disciplined knowing are exhibited. Yet such procedures are dangerous if they are conceived as self-sufficient tasks independent of the whole field of human knowledge. Because of the subtlety of the psychological and the logical tendencies involved it is easy for the inquirer to fall prey to the idea that the physical realm is to be equated with truth and that the principles of disciplined knowing are confined to the sciences, or to the implications of the sciences such as "the philosophy of science." The philosophy of science according to the second use of the term, which is correct, is the interpretation systematically of the facts, principles, and implications of science in the light of the whole of knowledge. Science is thus lifted up for inspection, interpretation, and evaluation into the full light of all its relationships. Such a procedure benefits both science by its seeing itself in the light of the general consideration of method and of the whole content of knowledge, giving it suggestions for its own work, meaning, and direction; and also philosophy by its seeing its total content and vision enriched by those who, although they have taken the general perspective as an orientation, have yet devoted their major effort to the understanding more fully that section of reality which is represented by science. Such inquiry is open equally to both the scientists and the philosophers with the proviso that either side has to acquire hard-earned competence in the other field. The constant temptation, it is easy to see, is to be superficial on one side or on the other. But more and more we need thorough work within concentric circles. The circles of science and philosophy need hard working by men who have spent years in the cultivation of knowledge, of critical method, and of creative imagination.

If we now turn to compare the field and function of philosophy with the field and function of religion we find that as far as fields are concerned they are identical. To be completely accurate we should perhaps use the terms "philosophy" and "theology." Philosophy is the interpretation of the whole of experience *centering* in the here and now; theology is the interpretation of religion, that is, of the whole of experience, *centering* in the complete combination, obviously only partially here and now, of the most important and the most real. We have used the term "religion" up to this point, even with regard to its interpretation, in deference to a common usage, as, for instance, in the phrase "science, philosophy, and religion," and in order also to avoid all thoughts of particular theologies. From here on we shall more and more introduce the right word, but feel free to use the general term as the occasion may warrant. The term "God" or *"theos,"* whatever the right content may be, stands formally for what is ultimate in the interpretation of whole-response. As to the scope of their fields for investigation, however, there is no difference at all between theology and philosophy. Both interpret the whole of human knowledge.

The intensity of cultivation differs. That is due to difference in function. Later we shall see that it is also due to difference in standards. As far as the difference in function goes, philosophy is knowledge for its own sake regardless of its uses and implications. Scientists, artists, philosophers may and, indeed, should, as persons, be constructively interested in the total uses and implications of their fields; they should be responsibly religious. But we must not mix this idea into the question of the specific function of each discipline of knowledge within the whole field and function of human knowledge. Theology is the interpretation of whole-response. It can never take the place of science or of philosophy.

It needs them. They supply it with knowledge. They, in turn, need theology, at least indirectly, as we shall see, for total direction, for the authority of the truth which is based on the full combination of faith and rational knowledge, and for the motivation that will keep civilization orderly and creative. Religion, constructively clarified, gives individuals and society both lift and leading. We have now anticipated later discussions, but only in order to clarify necessary distinctions.

We can illustrate this difference in function by a brief discussion of five or six major fields of philosophy. The fields we choose are epistemology, or how we know; logic, or the laws of thought as thought; cosmology, or the kind of world we have; ontology, or what is the most real; ethics, or the analysis of values and the laws of conduct; and religion, or what is both most important and most real. We begin with the first two: epistemology and logic.

The problem of knowing in general is crucial for philosophy. The long centuries have witnessed debates between realists and idealists, or between empiricists and rationalists. The ages have seen, and will no doubt keep seeing, an indefinite number of variations of these critical questions. But religion is not concerned with how we know as such. Only as the mode of knowing affects the content of religious knowledge is religion as religion concerned. Religion must explore all denials of its high claim that the most high is ultimately the most real. But the question of knowledge is not to be equated with the question of religion. Many able thinkers would consider that the limitation of reason with regard to ultimate questions leaves the more room open for faith. The ultimate cannot, of course, be logically proved, they say, except for being confirmed in its own terms, without making something else more ultimate. The final judgment as to what is ultimately most important and most real must consequently always be a faith judgment. The infinite cannot be grasped as it infinitely is by the finite and accordingly can be known only if it makes itself known to the finite—for instance, as spirit. Thus reason curtailed is more helpful than reason exalted. Reason debased is revelation enhanced. *Thus reason many*. Religion has vital interest in the bearing of knowledge on salvation. It has little interest, or may even be un-interested, in philosophic problems of epistemology as such. The function and intensity of cultivation of the problem of knowledge differ. The philosophical task will obviously be more appreciated by other religious thinkers who use an inclusive definition of rea-son, who refuse to confuse the form of reason with any concrete content, who want to rid reason of its identification arbitrarily with reductionist standards, and who agree with Bonaventura that "reason must be radically good since we have it from God."[2] The fact remains, however, that though the problem of knowing is a field both for religion and for philosophy, the function and in-tensity of cultivation do differ. The former is interested in knowing in so far as it refers to man's ultimate salvation and his conduct in this perspective and with this motivation. The latter is interested chiefly in knowing for its own sake. The former is inter-ested in epistemology for the truth that saves. The latter, for the truth of the knowing process itself.

Similarly, and even more so, religion is little interested in logic for its own sake. What difference does it make to most of theology how precisely logic is defined? The logicians may get heated over the question of traditional *versus* Hegelian logic, or *versus* sym-bolic logic. Obviously Hegelian logic, coming close to metaphysics, bears rather directly on the religious issue. Exact, algebraic logic, shunning content and intention, has little bearing on theology—except as this logic is made into a metaphysics negatively, like logical positivism. Yet inductive logic, being part of the general development of scientific nominalistic method, has real bearing on religion in so far as it has bearing, albeit negatively, on the super-spectively deductive nature of religious knowledge, which we are shortly to discuss, and on the entire question, for that matter, of the nature and standards of truth. Theology cannot be indifferent to logic; it must know logic; it must learn much from it in order to acquire accuracy of thinking; and it must be able to select the most adequate theories and to challenge the presuppositions of any false logic that would deny arbitrarily its highest claim. Philosophy

[2] Gilson, *The Philosophy of St. Bonaventura*, p. 93.

is interested in logic as logic, as the science of abstract thought (although even the logicians cannot agree on a definition because, again, of the relation of logic to the whole field of human knowledge!). Yet theology is interested in logic only in so far as it has a bearing on whole-response. Logic to theology must ever be related to salvation, that is, to the correct pattern of whole-reason within whole-decision. As far as the content rather than the form of truth goes the concern of theology is with whatever light the laws of logic, or correct thinking, can throw on the competency of reason to deal with what is most important and what is most real and to what extent they are ultimately one and the same.

With respect to cosmology and ontology the question is different. They affect religion critically. The questions of history, of progress and evil, and of all the countless implications of cosmology have vital bearing on religion. Especially is this true whenever cosmology is made into ontology, that is, whenever the world the way it now is, is made the standard for truth. Religion receives its content from cosmology as well as from the nature of the self and from its thinking beyond cosmology. The fields are the same for both philosophy and religion. The function is also partly the same, namely, to understand the world in which we live. Religion cannot react rightly without knowing rightly. Yet the functions differ with respect to ways of cultivation and the areas of *intensive* cultivation of the same field. Just as psychology is chiefly interested in understanding the self while religion is chiefly interested in changing and saving it, so philosophy has for its chief task the understanding of the world while religion has for its chief tasks the changing of the world in so far as it can be changed, and the interpreting the world with a view to what is most important and most real. Right religion relates the superspective reality, which receives its content from the highest instance of historic occurrence, but understood as prior to our history and as extending uncomprehensively beyond it, to our present historic situation with a view to the conserving of what is best in it, the changing of what is wrong with it, and finally the saving of the whole of history for the sake of, and by means of, the full combination of the ultimately most important and most real. Harold Bosley rightly says that "philosophy endeavors to systematize our knowledge of the world, whereas theology attempts to relate such philosophical first principles to human needs."[3] That is one side of theology's interest in cosmology. The center of the perspective, however, lies elsewhere: in the grounding of cosmology in an adequate ontology.

This question of ontology, moreover, is crucial. Much of the rest of the book will be devoted to it. Here *the field* of philosophy and theology are the same—to discover what the real truth of our experience is and indicates. *The functions* differ in that philosophy is speculative or interpretative while theology is through and through existential, that is, completely concerned as unavoidable whole-response with the question of man's nature and destiny in relation to what is most important and most real. The method must constitute the chief difference between theology and philosophy. The method involves standards. In the second half of this chapter we shall see how the two disciplines differ in these respects. But even here, if we keep in mind that the main function of philosophy is to interpret the field while the main function of theology is to obtain the authority and the motivation which, being rooted in the truth beyond the actuality of experience, can change it in satisfactory directions, we can see how the kind of cultivation and the intensity of cultivation in certain areas would differ. The most important aspect of ontology for theology is that reality, inasmuch as it includes actuality, is of such a nature that it can be radically changed. Were this not true, religion in its highest claim neither would be true nor would it matter.

The standards of science and philosophy are obviously quite different. The standards of science we have described at length in the last chapter. Science deals, as far as possible, with measurable sense data. Its method makes quantity a determining condition. Quality must somehow be translated into the language of quantity. By quantity we do not mean "stuff," but "measure." Measurableness is a condition of method in science. Science is highly interested in measuring. Science is concerned with numbers and meas-

[3] Bosley, *The Quest for Religious Certainty*, p. 46.

urements. Its concern with individuals is mainly as it exemplifies the many; with individual aspects mainly as they typify general aspects. Science is thus interested in such abstractions as are at any time capable of being illustrated by appropriate particulars. It is concerned with hypotheses, theories, laws. Science is concerned with concrete operations illustrating the characteristic nature of things. Its theories must be capable of direct demonstration in function or in fact, or in the relation of function and of fact, by controllable operations constantly confirming the theories. It is concerned with description leading to prediction, and with prediction that can constantly be checked by new description. Science centers on the notion of the reading of theory directly out of fact, out of the function of facts, or out of the facts of function, and on the notion of the direct applicability of theory to fact or function.

The modern concern with the bearing of philosophy on science tends to re-emphasize the classical unity of knowledge. Science in this sense is the broad verification of the general aspects of sense data by appeal to the more general considerations of knowledge. It is for the most part contrary to the drift toward ever further specialization which has been one basic aspect of the scientific advance. On the other hand, there is still a strong modern stress on specialization, on positivism in science, on the independence of operational fields of all philosophical considerations and of all obligation to harmonize the findings of any science with the whole field of human knowledge. This emphasis tends more than ever to stress direct applicability rather than general coherence. Obviously both applicability and coherence or validity and adequacy are present in any intellectual inquiry. Yet science is peculiarly dominated by applicability, or operational capacity, while philosophy is peculiarly dominated by its search for full coherence.

In one sense science is the only pure knowledge we have. True science, contrary to its logical and psychological, abstractionist perversions, is interested in the individual. If there were only one instance of one thing, true science would describe it for what it is. It would simply say, "That is that." It would record the fact.

Naturally it would try to relate it to any one science, and to every science that could study and classify it. But if the exceptional happened—that this instance of fact had no continuity with the rest of nature at any point except physical location (a farfetched and rather inconceivable example), true science would leave it for what it is. Philosophy would have to try to relate it to the whole. It would have to ask itself the question why it is and is there. For philosophy *as philosophy* the interest would be completely in its relation to the whole. We must not, however, distort the difference. Philosophy is not concerned with mere generality, with merely the relations of and within the whole. Science and philosophy would both be curious to interpret it for what it is in itself. Both would try to relate it all they could to other knowledge within their fields. But science, having failed, would be less upset than philosophy. Science takes for granted the general unity and continuity of its field. It works within a universe. But its main interest is pure description, direct applicability. Of late it has had to wrestle with discontinuities. As science it can simply recognize that there are such. It will always try its best to relate them to general chains of causation. If it fails, however, it has merely to record its findings and to leave the question open. Philosophy, however, being the interpretation of the whole, must wrestle for its very life with the questions of discontinuity and must ever seek to weave what is partially discontinuous into fuller relations and meanings. In this sense science is interested in the particular and philosophy in the whole of experience. In this sense the standards of science are pluralistic while those of philosophy must be universal. In this sense the standard of science is direct applicability while that of philosophy is coherence.

The circle of philosophy has three main standards. These are taken from its history and its nature. The first is inclusiveness. Philosophy deals with the whole of experience. It deals with science, with history, with religion, with inner reactions and reflections, with outward behavior, with the description and with the standards of conduct, with actuality, with possibility, with reality

—in short with all that can be known. No philosophy can be considered adequate which accepts partial evidence or starts with a preconceived or arbitrarily selected line of inquiry. Specialized philosophies, like those of aesthetics, of religion, and of science, lack full perspective and meaning if they are confined to the perspective and to the function of their special subjects. They must rather all view their special subjects in the light of the whole. The philosophy of religion, for instance, is not merely the systematic development of the presuppositions of one religion and their application to all areas of interpretation and life; it deals rather with all religions and with what is inclusively true of the whole subject of religion. This fact has led some philosophers to claim that the philosophy of religion, since there are no congruent areas of interpretation among the several religions, can deal only with the formal nature of religion. If this claim were true, then philosophy would indeed be limited to the formal nature of religion. We have, however, already analyzed and dismissed this false claim. The point is, in any case, that philosophy deals with the whole of knowledge and that this whole itself constitutes one of its strong standards. If special fields of knowledge are treated by philosophy proper, they must be seen in the light of the whole. Inclusiveness is a necessary standard of philosophy. Philosophy deals with the interpretation of all that we can know and whole-knowledge has a definite bearing on all partial knowledge.

The second standard of philosophy is coherence. The whole is not only inclusive. It must also be systematically interpreted. Philosophy lives in a universe. It seeks to know the necessary relations among the parts. It endeavors to unfold the underlying unity. It tries to understand and to fit together the parts as they cohere, stick, cleave, or coexist one with the other and with the entire sum and substance of things. Naturally philosophy has no right to find unity or continuity where none exists. It cannot read it into its interpretation from its presuppositions. It must not be schematic or forced. It has no right to be artificially constructionist. Whatever unity it finds must be natural; it must arise from within the very nature of the field itself. Discontinuities cannot be smoothed over into artificial unities by means of slippery methods. Yet neither may philosophy stress the fact of discontinuity to the point where the obvious relations we observe everywhere are lost or distorted. We do see and experience things together and so far, at least, they are together. The dispute between external and internal relations, for instance, has been largely due to the infiltration into philosophy of scientific method, standards, and attitudes.

Coherence is a necessary standard of knowledge intrinsic and inviolate to philosophy as far as the facts warrant. The term means more, of course, than formal consistency. It includes the givenness of experience. If it is adequately understood, coherence does not evaporate away the stubbornness of the concrete fact into logical relation. It recognizes the incoherent: for instance the fact of evil when viewed from a perfect rational perspective of good. Philosophy is coherent in the sense of the systematic, or the self-consistent, interpretation of our whole present experience. From this point of view it naturally meets many vital problems hard to fit into a coherent interpretation, like becoming, creation, etc.[4] Yet philosophy is under the obligation to be as coherent as it can be in view of what it has to interpret. For this reason we shall see that adequate philosophy points toward religion; that reason seeks its completion in faith. Hartshorne feels so strongly about this that he claims that "metaphysics evaporates into thin air, or it leads us to religion."[5] Erich Frank is similarly positive on the subject even to the point of making it a basic theme of his book, *Philosophic Understanding and Religious Truth,* that only by faith can reason arrive at the premises and perspectives which destroy its own frustrations.

The third standard of philosophic knowledge is objectivity. To think philosophically is to think *sub specie aeternitatis.* It is to

[4] If the dialectics of becoming, beyond the have-become and may-become, is included in coherence, the definition has gone beyond the realm of rational knowledge in the sense of self-consistent inclusiveness and continuity. The problems accepted, in that case, explode the basic function of philosophy and eventuate either in rationalization, we shall see, or in religious faith.

[5] Hartshorne, *Man's Vision of God,* p. 346.

view all times and all existences in the light of eternity. Philosophy is essentially public knowledge. In a certain sense there is a "cold light of reason." Methodologically there is a place for the part-seeing where reason is freed from the drives of the emotions of a participator and from the demands of immediate action, and can therefore look, as far as it is humanly possible, at the whole question of truth theoretically or disinterestedly. The modern revolt against the "balcony" view of life, as John Mackay calls it,[6] is wholesome to the point where it restores whole-thinking to the center of truth, but destructive when it decides to do without all the many methodological cautions and devices which whole-thinking requires to be truly whole. The scientist can be no more objective than the true philosopher ought to be. In all true philosophy there must be divine serenity and vast stretches of intellectual horizons. Existential philosophy is a contradiction in terms. Religion is existential. Yet religion cannot be equated with existential philosophy or claim an existential logic without either forfeiting its true nature as *religion* by becoming rational knowledge in content, however existentially apprehended, thus denying that truth is the full combination of the most important and the most real; or else abandoning the standard of philosophy, that is, rational knowledge centering in what is here and now actual, and thus not being existential *philosophy*. Existential philosophy has talked about truth being subjective, and has tried to show how superficial and peripheral, indeed distorted, objective knowledge is. It has often appealed to individual and social relativism to destroy the old objectivist philosophy. Nevertheless if general public knowledge is impossible and unreliable, so is philosophy. If the term "philosophy" is not to degenerate into mere opinion or into purely personal preference, subjectivist philosophy is a misnomer. Indeed subjectivism without firm foundation in objective thinking destroys all knowledge. Those who mean to strengthen religion by destroying philosophy know not what they do. Naturally every philosopher uses his own experience; he cannot escape from it; so

[6] Mackay, *A Preface to Christian Theology*, Chapter II, "Two Perspectives: The Balcony and the Road."

does every thinker. But such use of private experience, in whatever sense, if there be such, must always be checked by its systematic, coherent, inclusive relation to the whole of public knowledge. Unless knowledge can be objective in the sense of trans-personal, open to public inspection, then is nothing worth dignifying by the name of knowledge. "Existential philosophy" has seen and seized on one of the inherent limitations in philosophic method. The limitation points to a realm beyond philosophy. It cannot be eliminated from within philosophy. Just as science becomes better science by the acknowledgment and the heeding of its inherent limitations, so philosophy becomes better philosophy by the acknowledging its own inherent limitations in the finding of whole-truth through whole-response. The logical and the psychological tendencies of philosophy, inextricably intertwined, are to make philosophy the main, or even the sole, road to truth. It is no use, however, to destroy the strength of the proper function of philosophy in order to extend both falsely and distortingly its own legitimate method. Philosophy is good and needed as philosophy. But philosophy when true to its proper task is definitely not theology. Good philosophy, as philosophy, becomes, when taken as theology, both bad philosophy and bad theology.

We have given the three main standards of philosophy: inclusiveness, coherence, and objectivity. Naturally we include as intrinsic to legitimate philosophic conclusion applicability to fact and workability. These are not primary standards of philosophy, however, but rather presupposed conditions of the stuff with which philosophy works. But the proper task of philosophy is not to record or to establish either fact or function. It is rather to understand meanings and relations of, and in the light of, the whole. The function of philosophy in the economy of human knowledge determines its standards. Those who make applicability to fact or operational capacity central as the standard of philosophy usually think in terms of sense knowledge. They want philosophy to be exact, public, demonstrable. Public verifiability, as we have seen above, and common communicability always pull toward the regular, measurable, controllable world of sense. The logical and the psychological temptations, or the natural locus of distortion, are therefore away from adequacy of interpretation, which is the proper function of philosophy, and toward the validation of fact which is the proper task of science. The philosophies that stress applicability as a primary standard of philosophy rather than as a presupposition of its data, are, therefore, usually those that tend toward a naturalistic metaphysics. They are the product of philosophers with both their head and their heart pretty much in the department of science.

Before we go on to compare more fully the standard of philosophy with that of religion we pause to point out that rational verification goes beyond the empirical in the directly factual sense. The full-blown empiricist, as he chooses to pre-empt that term, demands that we get back to specific end referents in terms of sense data in every instance that we claim to deal with demonstrable truth. The rationalist rightly insists, however, that there are realms of truth that can never be reduced to sense. There is the whole-truth of the past which as past cannot be sensed. There is Plato's idea of difference itself which cannot be sensed. Hume's treatment of the spectrum pointing out that the mind can construct shades without direct dependence on sense still haunts us. Today there are discontinuities in science which break through all explanations in terms of an all-pervasive causal continuity, quantum theories, non-Euclidean space, etc., forcing attempts to redefine concepts like cause and continuity. There is the basic fact of mind, of consciousness itself, which after all is not sensed, and is yet the very basis and means of knowing. There is the whole life of hypotheses, right and wrong, but not as such sensed. Why are there not also implications from rational knowledge, like the postulated realms of Kant and Fichte, practical or theoretical postulates, which follow from the dependability of the accumulated structure of knowledge as surely as Galle could find Neptune from the mere mathematical calculations of Leverrier (or John Couch Adams come independently to the same conclusion)? There is, furthermore, the whole question of origins, of adequate explanation, and of the nature and meaning of purpose—all of which cannot be sensed. It is therefore necessary to keep firmly in mind that philosophy does not have fact as a standard, in any reductionist sense. Philosophy deals with realms of truth where there are no proofs possible in terms of present fact. Philosophy, we repeat, must presuppose the facts of science, unless it turn science to verify its own facts, in which case it is no longer philosophy. It is not, however, limited for data to the realm of scientific fact. We have definitely to think of rational truth as extending beyond "the empirical" and as having standards of its own. Philosophic truth is the fullest possible synthesis of adequacy and validity. Philosophy is the sum and substance of rational knowledge. But knowledge is not prematurely to be equated with truth. For the very content of knowledge, we shall shortly see, points to its own inconclusiveness. To equate knowledge with truth is to be guilty of an arbitrary faith judgment. Philosophy points toward religion; knowledge, being dynamic and from within a stage of process, points toward faith; but truth cannot be fully known, for to us it is not yet fully here. In the next chapter we shall develop at some length the nature and standards of religion, but in order to complete our discussion of philosophic method we now anticipate, by mere suggestion, of course, by comparing it with religion before we have explained and established our use of religious terms.

Philosophy is inclusive, coherent, objective; religious interpretation is inclusive, coherent, and subjective. Is, then, the only difference between philosophy and theology, except for the subjectivity of the latter, the difference in stress? We have said, after all, that the subjective yields no knowledge which philosophy cannot have. Or, if the subjectivity of theology is the only difference, besides emphasis, is philosophy *the interpretation* of the whole and theology the practical and emotional, *the motivational*, side of philosophy? Peter Bertocci, in a challenging article, has taken this point of view.[7] The fact is, however, that philosophy and theology are different not only in function but also in actual standards of truth. Subjectivity is not the only difference. Philosophy and theology

[7] Bertocci, "Faith and Reason: The Implications of Dr. Ferré's View," in *The Review of Religion*, May 1944.

have different standards of coherence and inclusiveness as well. Philosophy is the sum and substance of rational knowledge while theology is the synthesis of faith and knowledge. Philosophy is the synthesis of validity and adequacy as far as the present evidence goes. Theology is the full synthesis of validity and adequacy whereby the present stage in our process is seen retrospectively from the end, or in the light of the final fulfillment of our epoch of process (not of process itself). In this sense religion is "embodied and clarified anticipation."[8]

In order to compare philosophy and theology more clearly we start with the question of coherence. Both philosophy and theology are coherent, but the contents of their coherence differ. Philosophy is the coherent interpretation of the totality of our temporal experience. Its basis is the present stage of process. Its content of coherence is the here and now. Philosophy is the coherence of the actual. From the here and now philosophy can view the past and the future. It can predict certain possibilities and even probabilities in the light of past development and of present tendencies. But what is yet not actual is only possible, or at the most probable, from the perspective of rational *knowledge*. An ideal may be rationally realizable, that is, fit the needs and conditions of experience, and show much potency prophetic of its eventual further realization; but given this world as it is, there is no knowing that it will eventually be fully realized. From the point of view of rational knowledge God is finite. The reality of evil is a fact that cannot be sidestepped. Much confusion has entered our thinking because some philosophers, being personally religious beyond the rights of their philosophies, have failed to distinguish between critically philosophic thinking and the needs of their own hearts. From the point of view of coherent, rational knowledge based on the actual evidence of what is, religion has no right to combine completely the most high and the most real. It may hope, and have even some grounds for believing, that they will eventually coincide.

[8] Hocking, *Living Religions and a World Faith*, p. 230.

But if truth is to be equated with rational knowledge, and nothing more, religion is simply not fully true.

Religious interpretation is also coherent; else it is not knowledge. But its content of coherence goes far beyond the present stage of process. The center of the context of philosophic knowledge is the here and now. The center of the context of theological interpretation is the finished process (not the finish of process), as indicated by the highest instance within it. The confirmation of this claim will require a long, careful chapter, but we go on, nevertheless, to suggest the difference between philosophical and theological interpretation. Religious thought is coherent, not with what is here and now actual, but with the highest selective actual within the process, pointing beyond itself to what is more real than itself as an aggregative whole, to what is here only partially real, and therefore not yet realized in any fullness. The higher the selective actual is than the present process as a whole the more the difference is brought out between the coherence of the actual and the coherence of the full combination of the most high and the most real. The difference is not only between the aggregative or *mean organization* of the whole and the *hierarchical organization* in terms of the most important and the most true. The difference is between the total attainment or realization of the most high, the completion of the coherence of the fully best, and any standard of coherence which is rooted in the process that we now know. The difference lies between ideal coherence anticipatorily attained and partial coherence as exhibited by rational knowledge. That our highest selective actual is the final selective actual possible or necessarily the highest possible indication of what is the most real cannot be proved from within the process. This problem will have to wait. It will be touched on a bit more in this volume, but we hope to take it up in earnest in the next volume. If our basic intellectual and practical problems are not now ideally solved, actual solution being a conditional matter within process, religion still points beyond itself. It still seeks the full revelation. If they are ideally solved, at least suggestively, provided we see the problems deeply enough, we have the key, although it will be hard actually to turn fully around both in theory and in practice.

The basic question has to do with the content of truth. The problem concerns what the ultimate is. This we can know only from within the process. All knowledge is somehow from and through experience. Reason is the interpretation of that to which we react including our own reaction by any and every means whatever. Formally speaking there is no problem between faith and reason. The real question is rather what the content of experience is which rightly constitutes the criterion for what is ultimately real. Truth is ever basically a faith judgment inasmuch as the ultimate cannot be proved. Appeal to a higher ultimate in order to prove the ultimate would in effect make the court of appeal the ultimate. The ultimate, however, can be confirmed by reasoned experience, and contents which are not truly indicative of the ultimate can be shown to be self-contradictory as ultimates or at least less conclusive than other contents. The ultimate is ever a matter for existential decision, including, of course, our best reasoning concerning it. Our question is this: What is the least arbitrary and the most confirmed content of experience that indicates to us the nature of the ultimate? Truth, in the last analysis, is an existential ultimate. It is a religious judgment involving integrally both faith and reason. What is the content of experience which constitutes the best criterion for our existential ultimate?

Philosophy becomes a religion if it makes the coherence of the actual ultimate. Rational knowledge accepted as ultimate truth, in whole-response, becomes the content of religious knowledge. All, as we have seen, are religious. There are no atheists in the sense of human beings without religion. There are only true worshipers and idolaters, the makers of less or more true whole-responses. Religion claims that the most high, our best moments—our most creative and redeeming insights, the best man in history, the highest truth, the best whole-response made—form the content of experience, the selective actual, which best constitutes the criterion for our existential ultimate. Since, however, knowledge based on present process, whether it be organized aggregatively or hierarchically, falls short of the religious standard of coherence, inasmuch as this standard is not yet more than partially fact or fragmentarily verifiable by experience, faith completes the coherence of truth. Faith is the vision, suggested but not verified by the nature of process, of the final full realization of the purpose of our process. Faith is thus a conviction both of that which we have seen and of that which we have not yet seen. If the coherence of the actual is made an existential ultimate, it denies the full claims of religion. It denies that faith sees truly. It freezes present process as the content of the ultimate. Both philosophy and religion cannot be true *as religions*. The ultimate is like one or like the other. It is either wholly or partially good. It cannot be both at the same time. If it is wholly good in all respects, it cannot be partially good. If the good is wholly true in all respects it cannot be only partially true. If the absolute is inclusively good all the relations within it must be good. Imperfect relatives must be explainable, as we shall see in our next volume, as the freely and fully willed purpose of the Perfect in line with a perfect purpose *for them*. The full combination of the most important and the most real precludes the ultimate having only a measure of either, as indicated by the coherence of the actual, if that is made the content or criterion of our existential ultimate.

The coherence of religion does not deny fact as fact. The writer, in lecturing, has often taken the illustration of an airplane. Topography viewed from the ground differs from topography viewed more fully and in better perspective and proportion from the air. Yet the *superspective* of the air does not change any facts on the ground. A new dimension changes the appearance of a picture but does not change any fact in it. A new context of meaning leaves the basic facts the same *as facts*. Yet even this approach fails to bring out the full truth. It is too static and too centered in the actual. To see the process *superspectively* is less than the seeing of it *retrospectively* from the point of full attainment. Our highest selective actual is not the center of interpretation; it only points to the center of coherence. To see things religiously is not thereby to change facts, but to understand that present fact is only the temporary concretion of process. Be we ever so fired by religious seeing to change facts, our personal power to change the process is utterly limited. The facts are not yet in for religion; philosophy interprets, as far as it can from its perspective, the facts. It is rational *knowledge*. Religion sees things more than in full perspective and meaning, for even to see meaning fully in the present is also at the same time to see the frustration of that meaning. Theology is both the seeing superspectively, that is, the seeing facts and their fuller meaning including their present partial, perverted, and frustrated condition; but also, and this is the primary perspective, the seeing retrospectively from the point of the full realization of the fully best, having attained in vision and commitment to the end of the process as indicated by the highest instance, the best selective actual. Theology is thus the seeing our present actual process through faith as *the substance* of things hoped for. Faith is the selective seeing within process which by the alchemy of its *new coherence* turns present process itself selective.

Theology and philosophy do not clash so long as philosophy adheres strictly to rational knowledge for what it is, the coherence of the actual, however specifically organized. They clash unavoidably when rational knowledge is confounded with truth, is made the content of our existential ultimate, is made the intellectual content of religion. Then they clash not as to the nature of fact, but as to the nature of our ultimate faith judgment. Philosophy, as we have seen, cannot prove our process in its present stage to be ultimate. As a matter of fact present process points beyond itself. This we shall examine at length in our next chapter. Philosophy, because of the nature of its standard of knowledge, is always under heavy temptation to freeze process and to make ultimate the coherence of the actual, or even some lesser idols. Because theology operates with the same content of knowledge as philosophy, theology is often, actually, under the same temptation; and much theology, obviously, both historically and contemporaneously, is far worse than any adequate coherence of the actual. Most actual theology needs to be rethought and reformed in the light of its own basic principles. The way out of our perplexity is to restore both philosophy and theology to their rightful tasks. The coherence of religion when right does not deny either fact or the coherence of the actual. In the light of its ultimate vision of truth as indicated by process through the reaction to it by the fullest combination of thought and faith, religion denies that present facts are final, and thus indicative of final truth, and that the coherence of the actual constitutes the truest content, or most dependable criterion, of our existential ultimate. Philosophy can be a most helpful check and needful challenge to the content of faith; it is no adequate substitute for it, not only on the ground of function, or of motivation, but also from the point of view of the standard for truth. Later we shall look closely at the inherent difficulties in making the coherence of the actual, in any form, the content of our existential ultimate. Till then we have suggested that the centers of the contextual contents of philosophy and theology differ because they have different functions within the economy of human knowledge. The contents of their coherence differ. Their organizing principles differ, functionally to their mutual advantage, existentially to their mutual damage. Philosophy interprets rational knowledge; religion is more than rational knowledge; it is "the vision of something which stands beyond, behind, and within the passing flux of immediate things; something which is real, and yet waiting to be realized."[9]

The second standard of both philosophy and theology is inclusiveness. We have said already that faith is selective seeing within process that by the alchemy of its new coherence turns present process itself selective. Philosophy is inclusive with the coherence of the actual as the center of its inclusiveness. It reaches out from there as far as possibility can go. Theology is inclusive in the different sense that the most high, the highest selective actual, is the center of its sytem of inclusiveness. The most high, however, is not centered in the coherence of the actual. As we have already seen, theology is centered in what in its fullness goes

[9] Whitehead, *Science and the Modern World*, p. 275.

far beyond this actual world. Even the highest selective actual, therefore, is merely indicative. It is an arrow pointing to an indefinitely distant center. What is meant by distant is that, although the ultimate, to be known by us, must be within our actual world in a real sense, the finite mind can grasp the fullness of reality qualitatively only as "through a glass darkly." "For as the heavens are higher than the earth so are my ways higher than your ways, and my thoughts than your thoughts."[10] And quantitatively this world of rational knowledge, the history of our universe, may be less than the smallest fragment of the smallest pebble on all the beaches of the world in comparison to God's worlds. We must be done with Ptolemaic theology. We must be done with anthropocentric narrowness. We must have room to breathe. Our spirits suffocate if the stretch of reality does not far outrun the stretch of our largest and greatest thoughts, which we feel to be puny in comparison to Truth. We must be done with the putting of our present actual world, however central it must be to the content of our knowledge, in the center of reality. If time can be thought serially in relation to eternity even from one point of view, the time of our history, even when *completed* in terms of our cosmos, may be shorter than the fastest tick on the fastest watch in comparison to all the sidereal years that all the astronomers together have ever added and multiplied together. Enough of this. The point is that we need to be freed from small perspectives by spacious thoughts. We simply cannot begin to fathom the eternal mysteries of ultimate reality. Theology points to an indefinitely distant center in order to be as inclusive as possible. Faith glories beyond knowledge.

Philosophy is not limited, to be sure, to the here and now, even including the past of our cosmic process telescoped within it. It can deal with the future and the possible, but not as real as and *more real* than the present and the actual. Spinoza spoke about this world as being merely two attributes, thought and extension, of all the countless attributes of God. But this is not even a matter of knowledge. It presupposes illegitimately the equation of thought

[10] Isaiah 55:9.

and being. In so speaking he spoke rather as a man of faith, though without an adequate reason for his speaking in reasoned experience. There is no way of proving his contention in terms of reasoned experience. Later we shall briefly examine the ontological argument—but we can say now that the classical identification of thought and being and also of goodness and being was pre-critical; it could be used, that is, far more easily before than after Kant's critical philosophy. Philosophy can indicate *possibilities* and *probabilities* based on the knowledge we have. Its inclusiveness, however, is the knowledge based on present process including all legitimate extensions from it. Theology takes the most high (which, in order to be the most high, as we shall see in the next chapter, must be the center of the circle of all truly coherent knowledge, since even what is discordant with it points to it for its eventual harmonizing with all else), and shoots this center out indefinitely, eternally, or infinitely, and then draws the circle of all there is which includes as the smallest dot our history. In this infinite circle our history will not be as the center, but as surely as our history is an organic part of all there is, what is truly central in our history, known or to be known, will ever be central everywhere. Of our history our present stage of process, including its whole past, is even so but a part. Religion, however, includes even now prospectively telescoped within the present our whole future, not in detailed realization, nor in a predetermination of parts excluding freedom, but in the sovereignly controlled conditions for its general and all-inclusive actualization. In this sense religion is "anticipated attainment"[11] intellectually as well as existentially, in thought as well as in decision. It is "realized eschatology." This more limited inclusiveness of cosmological attainment, as over against metaphysical or theological universality, is exceedingly important in that it is only in its terms that we shall find a solution to the problem of evil. A distinction must be made between our whole-process and eternity. This will task our minds in the last

[11] Hocking, *The Meaning of God in Human Experience,* p. 31. Cf. also p. 439: "The meaning of the mystic experience is prophetic. It anticipates an attainment still to be won."

chapter of the next volume. The basic category as far as religious knowledge goes, in so far as it includes objective thinking, is the relation between the realizability of the most high and its actual realization. This category has no meaning and the fact of historic development is illusory unless the distinction between process and eternity, called for by the facts of history, is carefully made. In the meantime it is well to keep in mind our general distinction that philosophic interpretation starts at the center of the actual whereas theological interpretation stems from the center of a Purpose of which all of our present process and our whole process are but parts.

Philosophy, then, has as its standard the inclusiveness of rational knowledge; theology, the inclusiveness of the full synthesis of faith and knowledge—the most adequate interpretation, as we shall see, both theoretically and practically, of our whole-response to truth. Truth must by its very nature be a dynamically inclusive term that cannot be proved—for it refers to the ultimate. The full inclusiveness of truth escapes us. Knowledge can only say: I see thee but partly. I cannot contain thee. Faith can only say: I already see thee in a fullness far beyond what I can know of thee, but not yet having attained thee, or rather, not yet having let myself be fully found by thee, I cannot fully apprehend thee. Therefore I must keep seeing as through a glass darkly, seeing the better beyond the glass of the present yet also obscured by it. Thus even I, faith, must live before thee in hope and love.

The third standard of philosophy is objectivity whereas theology is definitely subjective. This does not mean, of course, that theology can dispense with objective knowledge. It must not mean that whole-response is without whole-reason. Whole-response to be right must ever include right whole-reason. Right whole-reason, moreover, must take advantage of every methodological device that will give it full insight. It must ever seek full evidence upon which to make intelligent choice. Theology needs a carefully objective philosophy with regard both to method and to its content of knowledge. Yet theology is always subjective in that it is whole-response, the interpretation of actual whole-response. It is ever a matter of critical, personal decision. It is the recording of the thought in our inescapable reaction to *the ultimate*. A philosopher can, perhaps, serenely interpret the world in one way, and live in another way. The personal problem that may arise, or may not arise, at least openly, because of our being partially disconnected beings, is incidental. His philosophy, as philosophy, is right regardless of personal commitment to it the way a mathematician's answer is correct regardless of his morals, or the way an artist may catch beauty of landscape without having beauty of life.

Theology is not so. Theology is the interpretation of religion. Religion is our actual whole-response, including our thoughts involved, to our inescapable ultimate. Theology is ever the thought of the whole man thinking. When the whole man thinks, if he is normal, he cannot come to dominant conclusions intellectually and then dominantly live in a different way. The first kind of thinking is not religious. It is philosophical. The thoughts involved in his different dominant living are his theology. Just as there are bad and good philosophies, there are good and bad theologies. Just as every man in so far as he speculatively interprets the world is a philosopher, so every man in so far as he is ever aware of the thoughts of his whole-thinking is a theologian—although we seldom like to dwell on our whole-thinking since we prefer to think that we are better than we are. When a man as disinterestedly as possible decides what ought to be done, or half-gropingly comes to see it through whatever ways or means, and then acts differently out of basic indifference or basic selfishness, he does the first as a philosopher and the second as a religious man. In so far as he rationalizes the second, his actual conduct, he is a theologian. Naturally he is not thus far split actually, but identifies himself in thought with the first theoretically, though not to the point of costly participation, and idealizes his actual choice, or inhibits as much intellectual interpretation as possible, perhaps even suppresses it altogether, except as thought is short-circuited into the subconscious to make there for restlessness and anxiety, which he in turn, in order to cover it up, may blame on concrete fears which have little or nothing to do with the original suppression. All normal men, however little of either, are altogether likely both philosophers and theologians. The professional philosophers and theologians are only exceptionally responsible because they have the advantage of knowledge and the time to think; but since they also live they are perhaps as much and more subjected to the same temptations which all men have as philosophers and theologians.

Theology is never objective, though it must use objective information. It is ever existential. This means that the whole person is involved critically and costingly in the thinking. The whole life is at stake. Theology is the interpretation of religion, and religion is the way we react to the ultimate. It is never a mere theoretical combination, however full, of the most high and the most real. Such a combination is a philosophy of religion.

Religion, however, can never rest satisfied with any intellectual solution in terms of knowledge. "This search for something to complement the finite and relative is nothing less than the most awful demand in the nature of man, that which has been expressing itself in every age."[12] A surgeon examining a patient in whom he has no immediate personal interest can give an objective diagnosis of a case. He many say that the operation has certain chances of being successful. The more skilled and objective he is, the more he can rightly, objectively state the objective aspects of the case. We need such knowledge immensely. Objectivity is placed so high as a quality by men of medicine that they do not like to diagnose or operate on those for whom they have intense personal affection, like members of their family. This objective knowledge is like that of philosophy. But for the person to be operated upon, "the case" is *a situation of personal crisis*. He must choose life or death; he must choose critically whether the chances of success for him and for those whom he loves are high enough to warrant the operation. Such existential use of knowledge suggests, however inadequately, the existential nature of theology.

Religious knowledge puts a demand on us to the very present and last breath of our lives. Theology is the interpretation of continuous personal crisis as we seek in vain to become self-sufficient; or the

[12] Maurice, *What Is Revelation?* p. 465.

interpretation of personal victory through faith and grace as we find our security in God. Most of the time, in whatever measure, it is a mixture of both experiences. Theology is the constant standing before death and life; it is the dying and the living daily; the dying to live, or the living to die and not wanting to die. Theology is ever as vital, if we can uncover it, as our will to live. Theology is the wishful thinking of all who fool themselves about the seriousness of life, or who want its sweetness without its suffering, as well as the wishful thinking of all those who accept the seriousness of life and find through and beyond its suffering the sweetness of life. Theology is the interpretation of all our actual choices—how we treat persons, property, ourselves, our talents, how we live all in all—in the light of the inescapable reality to which we must react and keep reacting. Kierkegaard may be right that we learn truth in proportion to our suffering.[13] Suffering is our participation in the costly decision of life without which, whether self-chosen or imposed, we never come to the critical self-despair which can lead us out of our individualism to fellowship, and out of personal self-sufficiency to worship. Suffering leads to empathy and should lead to sympathy; although it may harden lives on the surface, there is a crying understanding within which may be so sore that it may recoil from even looking at further affliction. Yet such understanding is the preparation in the fullness of each man's life, wherever and whenever, whereby the self ceases to be a dot and becomes a cell, ceases to be an individualist and becomes a responsible member of a society. Without the shedding of blood, that is, without suffering, without self-giving costingly, there is, at least, no salvation from self, and no remission of sin.

Philosophy may solve the problem of evil in the religious perspective by producing levels of solution in terms of God's ways and faithfulness. Suffering may even be the cornerstone of this solution. But no solution is fully religious, and no interpretation

[13] Cf. especially "Existential Pathos," *Concluding Scientific Postscript,* pp. 386 ff. Cf. also *Purity of Heart,* pp. 132–159. Cf. also Unamuno, *The Tragic Sense of Life,* p. 192: "Suffering is the substance of life and the root of personality, for it is only suffering that makes us persons."

is theological, unless it also springs out of the depths of personal struggle and the personal overcoming of evil. A smooth theology may be shallow or it may be the smooth surface of the deep that has found stillness in its depths. The theologian's life, however, is inevitably involved in the solution, for theology is the interpretation of the whole man thinking which can be understood only from within, that is, subjectively. The objective criticism of religious reactions is philosophy. Theology is never objectively systematic. A theologian's competence is in proportion to his self-surrender, his whole-surrender to the truth of the common good in the ultimate perspective. All impersonal solutions are philosophical. A person's theology, as Douglas Steere pointed out, is to be understood in terms of his devotional life: "Great theology springs from devotion. . . . Great theology may only be understood through the aid of this background of devotion."[14] Theology is the seeing subjectively the relation between the realizability and the realization of the good over evil. Theology is ever a matter of our struggle with evil. However inadequate in content such theology may be, it is yet deeper and better than one good by content held by someone who denies in his own personal participation the claims of religion. There is something incurably individual about religion. It is personal to its very grass roots. Religion rightly revolts people because its actual theology as lived by its devotees falls so far short, even often radically denies, the theories, the professed theology, which it teaches. The preacher who demonstrates what he witnesses to, though he be more modest in his faith-claims, has more power to convince than the preacher who claims the whole New Testament in words and shows by his deeds that he does not believe it. People know, deep down, what his religion actually amounts to. Rightly to teach theology, or to learn it in one's own life, is to gather all knowledge and wisdom from every method, but, further, it is to find personal insight and power through life as a member of a constructive kind of fellowship which frees the self for creative co-operation. Right theology learns all it can from both science and philosophy. It insists on methodological objectivity in

[14] Steere, *On Beginning from Within,* p. 88.

the establishment and interpretation of knowledge as such. But beyond that, theology is the interpretation of our whole-response in all the issues of life and death. As such it is completely and constantly subjective. It is irrevocably existential.

Perhaps from the point of view of this analysis it becomes clear what the relation between the philosophy of religion and theology is and the relation between philosophical and theological ethics. Remsberg points out that "faith tells us more about God than reason can. Reason tells us more about the world than revelation."[15] The tension between what ought to be and what actually is, or between the eternal purpose and its partial historic realization, is beyond the capacity of man to bear unless he himself be borne up by a power greater than his actual self. Clearly to see and deeply to desire the full world of faith is an experience of anguish, at least without the full faith of God's peace. Few ever dare to let themselves be drawn into the middle of the whirlpool of the world's remaking. Whole-surrender in responsible existence is despair. High religion is "comforted despair." To live creatively and redeemingly throughout the constant decisions and relations of life is to be torn within and to be beset without. Practically all people, quite understandably, decide not to trouble trouble, to let things slide, to let things be as they are, or at best to smooth them over a bit. Few dare stand at the fulcrum of faith. Few dare stand in the vortex of redemptive living. To take up the cross of the world's remaking daily is not easy in spite of the peace which the world cannot give. The natural man seems to have the lives of a million cats. To live for truth and right is daily to be crucified to self-concern and even our resurrection moment by moment must often follow bitter anguish of spirit, at least until we have attained the full-grown stature of religious maturity.

This situation of continual crisis, however fulfilled in the fruits of the spirit and in the peace that passeth understanding, is easily dodged. Particularly easy is it for comfortable, professional people,

[15] Remsberg, "The Relation of Faith and Knowledge in Aquinas and Luther," in *Lutheran Church Quarterly,* Jan., 1942, p. 17.

paid interpreters of truth, to dodge it. It is far easier to enjoy the steady income, the long vacations, the chance for travel, the prestige of position, the authority of knowledge—to become self-pleasers and men-pleasers, however rationalized—than to stand in the breach of the struggle for a new world where God's will is done on earth as it is in heaven. The temptations of the professor and the preacher to talk about but not do the truth are more severe and steady than most of us like to think.

The temptation of the philosophy of religion is the temptation of philosophy, namely, to make this world central in interpretation and thereby to remove the tension from another world which declares this one to be but a factory under reconversion. This truth was well put by the writer's son, Frederick, then eleven years old, after hearing a sermon that declared the present to be a bridge between the past and the future: "Instead of a bridge it should be a factory where the whole world is remade." The means of production of our entire common living need to be radically retooled; and the people who use the tools must be basically reoriented and transformed. We and our institutions, both, need to become changed in depth purpose and direction. The philosophy of religion should interpret the world for what it is. Our world is a stage in process. Thinking, none the less, is at its deepest wholethinking; for those who are not fully surrendered the temptation is, therefore, always strongly at hand to interpret the world in such a way that the tension within it between process and its purpose is lessened. This happens whenever the possible becomes optional and the great claims of faith are declared ideal but not compulsory. This removes the challenge of the cross that always threatens the saviors of mankind; but it removes also the authority and motivation which alone can change the situation that makes crosses for the good into situations where the good is itself crowned to the glory of God. Whenever the coherence of the actual is made ultimate, the full force of religion cleansing the inward parts of self and society is gone.

Theology, on the other hand, always reflects the interpreter's actual commitment. It may show him to be a philosopher interpreting speculatively a world that he has not himself fully entered. His theology so-called is likely to become an ideal realm without direct and all-demanding claim on the whole of the present; first of all his own. Theology actually tends to sink more and more toward the actual and thus to become more like philosophy in content, that is, to be centered in this actual world. It tends to become reduced to the power of rational knowledge; or else it tends to become an ideal, other-worldly realm, for contemplation, for future existence, or for general escape from present responsibility. Theology thus does become a most destructive opiate. Since this common tension between Reality and the actual touches both philosophy and theology they need each other. The philosophy of religion needs right religion, i. e., true theology, in order to be free to interpret the world truly and clearly. Right religion involves full surrender to truth, as we shall see, by the finding of freedom from fear. Philosophers who are religious in the fuller sense, who are men of a high and noble faith, are thereby better philosophers. They are delivered from defensive pressures to rationalize. They escape the insidious attacks of all the psychological tendencies to perversion that beset all human thinking. Theologians who are men of faith, on the other hand, will dare to see the actual world for what it is and yet also the existential claims on it of what eternally is and actually ought to be. The more richly religious they are, the more use they will have for philosophy. They can use better than otherwise the works of the philosophers of religion.

The work of the philosophy of religion, moreover, is not to bring out the implications of one religion; philosophy is inclusive. Nor is it to find a common denominator among the actual religions; that would be to deny the full claims of religion because of man's general failure to accept them and to embody them either in system or in life. The philosophy of religion is, rather, concerned with all the realms of religion from the point of view of rational knowledge, as far as that can possibly go. It wrestles with all the problems of the actual in its bearing on religion. As far as method is concerned, for instance, that is the work of philosophy. And how urgently we need it! Would there be need of this, moreover, if it were not for our *actual situation* as human beings? Those are right among us who claim that religion as religion is not much concerned with knowledge in our actual sense of it. Knowledge in this sense will be done away. Knowledge is needed in all whole-response but religion "passeth knowledge." This volume is a work in the philosophy of religion, not in theology. Theology deals with the full light of purpose, not with the complexities and problems of pedagogy or partial process. Theology presupposes the highest to be the most real. "Faith is the creative power in man,"[16] not the critical. In the next volume we shall establish the nature of the most high and the most real. In the following volumes we shall simply start with this as a basis and perspective. Theology is seeing within the atmosphere of the fullest faith possible. Faith does not argue. Faith witnesses. The reasons for the faith that is in us are not the reasons of philosophic analysis, but, rather, the witness of our experience and reasoned faith of what has been done and can be done for us. Method and apologetic belong to the world of philosophy, not of theology. Theology is didactic and exegetical. Theology deals with right whole-response, and the interpretation of it. Theology is the voice of the Spirit from the world above. At its highest it is like the New Testament.

Philosophy deals with the content of religious knowledge in the light of knowledge as a whole. Both to clarify its own content of knowledge in relation to the actual world and to relate itself to minds which have had no opportunity to see, or have failed to see, the fuller truth because of intellectual road-blocks, theology needs the work of philosophers of religion who can point out in terms of knowledge that knowledge points beyond itself and who will build bridges of understanding by showing the relation of faith to knowledge, thus helping both the unbeliever who is ready to see and the believer who is confused on these questions. What we need in the future is a far more effective philosophy of religion. The attack on it by some modern theologians is well meant, we believe, though it may be also partly defensive, but it is mistakenly directed. The task and function of the philosophy of religion is

[16] Unamuno, *op. cit.*, p. 192.

almost unlimited. It becomes destructive only at the point where it makes itself into a substitute for theology. To do so is to reduce religion to knowledge and to clip its strong wings until it can no longer fly. It is to forfeit the motivational power that can change the world. Today we need both more faith and more knowledge. "The concepts of faith, to modern man, become understandable again in their real meaning and in their truth only when he encounters the limits of his factual existence and realizes that even the scope of his theories is definitely limited."[17] Faith we need. But faith has no body to fly if it lose its body of knowledge. For the sake of truer perspective, for the sake of better application of knowledge, and for the sake of actually keeping in the center of the stream between the world which is and the world to be, we need the fullest possible stress on both the philosophy of religion and theology. Both like close brothers must work together in different ways, but to the selfsame end.

The same thing holds true with regard to the relation between philosophical and theological ethics; only even more so. Ethics is the science and the art of conduct. It is the description and the prescription of conduct. Prescription that is based on average description would be useless as far as changing the world radically for the better is concerned. One that is based on the best that knowledge can find, however, is the best rational ethics that we can have. All that we can know in history and in experience is accessible to knowledge. Philosophical ethics can thus deal with both description and prescription from this point of view. All the questions of value, of the relation between value and truth, etc., are questions, moreover, which the philosophical approach must deal with almost exclusively since they have little or no meaning for theological ethics. Theological ethics is the stating of the ideal or the revelational norm and its full implications for life. It is the Sermon on the Mount part of theology. Theological ethics is not concerned with rational compromise or with prudential practicality. It is concerned with the full truth of God's ultimate will. Or, to return to our original language, it is conduct in the

17 Frank, *op. cit.*, p. 17.

light of the full combination of the most high and the most real. It is living as when the most high is fully realized. Our actual ethics and man's hardness of heart are not part of theological ethics, except as implications and backgrounds. Theological ethics is never compromised ethics "under the circumstances."

Between theological and philosophical ethics, therefore, there is ever tension; this tension is not so much theoretical as existential. To be sure, the logical tendency of philosophical ethics by itself is to reduce right to the practicable, humanly speaking; it is to reduce ethics to what can well be expected in view of our actual world being what it is. The logical tendency of theological ethics is to expound the ideal regardless of whether or not it can be realized. The theological teacher of ethics is, thus, under logical pressure to deny how seemingly inapplicable his ethics is to the actual world. These disparate logical leanings tend to remove the existential pressure at the center of action. Far worse and more powerful, moreover, is the psychological tendency in either case whereby the philosophic teacher is under personal constraint to ease the tension by declaring the theological ethics inapplicable to the world as it actually is, as known in terms of rational knowledge, and whereby the teacher of theology is ready either to make his ethics future or other-worldly, or oppositely, to compromise it down to the personally practical, or to accuse his philosophic colleague of cynicism or false pessimism. We all have seen how we Christians have tended to rationalize the race situation or participation in war, which is obviously almost the direct denial of the central core of Christian ethics in the perspective of eternity, where to lose one's life constructively and redeemingly is advocated as the opposite of defensive living and fighting, let alone aggressive and vengeful slaughter. The point is crucially that we tend to deny in thought the need for the full function of both theological and philosophical ethics in order to escape existentially the standing in the middle of the world's remaking, or else to escape standing aside with hurt consciences. We may differ on how concretely to stand but right religion will not let us accept the wrong situation either by inaction or by rationalization. Religious ethics, as we shall see later on in another chapter,[18] is a constant force for changing and for healing the world. And if the body is to be saved the white corpuscles cannot think first of all what happens to them.

We need philosophical ethics to make a thorough inquiry into the actual human situation and into the prevailing modes of conduct. We need a disinterested, objective investigation into values and into practical courses of action. We must know how best to deal with all who will not accept in thought or conduct the full claim of religion. The question of our actual situation is deep, comprehensive, and stubborn. Theological ethics cannot do without the philosophical and be adequate in its full task of application. Theological ethics is confessional in the full sense and we are faced with a general refusal to confess in truth and deed. We therefore must have wise pedagogical ethics and that, on the objective side, is the task of philosophy. Yet we must have the fullest possible development of theological ethics, the exploration of the kind of conduct which we shall have when the perfect fellowship is realized. This by itself, however, would be a philosophical ethics. This would still come under rational knowledge. It would be the highest possible known mode of conduct. Theological ethics, however, speaks from the perspective of perfection, yet also out of the actual conflict with evil. Theological ethics cannot be objective; it is subjective. It is under the eternal and absolute compulsion of God to live now, moment by moment, the full ethics by a strength beyond our own. It demands that we surrender every personal fear and lack of faith to live by and under God for the whole world regardless of personal fate. Theological ethics is rooted in whole-response to what is beyond us. It is from within whole-surrender to the completely realized combination of the good, the right, and the true beyond this actual world that they may become realized in it.

In the next volume we shall have a special section, though short and merely suggestive, on theological ethics. Both philosophy and theology have to apply to the actual world. Theology has no basis for its selection of the most high except as this can explain

18 Volume II, Chapter 2.

satisfactorily and change desirably the process of our history, and, nearer, of our individual lives. But philosophical application is rational; theological, existential. And, as we shall see, beyond rational knowledge, life demands daring existential decisions. There are few smooth edges where the rational ideal and the actual meet. In application, therefore, theological ethics needs the light of the philosophical, but can never find rest in it. Life surrounds ethical life with dark areas which can only be lighted by daring faith. And often faith must grope and keep groping beyond the focused light of neat rational choices.

When philosophical and theological ethics understand each other's task, and both are frank about their own inescapable obligation, they can help each other to meet where earth reaches up to heaven for help and heaven reaches down to help it, or where earth runs away from heaven in fear and selfish rebellion and heaven yet overtakes it, troubled and anxious, to offer it freedom from fear and creative obedience to the common good. Philosophical ethics can make the theological practical enough to escape being utopian; it can warn it of false solutions beyond the world by means of pseudo-philosophies. Theological ethics, on the other hand, can keep the philosophical from calling itself ultimate, thus offering an idol that cannot save, and from reducing the content of the most high in knowledge, the content of our highest instance of conduct in history, to such practical ethics that can be readily practiced but that cannot transform selves or society.

We end this chapter by saying that we shall surely not get to the truth that saves if we neglect either the full interpretation of fact or the full interpretation of faith. The former is the task of philosophy; the latter, of theology. But fact and faith belong together. Good facts must be established, improved, and multiplied; evil facts must be reformed, improved, and redeemed. In the chapter to which we now turn we shall try to show how knowledge and faith together in dynamic relation give us a dynamic truth. Such truth must see clearly what is, what ought to be, and the why and the way that what is can become what ought to be.

CHAPTER IV

The Circle of Religion

The ultimate, as we have seen, is existential. It is as inescapable as responsible human life itself. To live as a human being is to hang together, for better or worse, with the universe, to keep reacting to it continually, and to decide necessarily what in our actual choices constitutes the most important and the most real. Most of life is unexamined. We have little courage or energy to interpret critically, to weigh carefully, and to choose in the light of our most mature and most fully surrendered understanding. As we avail ourselves of knowledge, however, in as full and objective a manner as possible, we find that while science describes the physical world it does not deal with either our ultimate values or ultimate reality. When it is pressed into such service by unheeding logical or psychological tendencies, or anxiously invited in by ignorance, it offers only the stones of its own relative realm for the bread of ultimate truth. Philosophy, moreover, commands the whole world of rational knowledge; it interprets all the facts and meanings of our actual world. Like science it can inform and enrich us as long as it sticks to its proper task. Foolish or arrogant philosophy, however, confuses knowledge with truth, its distorted and partial appearance with Reality. That which can be known and demonstrated to be true in terms of our present process cannot save us; unless it can be so demonstrated, in a wide sense, it cannot be called knowledge; yet, as we shall presently see, it can also be demonstrated that knowledge can know that it knows but in part. The interpretation of our existential ultimate is unavoidably the responsibility of religion. Within and beyond present process, so brief in its passing and deep in its frustrations, there is, too, the permanence of Purpose, which though it cannot be fully known, being as yet only partially realized, can yet be significantly seen and freeingly believed. Our existential ultimate to be both true and saving must be the fullest synthesis of the most important and the most real, arrived at by faith and knowledge in dynamic interaction, critically and creatively.

That is the thesis of our chapter on the circle of religion. Our first task will be to describe the specific standards of religion, not those of disciplined knowledge in general, nor such as it shares in a general manner with science and philosophy, like applicability, coherence, and inclusiveness, but those which characterize religion, those which are peculiarly, though not by intrinsic need exclusively, its own. The second part of our chapter will be used to establish our right to these standards in terms of knowledge in general. Theology, like philosophy, "should follow the example of science at least in respect to formulating its proper problems, articulating its own objectives, and establishing its peculiar methods."[1] If religion is to cultivate the field of human knowledge in co-operation with other fellow workers it must, to win proper credentials, show to them, not that its crop can be cultivated equally well by them, for then it would be rather useless, but that it has a most important crop of its own, needed for proper nourishment by all men, that cannot be raised except by taking proper account of its own nature.

The corroboration of this claim will demand both volumes of this book.[2] Yet in the end, no matter how much objective cor-

[1] Welch, *The Philosophy of Edmund Husserl*, p. 113.

[2] In this chapter, after the description of the standards of religion, we shall show that the best explanation of the meaning of process in terms of its own origin and origins can be had in terms of religious truth. In the next volume, after having completed our formal investigation of religion, we shall have three chapters dealing with the concrete content of religion, or with our existential ultimate, and how that confirms the conclusion of our formal analysis. The first of these chapters must be devoted to the selection and the establishing of the content of religious truth. The second will show how this meets our practical needs as individuals and as society. The third will deal with the solution of the problem of evil beyond the

roboration, how much knowledge we may have, our truth must still be thoroughly existential, a dynamic whole-response of faith. For the finite there is no finished knowledge. For that matter, wherever there is finite freedom there can be perfect, specific knowledge of finished process for no one, not even for God. We may find Him to have, as far as we can see it, the possession of perfect, general prediction of process and the final general control of it by His purpose; but our knowledge, however seemingly whole, is yet bit by bit. There is much wisdom to be pondered in Augustine's observation: "Now everything that we know, we may with reason perhaps be said to believe, but not to know everything which we believe."[3]

Our first task is to indicate what we take to be the five characteristic standards of religion.

1. The first of these which we shall try to describe is the *selective ideal*. By this term we mean that religious truth is to be understood in terms of the highest instance of the good within actuality. The most high is at least the best indication we have of what reality is, the best pointer to truth, the most adequate content, or criterion, of our existential ultimate. But how is the most high to be selected? How is this ideal to be chosen? If the mean, or average, description is not taken to be the standard, if the whole as a whole is rejected as the best guide to truth, what right do we have to pick out any selective ideal and make this the criterion? Our reasons for using it as the content of our existential ultimate we shall give in the second part of this chapter, but the following requirements define its nature, that is, give the conditions which will have to be met by the selective ideal if it is not to be arbitrarily selected and arbitrarily set up as a standard

limitations of rational knowledge, which is based on present process. It will suggest that religious truth is not arbitrary because beyond its power metaphysically to explain the origin and origins of process, and beyond its pragmatic value for present process, it can also deal with considerable suggestiveness with the vital problems which are connected with the end of process.

[3] Augustine, "Soliloquies," in *Nicene and Post-Nicene Fathers*, Vol. VII, p. 539.

for religious truth. Unless it fulfills these requirements it cannot be considered to be the necessary interpretation of right whole-response. The selective ideal must, then, meet man's deepest needs, as far as anything can, in all respects. It must constitute the fullest all-round answer to man's craving to interpret his whole-response and his need to do so in order to react in the most satisfactory way possible. This means that the selective ideal must have the capacity for fuller intellectual explanation of the entire process than any other available content of experience, selectively or aggregatively. If, given all possible, legitimate methodological aids, it does not satisfy the needs of our minds to explain critically and creatively, as well as and preferably better than, other principles of explanation, it has no right to the claim of truth. We must not belittle the legitimate demands for rigid reasoning.

The selective ideal must also be the key to the solution of our practical problems, individually and socially, unrivaled by any other approach to them. This means that it must not only shed light for adequate planning but also provide the power for the effective carrying out of those plans. It must meet the crucial tests of authority and motivation. It does not mean that it is not conditional on man's freedom. If it were automatic it would contradict experience. But it must give power to those who sincerely see and accept it; and it must be integrally related to the needs of all men, so that not to accept it is to walk in that much darkness and in that much frustration of life.

The selective ideal must thus be organically and inclusively related to the whole of the process of which man is a part. If the selective ideal is to be considered more true than the aggregative actual and than the actual hierarchically organized by means of the selective ideal itself, it must possess adequate suggestiveness for the solution of our intellectual problems concerning the actual and also indicate by its own nature how and whereby that actual can be ideally transformed. The selective ideal must thus mediate the source of the world's transformation as well as constitute the truest principle for its explanation. It must be related to the actual as its savior. The needs of the whole test the standard but the whole is not therefore the standard. The whole establishes the selective ideal by the way that ideal is inclusively and redemptively related to it. The whole is, nevertheless, not itself the standard because it establishes and tests it. Since the selective indicates which way the process is going to go, points to what the actual will become when the ideal is realized, or, to say the same thing, when the Real is actualized, this selective, however much confirmed by the aggregative, is itself the best indication of truth. The whole is more subject to transformation than such parts as have already become transformed.

It is the forward thrust of the process which points where it is going. It is the ripest part of the fruit which indicates what the ripe fruit will be like. The process, moreover, by where it is going indicates its own ultimate source, power of being, and direction for going before it has itself gone there. The fruit indicates the nature of the tree. The best man indicates better the essential nature of man, not the actual nature, than does the average man. The average man is the standard for man's actual nature in so far as an abstraction can be made of it. The best moment, insight, action, of the best man's life indicates better the nature of truth than does the average moment, insight, or action of the best man— unless, of course, he was perfect. If the purpose of process is the becoming of good being, the fullest truth within process resides in that which has most fully become good. Later we shall try to indicate why we believe this to be true, but right now we think that the description of what we mean by the selective ideal is sufficiently clear. We may consider Bergson's well-written suggestions along these lines:

> The men of moral grandeur, particularly those whose inventive and simple heroism has opened new paths to virtue, are revealers of metaphysical truth. Although they are the culminating point of evolution, yet they are nearest the source and they enable us to perceive the impulse which comes from the deep. It is in the studying these great lives, in striving to experience sympathetically what they experience, that we may penetrate by an act of intuition to the life-principle itself. To pierce the mystery of the deep it is

sometimes necessary to regard the heights. It is earth's hidden fire which appears at the summit of the volcano.[4]

2. The second standard of religious truth is the *selective actual*. The selective ideal and the selective actual are one and the same thing, but from considerable experience the writer has found the advisability of giving it in two forms to stress two different basic aspects. The ideal brings out the point that the selective points beyond itself as well as beyond the aggregative actual. The ideal suggests that, not only is the selection at the peak of the height or at the front of the process, but it is also a peak that points upward to the illimitable heights or an arrow that suggests the unpredictable distances ahead. But the word "ideal" by itself is too closely associated with theory, with something that is not real, with something that is not actualized, but would be desirable if realized, or good if true. The actual, however, stands pat for the fact that no theory as such can solve our problems. No hypothesis based on an abstraction of mind will do for the content of our existential ultimate. The selective ideal will have to be taken from, and as a matter of fact, *found* among the actuals of process. To satisfy whole-truth, which can be obtained only through the whole-interpretation of whole-response, nothing less than the content of an actual whole-response, rightly interpreted in its relation to the whole, will do. The selective actual in order to indicate a realm of reality far more true and real than the process as a whole, particularly in its present stage, must be solidly actual in the first place. It must possess the power of actualization and the organic relatedness and direction of concretion if later it is to solve our problems of actualization and concretion even indicatively, signifying even by its partial fulfillment of process, because of its representative character in its organic, fulfilling relation to the rest of process, the final fulfillment by purpose of the whole process. Reality is exemplified within actuality by a true, selective actual. Or it is actualized with such fullness as to testify to its eventual complete realization. (We can now look at the problem

[4] Bergson, *Mind-Energy*, English translation American edition, p. 32, in Baillie, *Interpretation of Religion*, p. 465.

either as the real becoming actualized or as the real becoming realized within, or in, actuality, though later we may draw fine distinctions between the two terms.)

Religious truth, in any case, is not built upon mere theory, abstract ideal, or rational persuasiveness. It is built upon the concrete. Theology is incarnational. Philosophies have been built upon rational consistency beyond concrete exemplification. These are legitimate in so far as they are the inferential adumbrations, or penumbra, of knowledge in the stricter sense. The regulating, all-embracing pattern of true theology, however, is always the concrete event, the actualization of the ultimate, the Word made flesh. Much confusion may arise in our thinking if we forget to keep clearly in mind that the selective ideal is at the same time also definitely actual.

3. The third standard of religious truth, that is, truth in the ultimate sense, is the *existential ultimate*. We have already discussed this at length, both indirectly and directly. Here we need, therefore, only to sum up the gist of the meaning. The ultimate means that which truly is most important and most real. The ultimate is the dominant nature of the universe with which we hang together. It is the intrinsic nature of the world to which we must react. The ultimate is that which is necessarily out there, no matter what, whether in being or in value. Yet the "necessarily" in the last sentence cannot be interpreted as a static real, or as an independent realm, or yet as a world known apart from our own reacting. The "necessarily out there" must be thought of existentially. The ultimate is the interpretation of whole-response. It is out there inescapably for us. The "no matter what" phrase is similarly to be through and through existentially focused. No matter what we do we must react to that as the strongest, the most important, the most real, the most true. Whatever we do, in service or rebellion, our basic decision is with respect to that ultimate. The existential is as unavoidable as our own existence and as important as our own existence. Our existence is defined in relation to it. The very content of our existence depends upon the dominant nature of that to which we respond.

The existential ultimate is the content of our reaction, not in mere theory, but in whole-interpretation. It is the god we actually worship. It is our whole self as actually living and lived. We may interpret wrongly, ignorantly worship or willingly serve idols. But they are, in fact, our real gods. They are our existential ultimates. Whole-response, unavoidable, critical, personal, actually dominant —these are words which characterize the existential. The ultimate must be as compelling as our positive will to live and our negative fear of death. It must be the strongest drive in us, our depth decisions, our whole-reason, the light on existence thrown by the deepest burning of our lives. The existential is individual, deeply inward. It is the decision where the martyr must face death rather than deny or recant; it is the depths where the prophet must stand, if need be, alone against the world. Or it is the decision whereby the traitor betrays his dearest cause, as he *thought*, rather than lose his own life. Surely the existential ought to use every scrap of information, every bit of objective knowledge, every ounce of wisdom, social or personal, historic or contemporary, but in the end, faced with life or/and death, he must choose, and he alone.

> You cannot, as some agnostics have supposed you can, keep simply to the ground of ascertained facts. . . . Supposing we were spectators only of reality, and not also makers of it, it might be possible to remain purely agnostic; but the moment you act, you have to be guided by some judgment of value. . . . And the question what is good, what ought to be, depends very much on the question: What kind of universe is this, what is the Ground behind the phenomena.[5]

The existential ultimate is the depth decision of our lives, as inescapable as life on the human level itself, concerning who is our God and how we are to serve him. It is more than the question: What is my life and what will I make of it? It includes the further and more important question: Who is my God and what will be made of my life?

4. The next standard peculiar to religious truth is the *reflexive*

[5] Bevan, *Symbolism and Belief*, pp. 371-372.

superspective. The superspective is the perspective from the most high. It is the regulative pattern, the dominant motif, the molding form, the all-shaping principle of interpretation. It is the center of the focus of religious seeing. It is the main stream of process. It is the main outline of the theme. It is the central structure of the thesis. It is the most important crossroads of all thinking. It is the final, fulfilling dimension. It is the main fuse which lets the rest of the fuses work. Not all is to be reduced to the most high, but nothing is to be understood, in the end, apart from it. But the religious superspective is more than superspective; it is reflexively superspective. Not only is the process to be in terms of it and is it under obligation to be guided by it. Rather the process is in the end to conform completely to it. The process is to be understood in the light of the superspective having become all-dominant and all-inclusive so that what is now contrary to it is seen reflexively, retrospectively, from that point of attainment, as incidentally instrumental and as ultimately unreal. Only that partakes of reality within the actual, in any eminent sense, in any true and permanent sense, which accords with the superspective. Reflexively, or retrospectively, from the point of final attainment we can even now, albeit only darkly and hesitantly, understand the nature of the process as a whole. The reflexive superspective must by its very nature account for all deficient reality, that is, for every kind of actuality that we do have, inasmuch as this is truly a part of our present experience. The reflexive superspective is our perspective at the center of the selective ideal when this, in turn, is taken to be the center of all purpose and all processes. The reflexive superspective is thus constantly on guard against making the selective ideal, or the selective actual, existentially limited to our present stage of process. It is the barrier against making the selective ideal merely the organizing principle of the coherence of our actual, which is, after all, only a broken and distorted coherence. The reflexive superspective is the center of that final coherence which is based on the nature of the ultimate, at the same time transcending process yet also selectively actual within it. It is the light of eternity embodied within a historic event, and, seen from the opposite direction, a historic event affording us, existentially, a window opening out of our kind of time onto eternity. It is the unique stone containing the ultimate kind of language, telling the truest story, a story which we know in a garbled form in our actual world, but a story which must be more fully understood as we come to know the better version in a better language and as we ourselves act out the plot and direction of it. It is the key to our full release, but a key so incorruptible to any kind of change that if we are to be released we must fit the door to the key. It is the "anticipated attainment," the "clarified anticipation," the best sample of the kind of goods we are to get, the truest token of our destiny. The reflexive superspective is our seeing of the partial and perverted present process after our having already seen the fellowship realized, and after our having already seen all else conducive to the fullest and finest fruits of such fellowship. It is the seeing of the right blueprints for our present process and at the same time the seeing of our present building, both right and wrong, in the terms of that blueprint. It is the existential seeing of the most high as the prospectively realized center of all coherence, as the kind of condition universally understood and accepted, as God ruling in a perfectly good and willingly accepted sovereignty in the midst of His people—and the anguish of heart, consequent on such seeing, that this condition is now far from us.

5. The last standard we mention is that of *dynamic self-verification*. That religious truth is dynamic means, positively, that it is progressively self-verifying and, negatively, that its opposite is progressively self-refuting. This is true personally and socially, subjectively and objectively, theoretically and practically. Faith is existentially accumulative. It has a historic body as well as eternal spirit; it has horizontal unity and propulsive power as well as vertical standard and dynamic. Personally truth and grace enrich the individual life, giving light and steadiness to it increasingly. The spirit is self-authenticating. The ultimate compels the more intensively both the more strongly and the longer we look at it, listen to it, and walk according to it. Religious truth, when lived in whole-response, must convince more and more, until

all else seems groundless in comparison to it. Not being fully actual it cannot be proved *ab extra;* but it can be the vision that is knowledge, the feeling that is assurance, the power that is spontaneous, constructive action, the peace and total well-being, meeting the depths of our needs, that no other whole-response can give.

Socially, religious truth must be the locus of the most practical solution of our problems. The more religious truth is accepted and universally practiced the more the problems of society must be soluble and on the way to solution. Oppositely, the more religious truth is neglected or defied, or not learned at all, the more individuals and society must become increasingly thinned out, frustrated, tangled up, destructive, suffering lack of nerve, deficient in creative vision and joy—the more all life must become unsatisfactory. Naturally, as Plato observed with regard to the unjust man, only the just or the virtuous, or those who have once been just and good, can adequately judge what constitutes true happiness because the wicked cannot even understand the experience of justice and goodness.[6] "Wisdom" must be "justified by her children." "Faith is the proving of things not seen." We must be transformed in mind in order to prove what is good and acceptable. Nevertheless in a chapter in the next volume we shall find much to suggest even objectively the truth of the dynamic self-verification of religious truth both personally and socially. No neat line can be drawn, of course, between subjective and objective, theoretical and practical self-verification, but both must be met as fully as possible. Religious truth cannot, in any case, be objective and theoretical in the sense that it can be shown to be our only way out, for instance, as a civilization, and yet leave us subjectively unconvinced and uncommitted; it cannot be a matter of excellent theoretical demonstration which still leaves us, personally and socially, skeptical as to its practical power and relevance. Nor can it, on the other hand, be a case of subjective compulsion and practical conviction without solid basis in objective thinking and in theoretical vision. Dynamic self-verification must be a way of increasing seeing as

[6] Cf. "The Republic," in *The Dialogues of Plato* (Jowett, trans.), Vol. III, p. 97.

well as increasing believing and vice versa. It must be *truth* that works but also truth that *works*.

It is most important to realize and to keep constantly in mind that truth within process is inevitably dynamic. Truth is not for us final or finished. He who looks for static proofs must look in vain. Except as the proofs refer to structures within process, which must themselves partake in some way of the finiteness, fluidity, and plasticity of process, there are no proofs in terms of fixity of form. Staticness if absolutized is frozenness of mind, rather than of process. Process is fluidity of form. It is plastic. The form of process is conditioned in part by freedom. Regularity of pattern is not automatic. The form of men marching together is due in part to men having agreed. Process is a mixture, both muddled and purposed, of past and present, of confusion and vision, of evil weakness and constructive design. The most important aspect of religious knowledge is the relation between realizability and realization. Unless the religious truth is a true ideal for us as man and men, unless it can be for us a good way of walking, unless it is ideally realizable, organically capable of actualization, it cannot be the highest existential truth; it cannot satisfy whole-thinking on whole-response.

Unless, on the other hand, we have also seen it actualized, unless it has been concretely embodied, unless it has made a real difference in history, when it first appeared and now, unless there is realization of it, religious truth remains a matter of theory. Some men are more convinced by seeing, by rational cogency than others. Most men, however, are deeply convinced only when they see actual demonstrations of the way truth works. That appeals to whole-thinking. Righteousness is largely "from faith to faith," from right whole-response to right whole-response. Objectively there would be little to say for religious truth if the proportion of good and evil had always remained the same. If there had been no novel emergences, if there had been no new people with more ample ways of seeing and with whole-responses which created new facts in history, if, in the long last over the ages, there had been no in-breaking of the larger and truer good, if the relation of life's "marble and mud" had always been in constant ratio one to the other, there would be little if any objective reason for concluding that the most high was also fully the most real, that process pointed beyond itself to Purpose.

This is the reason that the relation between realization and realizability is crucial to religious thinking and to the whole question of ultimate truth. If religion is true, *faith* must produce new facts and faith must produce new *facts* that bear on the case. Dynamic self-verification cannot, obviously, be exact, open to strict, objective measures, but it must be based on such general facts as will stand up under strict, objective scrutiny. It cannot be automatic, individually or socially, for then the fact of freedom would be denied and violated; but unless we can see that actuality is a process, that it is going somewhere, and unless we can indicate in general the direction of its going, we have little religious knowledge, and therefore little right to equate religion with truth. Truth of process is fluctuating, conditional in part on freedom, ever bafflingly incomplete. It can never be absolute in a static sense. The ultimate must include process and be seen within the dynamic tensions of process. God always precedes the marching pilgrims. He is who He is in Himself but for us; if He is to be what He is, He must be mostly the God of the future.[7]

The dynamic self-verification of religion depends on the truth that only by going according to the direction of its nature, according to the purpose prescribed for it, can the conditions of process become satisfactory. Life wants satisfaction and is made for it. The general conditionedness and controlledness of process, still allowing for human freedom, rebellion, redemption, and growth, indicates dynamically, as we shall see, the verification of a truth beyond process. The history of nature and the history of humanity are but two aspects of one process pointing beyond itself. The fearful soul imprisons truth within history and is continually frustrated by its escape from him; the creative soul, the vibrantly free soul, however, finds truth a quest to follow. Often the trail it

[7] Cf. article by Edwin Ruthven Walker, *The Christian Century*, Oct. 21, 1942.

leaves is far from well marked; but in the creative adventure of following it the wanderer becomes touched by its spirit and marked by its strength. And though it leads through valleys and through rough places, not infrequently it leads to the mountain's top where the vision is wide and the air is brisk.

Explanation is native to the human mind. We crave to know why things are as they are. Within the limits and attitudes of methodology we may, of course, refuse to ask that basic question, or we may try to reduce the why to a how. Because the method which we use, and which we have assumed or presumed to be all the truth that we can know, is limited to description, we may contend that when we have accurately shown *how* things are we have also shown, as far as human beings can, *why* they are. To this position, too, we may cling in academic or social discussion. Yet we are not really satisfied with that! We want to know why. Our lives search restlessly for meaning. The process which we are in does not seem to make sense altogether. This process of ours is not self-explanatory. We want to know why it is as it is, why it is at all, and why we are in it in the way we are. To be human is to wonder. And beyond wonder there is worry. Besides curiosity, perhaps because of it, we need courage to face life. We are involved. The meaning of our own lives is at stake. We have to react meaningfully. We are men of purpose and inescapably we must respond to the world which made us. We know that the world came before us and that it has set us, who have purposes, into it. To act with purpose toward the world is by implication and indirection, at least, to explain the nature of it. Our purpose both describes and evaluates, or is based on description and evaluation, of an interactive situation between us and the world. The world must be such, at least, as to be open to, and affected by, our purposes. To act with purpose is to explain in a practical sense. It is to say the why of things in the language of whole-response. In purposing we pass on the question not only of how things are, but how things ought to be, and back of that question is always some kind of why of things. Value and being are not two discrete realms. They meet in us and point primarily beyond us. Purposive action refers beyond ourselves. Intention, as John Macmurray has well pointed out in *The Clue to History*,[8] combines reflection and action, making action issue out of some why of things. Purposive action is the interpretation of whole-response. It involves feeling, will, and thought as they have originated in connection with whole-reaction and refer back to the world which acts on us.

Explanation, thus, is native to the human mind more than philosophically, in the strict sense. We want, of course, to know for the sake of knowing. We are curious creatures in a mysterious universe. We are children asking interminable questions. Part of alert life is simply wanting to know. Explanation is also native to the human mind on a more decisive level, that is, theologically. Our lives are always in the making, making and being made. Life is reaction. It is a cumulative interpretation of how things are, why they are as they are, and how, therefore, they can be made different. Such practical explanation is existential. It is inescapably responsible. Whether or not we meet Purpose, as we think, we do meet purposes. Our dearest and most vexing judgments on the human level concerning family and profession involve whys. Beyond the social situation, moreover, is its meaning and the meaning of process as a whole.

If process, moreover, had always been basically the same, as far as we know, there would be little reason, if any, not to identify process with reality. There would then be no legitimate objection against reducing the why to the how. Then, indeed, such equation would be altogether natural. But the history of our cosmic process has undergone basic changes. Actuals have become radically different. Particularly is this true if the accounts of science are true. Mythology, too, stresses origins, the coming of the radically new. Religions, similarly, speak of creation, or of the coming of basically different epochs. Science, however, is to a very large extent an attempt at a disinterested, factual accounting of things as they are, and how and when they became that way, as far as we can know it. In so far as science describes this actual world and its history in the best way human knowledge can, we accept for substance of

[8] P. 7.

doctrine, without winking at its many mistakes and unfortunate fads, which are but part and parcel of general human foibles and fallibilities, its general picture of some kind of evolutionary process. We believe that as far as the relevant environment of human history is concerned there was a time when, for instance, there was no water, no life, no human life; when the time came that men could leave behind them some kind of permanent records, historical life, in a recorded sense, began. We know something about the beginnings of science, of men's first attempts to interpret this process philosophically (at least a beginning, or beginnings, or kinds of beginning, for there were very likely incipient beginnings long before we have any knowledge or any idea. Thomas Mann's idea of "coulisses" in *Joseph and His Brethren*, for instance, has probably much real insight).

From the existential point of view, however, our origins and their meanings have naturally first claim since these have to do with answers to our most insistent clamoring for the why of things, why we are, what this is all about. We understand that there was an inorganic evolution before there was life in our cosmos, then there was life of a low grade, then there was consciousness, later self-consciousness, later still, attempts at objective interpretation, later still, the understanding of the law of love as the constructive law of life—a fact as yet seen only exceptionally in terms of actual whole-responses, that is, in terms of such thinking as results from and accords with dominant living. There have thus been different actuals, different stages of process; particularly from the point of view of what is most meaningful to us, from our inescapable existentiality, there have been radically different actuals, all-important revolutions in the nature of the different stages of process. Something new has been added that makes all the difference to us, without which we should not even be here at all. If science is right, all this effort to know would not even have been considered, unless there had been the coming of the meaningfully new, which as such, at least, was not there before.

In terms of these facts, as facts go (for these facts are obviously not on a level with the existential fact that we are here now and

have to make decisive interpretations as to the meaning and becoming of things), what is the meaning of it all? What is the reason
for our being here? What is the purpose for our being here? Or is
there any meaning out there? Is there a reason out there? Is there
a purpose out there? What are we here for, or are we here for
anything, and what are we going to do about it all? In this next
section of our chapter we shall try to examine three possible explanations, all widely used. The three are the following: that which
came first, that which is here and now actual, the most significant
emergent or arrival in the history of process. The first two try to
explain our existence from within process, from within rational
knowledge. The last gathers all knowledge it can from process and
finds that this reaches out for the explanation of itself beyond
process. The middle explanation, as we saw in our chapter on
philosophy, tends to swing between the first and the last. Some explanations come more closely to science abused as metaphysics;
others to religion abused as mere knowledge. There are no clear
lines from one end of explanation to the other. There are, rather,
innumerable shades of explanation. These three, however, are both
basic and typical. We are not one bit concerned about names or
schools of thought as such. Our real, compelling concern, rather,
is to lay bare the underlying issues in order that we may learn to
see the issues for what they are and to co-operate to advantage
from within our respective fields of knowledge.

1. That which is known to have come first offers a common and
suggestive explanation of the origin of all that came later. We are
not now thinking about that which ever is, or which truly was
first, but about that which science describes as coming first. The
inorganic, for instance, preceded the organic. Because of this
fact it is considered reasonable to suppose that the organic came
from the inorganic, is somehow to be understood by attention to it,
is in some way or other to be considered an aspect of it. Some
simply say that the organic is nothing but an extension in kind of
the inorganic. Whatever sudden leaps there seem to have been, we
know that evolution as a whole has been a slow and rather gradual

process. We know, for that matter, areas where the organic and the inorganic are even now hardly distinguishable. Missing links, most likely, are only lacks in our knowledge. The process, we may suppose, is continuous, albeit we have failed up to now to find, or to understand, certain sections of its history.

Obviously this kind of explanation of origins is not science but metaphysics. Science simply describes. When the organic is reduced to the inorganic because the latter is known to have appeared first in our cosmos, pure description has given way to explanation; strict science, to philosophy; and, to whatever extent the self is critically involved, science, to religion. Our question, consequently, is whether this explanation is or is not good philosophy. While we can, of course, state and test only the objective side of knowledge, the philosophical, to do so is of utmost importance since knowledge in some form constitutes the content of our existential ultimate. In weighing the three main principles for interpreting the origins of process, we discuss meaningfully their relative rational adequacy. Is, therefore, this first principle rationally adequate?

The position that what we know came first explains what follows is now held more popularly than professionally. There are few scientists of thoughtful disposition and few philosophers who subscribe to this crude kind of naturalism. Nevertheless this position is held, though often assumed without much critical investigation, in large sections of educated and semieducated people. It has also penetrated into the unconscious presuppositions of the popular consciousness by means of the various indirect sources of modern communications and entertainment, and often from the very mother's milk of education, whether public or private. The upshot of this position is vaguely that since the inorganic came first it must somehow account for the organic. Whatever there was in the beginning according to our best knowledge must naturally be the source of all else.

This line of thinking is positively suggestive for two reasons. In the first place, it gets much plausibility from the general idea of chronological priority, which is a natural principle of interpretation. Which came first: the hen or the egg? If we only know which came first, so we reason, we should also know which had the prior claim to reality. Temporal priority is our common way of explaining things. Obviously it contains a basic truth. Is this truth, however, appropriately applied with respect to this first position? The second reason for the suggestiveness of this line of thinking is that of causal continuity. The reason that chronological priority itself has such a hold on us is that in the general cause-effect sequence, or at least in the general idea of it, the cause always precedes the effect. Ante-sequential causation, or purpose pulling from in front of the event rather than pushing from behind, is not a common way of looking at things. The modern attempt to re-define cause is esoteric as far as general thinking goes. For us to explain has been to refer to a cause, to some equivalent event in the past, whereas for the classical tradition to explain, as for in-stance in Plato, was to refer to a purpose. Thus chronological priority rests partly on this general sense of causal continuity in common experience where the cause precedes the effect, where that which precedes explains what follows.

Causal continuity, in a restricted operational sense, is also natural to the modern mind because it has been the overwhelmingly prevailing method of science; and science in this strict sense has come to be increasingly equated with truth. The content of science has become a metaphysics almost by default. It has simply been assumed, in most instances, as the whole truth of humanity. In the older mechanistic science, which in some quarters is still very modern, the exact equivalence of cause and effect was the corner-stone of knowledge. What is more natural, then, than to suppose that since we know that once there was a lifeless world, the life which appeared after the lifeless must somehow be reduced to the lifeless world that preceded it? Life may therefore be called an epiphenomenon. It may consequently be considered basically an unreal thing, an aspect of the inorganic, or merely a new arrange-ment of it. In any case the prior claim to reality is to be held firmly by that which we know had the prior existence. Spirit, freedom, meaning, and similar terms are terms without effectual reference; they are mere abstractions of the mind; they have no effectual existence in the actual world of real causes and effects. This is the position in general. We have tried to state it as accurately as we can for substance of doctrine. What now have we to say in appraisal of this first principle that what came first in our cosmos is the best principle to explain all that is now present in process?

The first, and perhaps most obvious, observation is that the mechanistic assumption which underlies it is itself false. It is an abstraction from a method which deals with only a part of our experience. For that matter, it is now no longer held by a good number of scientists. All the way from quantum physics to psychology there is much protestation that indeterminacy must be a part of scientific thinking. The concepts of organism whereby the whole affects its several members and can even substitute functions on the part of its different members in order to preserve the whole has invaded biology and physiology. Old localization theories in medicine of a mechanical nature have in many quarters become transformed to organismic, functional concepts. Depth psychology has found out much about the psyche and its effect on the operations of the body. Profound thinkers in this field, like Otto Rank, have even understood the effect that conscious willing has on the psychosomatic situation. Yet regardless of what the scientists find in their fields, by their methods, such primary facts of experience as purpose and freedom remain. They are as basic as our existential situation. They can be explained away by reductionist method or philosophized out of rational discourse, but they nevertheless remain at the very root of life and cannot be existentially denied. The very denial either is an attempt to escape a responsibility which is as inescapable as life, or else it is the ignorant yielding to the lure of the logical temptation of method to reduce life to forms that can be handled, to the quantitative contents of causal continuity. Then, too, "science" varies. Its theories come and go. Today it has its full measure of uncertainties and quick, revolutionary changes. It is also prone to fads, the way any human situation is, fads that are part-truths or distorted truths enthusiastically, but prematurely, proclaimed as the full truth. Then after a while. . . .

To try to explain everything in terms of the lowest forms of inorganic evolution because it came first is natural and suggestive to the uncritical mind, but the mechanistic assumption which underlies it is not warranted. If, as science says, to begin with in the world there were no persons, no freedom, no spirit, then something new has come into history; *that we know.* The power and prestige of the mechanistic method and its uncritical identification with all the truth that can be known has, however, so sucked the human spirit into its grasp that it has become actually possible for people to believe that only that which can be handled well by strict science and which is capable of exact, quantitative measures can be called truly the really real. It is a strange commentary on the power of method and on the gullibility of the human spirit that in order to justify this assumption people have been actually able to deny the reality of life, of consciousness, of spirit—to deny in fact the reality of the very existential situation which makes any interpretation possible.

The second observation is to the effect that to make what came first in our cosmos, according to our knowledge, first in reality is to be needlessly anthropocentric. Because for all we know it came first, it need not be first in reality. Our knowledge of the first is no guarantee of its being first. To equate the lowliest beginnings of our process with the fullness of reality, however, may not be anthropic enough, since this equation is amply contradicted by what we do know now. Yet in our defensive search for security we want to know everything. If all there is can be known by us in the laboratory we have increasing hope of knowing all about it and also of controlling it increasingly. Our knowledge becomes our power. Our control becomes our safety. We tend to become central in the universe. We can control the blind forces to our advantage. Thus we reason away, or try to reason away, our fears. As far as the facts go, however, we sin against them, we violate them by being thus needlessly anthropocentric. If we were less defensive we should dare to open our eyes to the mystery of creation, to the mystery of the new. Then man would have more meaning, status, and hope; in this sense he would be more adequately anthropic. But his hope would now lie in the larger reality which created him.

He would now have to look up rather than down; obey rather than control; follow rather than steer.

Obviously what comes into history, or into actual being, points to *some* prior ground. This may be a prior chain of causations or it may be the ground of being itself, that which always is, no matter what. Priority or ground can be within or beyond actuality. There is nothing wrong with chronological priority as a principle of explanation provided it does not amount to an endless regression where our stopping point is arbitrary. The child has every right to ask: "Then who made God?" There must be some reason for our existential ultimate. A famous philosopher said that only fools ask about first principles, but first principles cannot be chosen at will. How natural it is simply to accept the first of our process as the basic principle of explanation. Chronological priority filled with the content of the beginnings of our cosmos is, however, arbitrary because it lacks the power to explain that which came into it afterwards. Even though this principle is a natural assumption, it is still an assumption. It may seem to be the obvious explanation and the minimum explanation, but because it seems obvious and simple, we must be all the more careful that it is not specious. What came first is an arbitrary principle of explanation which may seem to make man's power central since the content of his knowledge can be increasingly controlled, but which, in effect, is needlessly and destructively anthropocentric, since by being more anthropic and rationally adequate in explaining the new, man can find a truth that can save him even beyond himself.

Our third observation is that reduction denies; it does not explain. It limits knowledge by presuppositions. It is a false, at least an *a priori*, way of thinking. Because mechanism is all that we can know by the strict method of science, as some thought, or is the content to which we have already confined this method, there can, therefore, be nothing else. Thus men limit knowledge to exact science and reality to knowledge. If there seems to be something else, it cannot be real; it must be mere seeming; it must be the error of mortal thought. Thus a most limiting rationalism, a false philosophy, takes the place of the adequate description which is based on the open-minded observation and the full reporting of all that is seen. An excellent scientist, holding an important position among scientists, even tried in this fashion to deny that there were any value judgments at all. He reasoned as follows: Science deals with all the truth there is. Value judgments are only seeming. They are simply the result of past experience and are completely mechanical in their operation. The strongest impulse based on past experience always wins. We want and choose that which was most pleasant to us in the past. Value judgments are nothing but our illusion of choice, while choice actually is determined purely by cause and effect and that is always purely a matter of fact. Man is thus a mere machine, an automaton. He is completely controlled by his environment, like a rock.

Here was a plain denial that purpose, conditioned, of course, by past experience and grounded in the nature and preferences of each person, is ante-sequential in its main drive. Yet we know that purpose *faces* the future predominantly. It is aim at value. This whole experience is simply explained away in order to make a certain method exclusive. Instead of seeking to explain the full facts, the defensive pull of method, whether logical or psychological, simply makes men take refuge in outright denial. The fullness of experience can, of course, be denied theoretically, but it can never be denied existentially. Purpose is simply part of life, laying us all under obligation to something beyond ourselves.

How large this reduction is can be readily seen by a comparison of the fullness of our process now with its most meager beginnings. This can be seen even objectively. And existentially! The difference is all-important. What difference does it make, basically, whether the new comes into history gradually or at a bounce? At a bounce the new is more startling, more easy to isolate, and more accessible to public demonstration. The more discontinuity is directly involved in the sense that the new can only very partially be explained in terms of continuity with previous chains of causation, the easier it is to prove the existence of the new. Yet the new is new no matter how or how fast it comes. "This is not that" is a basic intellectual judgment. It lies at the very root of our thinking.

The principles of identity and difference are essential aspects of knowledge. Life is not non-life. Consciousness is not non-consciousness. Reason is not non-reason. Justice is not non-justice. Love is not non-love. The coming of one of these, or all of these, into history may be gradual or it may be abrupt. But it came. It was not there before as such. It will not do to reduce the difference to common basic elements. It will not do to change the problem to one of mere arrangement. It will not do to make the new simply a matter of form. There is newness and there is difference. My child dead may be only a different arrangement of energy from my child alive, but I will defy anyone to say that the two are basically the same. The truth that matters lies in that difference of form or of arrangement, if *that* is what it is. If my child should become alive again and sit in my lap and play, the truth of the situation would be different and new, no matter how some chirped about the elements being basically the same. Whether the process would be gradual or sudden, within relevant limits of time, of course, would not be crucial. The crucial thing is this: is my child dead or alive?

This world of ours is not the same as the world before life came into it. There is something new and different. Whether evolution jumped like a chased squirrel or crawled like a drugged snail makes little difference now. Whether the change came in six days or in six sidereal years matters not basically. What matters is the difference. Objectively the difference is large enough to fill volumes upon volumes of scientific description; and existentially the difference is decisive. Suppose that a friend told me that a seed and the flower that later came from it were the same. I should naturally grant that there was a definite observable sameness of substance and function. By all means. But if he insisted that I was sentimental and superficial, not wanting to face facts, because I knew that the difference between the two was immense even objectively, I should simply keep thinking that his way of looking at things was prejudiced, abstract, lifeless. His truth would be of utmost importance in the study of the seed and in the care of the plant; in the botanical understanding of it. I should be no end thankful to him for his work. Nevertheless, if he asked me to believe that the seed and the flower were the same in the most basic sense, I should balk irrevocably. Objectively they look different and have different uses. It is true that one came from the other, but even so it would hardly have come from it if the flower, the full source, had not been there before it in some way, and the flower even then would not have come from the seed unless there had also been the sun and the soil, the food, the moisture, and the vitamins. That is the objective part of it. That the seed came first, that the flower to a great extent came from it, and that the process was one of gradual growth are true and important facts, but they do not, nevertheless, make the seed and the flower the same. Just let the scientist try coming home with a package of seeds for a centerpiece when his wife has asked him to bring flowers for her dinner party. Let him argue that the elements are basically the same. Let him say that value judgments have no relevance to existential truth. He may find out that truth can be learned in the kitchen as well as in the laboratory.

The beginning of our process is only the seed. Within it is unguessed power to become. Outside it there are the sun and the soil. The seed simply is not the plant, even in its long process of growing. The plant in the process of growing is simply not the full flower. How much we need to know about the nature of the seed and of the growing plant. That aspect of our situation must not be belittled. Perhaps we need to know more about the sun and the soil, about what there is outside the plant to let it grow. It would be folly to become so interested in the botany of the plant that we could no longer enjoy the life of the plant and its flower, in all its beauty. To reduce the fullness of process with its existentially essential differences to the meager beginnings of process is not to explain. It is to reduce. Whether such reduction is due to the logical tendency of the scientific method or due to psychological tendencies is unimportant as far as the truth of the situation goes. The reduction is a fact all the same. Only pseudo-science will explain away the new in order to make its method all-embracing. Only science so-called will falsify description and turn metaphysical in order to be able to call itself all the truth that can be had. By so doing it tries to have its cake and to eat it too. It claims to describe things as they are with utter honesty and yet violates most damagingly full description in order to keep its perfect security and demonstrability which is rooted in objective, exact, causal continuity. Such defensive thinking proceeds to describe the new only to deny that there really is any.

A brief summary, or restatement, of the first principle and its inadequacy to explain the full present stage of process may be helpful at this point. The principle is this: What science says came first in our process explains all else. What came first was some form of inorganic evolution. Historically we know neither pure matter and motion nor pure energy. These are abstractions by analysis. What we know came first was inorganic evolution. This inorganic realm must then itself be the reality and nature of things. All else that has come must be from and of it and is, therefore, appearance only. The manifold organic realm is simply a nonessential extension of this inorganic realm—matter, energy, motion, and whatever, in their most primal combinations. There is no essential or effective newness in history. Nothing now is which is not some combination of these primal realities, some form, or arrangement, of them, and which cannot be reduced to them or resolved into them.

This principle is accepted mostly on the grounds of chronological priority and of causal continuity in an exact mechanical, or equivalent, manner. These standards are obviously intrinsically necessary to certain levels of scientific investigation. They have at least been generally assumed to be so until lately. Priority and continuity, in any case, are essential elements of dependable rational discourse. We have, however, no right to fit history and description into the limits of method. Both objectively and existentially there is newness and difference. Whether this newness is gradual or sudden is not of basic importance. Between life and death, matter and consciousness, there is basic, although naturally not complete, difference. Even if human intelligence should learn how to produce or to manipulate life by the combination of elements, it still would be life, intelligence, that did it. Already man manipulates life, in connection with birth, sickness, and health, and in connection with death. If, however, a lump of coal should walk up to a laboratory and combine elements into life, or give caffein to a stopping heart, we should be more surprised, but even so, in the direction of *extending*, not of reducing, life and intelligence. The basic fact is that process is such as to contain life and to promote life. Life, too, seems to become more and more conscious of itself and of its environment; it is actually growing in reach even while it fearfully denies its own essential existence. Whether ultimately all life and purpose has some counterpart in outward appearance, whether bodies of some kind are necessary to intercommunication and creativity, is of interest and of some importance; but the deeper question is whether there is ground to believe that the life we know points to some fulfillment of process, to some newness of arrangement, if we will, to some combination of itself from within or from beyond itself, which means the fulfillment of the highest purpose we know and believe in because of the highest instance that has already appeared within process itself.

From within inorganic process there is, in any case, no explanation of the meaning we know, no reason for the coming of the higher. There is only blind chance leading the blind material. He indeed is blind, and keeps letting himself be blinded by his fears, who in whole-thinking, by heart, head, and hand together, can conclude that such content constitutes a more rationally conclusive criterion for our existential ultimate than other choices which we are to offer. The knowledge which he gives us we value. The religion which he makes of such knowledge we shun. For we must live by whole-knowledge meeting the needs of the whole man and not by the lifeless abstractions of a limited method, prostituted by logical and psychological temptations.

We agree with William L. Sullivan:

> If a man asserts to me that nitrogen and carbon can in certain conditions work out, let us say, Appel's equations for motion in a dynamic system; if he declares that, given the right conditions again, alcohol, bicarbonate of soda, and the enzyme that hydrolizes protein can write the Divine Comedy, I for one do not know what

he is talking about, and am quite sure that when he gives his theory a moral value by calling it truth he doesn't know either. . . . As for the "reduction" of the higher to lower, leaving the higher "explained" by the lower, it is to me the most perverse of all ineptitudes, the most empty of all fallacies. It is a feature of that flight from fact—that substitution of simplification for simplicity which will furnish to the erudite the best example of romantic "wishing" that they could find.[9]

Explain we must. The ultimate is existentially unavoidable. Mere description will not do. Moment by moment we must pass on what is the nature of the most high and the most real. What came first, falsely limited to the meager beginning of our process, cannot meet the requirements of the fullest possible explanation that will validly face all the facts and then adequately relate and explain them. We go on, therefore, to the second and more adequate answer.

2. The second possible principle for explaining our process, the second possible content for our existential ultimate, the second possible criterion of truth is this: all that which is here and now actual. We must be careful to remember that the actual includes all the ideals that we can know, whether they are actualized or only true potentials or possibilities. Truth is all that we now know. We may discover more truth but it can never go, for us, beyond our knowledge for that is our standard of truth. Truth can have no legitimate meaning other than knowledge. More we may find out day by day. More will become actualized, we may believe, but until we see it we can only believe it. "We have but faith: we cannot know; for knowledge is of things we see."[10] And faith is faith and not knowledge. It cannot convincingly be called truth. This is the general position of this point of view.

What is here and now actual, moreover, can be looked at either conjunctively or disjunctively, either as a unit or as an area filled

---

[9] "The Moral Will and the Faith That Sustains It," in *Contemporary American Theology,* Second Series, ed. by Vergilius Ferm, pp. 286–287.
[10] Tennyson, "In Memoriam."

with more or less discrete particulars, either as an organized entity or as a mere togetherness of things. The former view is more philosophical; the latter, more scientific. The former is more systematic interpretation; the second is more pure description. Both positions, however, make what is here and now actual as a whole, or in its totality, the standard of truth.

A. We shall begin with the latter view as connecting more easily with our first point. This view says simply that what is here is here, as it is here, and that is all that we can know. Truth is what we can know as we know it. It is accurate description of all there is. Further interpretation is futile, misleading, and an impoverishing speculation. We can describe pretty well, but as soon as we begin to interpret, we oversimplify. We change the actual world with its rich and full experience for bloodless categories and meatless principles. At the best we are left with nothing but a skeleton; but most of the time we have only bones picked more or less at random and rigged up as a skeleton, and then, of all things, labeled the full body of truth. Description is all the truth that we can have except as inference must perhaps occasionally fill out the picture. Yet it must do so as sparingly and as grudgingly as possible. We must stick to the facts. If inference preserves rational discourse in the strictest sense or leads to new facts, or to their effective, extended operation, we may use it; but no further. Even this point of view, the disjunctive, the one that treats all the facts on a par, as equally true if they are really here to be known, even this point of view divides into two parts: Some say that pure description is enough regardless of origins; others try to cover the problem of origins by recourse to possibility or subsistence.

a. Many say that all we can do is to describe. That is the truth. If certain things were first in history, that is that. If others appeared later, that is that. It is vain for us to explain why and how the latter came into history. We do not know any ultimate origins. That problem goes beyond the competency of the human mind. Let us stick to facts and say that this is this and that this came then and then. That is honest and that is enough. Why reduce what is later to what went on before? The two are not the same.

That is to stop describing and to philosophize. Neither let us say what will happen. We do not know. Our minds must be open at both ends: both concerning origins and concerning ends. There is newness. There is difference in history. There is emergence, and emergence is simply a fact like other facts. There are novel emergences. Some are more continuous with what went on before. Some are less so. Yet change is real. Not to admit it is to deny true description. Those who reduce everything serve the cause of science ill. Science gives us truth when it sticks to facts and refuses to philosophize. Those who reduce description by explanation are defensive about their method, and because of this become unduly offensive about their exclusive way to truth.

Positively this viewpoint is well taken. It is the finest flower of the scientific spirit. Negatively this view is disastrous. It denies the need to interpret, the need to select. Life, as we have seen, demands decisions. To live is to exclude more than we directly include. We must act and keep acting on what is most important and most real. Whole-truth comes through whole-response, through living decisions. Methodological tentativeness and non-commitment in the descriptive realm are virtues. In whole-response they are both impossible and irresponsible. Life demands interpretation. Our lives must have unity. Civilization needs guidance. To sit aside after scientific description has made life potentially a possible hell or a possible heaven, comparatively speaking; to sit aside while civilization builds castles of co-operation or destroys itself and its home in the cosmos is simply criminal negligence. Truth matters. Truth helps or hurts. Truth wounds or heals. Truth kills or helps life to grow. And saving truth can be found.

Simply to say: description is enough; we shall make no choice; we have no faith in value judgments or in the selective interpretation as truth; we shall wait and see what is around the corner for us to describe—simply to say this is fatal negligence. It is driving so as to endanger. For drive we all do. Our lives move and make a difference. Life is no placid sitting behind an experiment. Real, full life, personal or social, is decisive action based on the best and the most true interpretation we can find. It can be found if we patiently and openly search for it with all our lives. We need, of course, all the description that we can get. The more and the more accurate description, the better. There is a truth of description. We need it vitally. Even so, description will not do for prescription. Mere knowledge cannot substitute for knowledge wedded with creative faith to produce truth. Existentially scientific description substituted for the full truth is in fact an evasion of the problem regardless of intent.

Then, too, this evasion is also treason to reason in its fullest reaches. For reason, to a large and most significant extent, can explain. The fact that we are not all-knowing dooms all knowledge alike. That would doom description too. We must know in part, but in part sufficient to describe for our purposes from our point of view, and for us to be saved within our situation and from the evils of the situation in which we now are. Mere description does not push reason to its utmost limits, and man must ever be up and alert to scan his horizons of thought. Naturally we are not judging people but positions. Some who hold this position theoretically are most alive and different existentially. Actual people are very busy creatures who think little and who seldom mean merely to be perverse or to be inadequate. Most of them surely are not conscious of evading responsibility or of being traitors to reason in its further and more important reaches. They just live and do their day's work, full of little joys and sorrows, of vexations, of encouragements, of disappointments, of hopes for a better day. They decide enough actually. Many have deep religious faith existentially. Yet they cannot see beyond their narrow pet, or professional, theories.

It is easy to say that science deals with truths, not with Truth. Yet science assumes a universe. It assumes the reliability of concepts, of theories, of relations. If everything were a matter of unrelated facts, of discrete truths not implying and involving one another, we should not be conducting scientific experiments based on centuries of common thinking in a common world using inherited and gradually accumulated knowledge. We should not be comparing notes either as scientist or as scientists, philosophers, and theologians. We could not even live and talk together at all.

Experience itself is based on the repetition of our reactions, the regularity of occurrence, the dependability of memory. The world is threatened today by the fact that while we hang together as a physical universe and as social beings within that common universe we do not hang together as thinkers and as men of religion. In order to defend a limited method or in order to escape the demand not of religion, but of God, we turn glibly agnostic and deny all togetherness. We talk about truths, facts, observations as if there were no common background and knowledge needed for the understanding of those facts. The whole approach would seem sophomoric and comic, to be laughed at as a fit of professorial absent-mindedness, as the wearing of rubbers on a sunny day, as something incongruous, at least with real life, if our situation were not so utterly serious. Perhaps we ought to laugh such impossible agnosticism out of court. Perhaps we are foolish noticing such drivel. Perhaps irony alone will bite on such sophistication. Perhaps such academic tripe ought to be roasted on the hot fires of sarcasm. That is unfortunately not our nature. We long to be constructive and to honor every point of view. Yet one wonders, truly wonders, if those can be sincere who deny brazenly the power of reason to deal with anything but the description of particulars and then set out to make universal affirmations about it expecting to have the very reason taken seriously which they have just denied. Existentially speaking the situation is tragic. How can a method or personal irresponsibility lead people so far away from the plainest truths of whole-response, namely, that we can talk intelligently together and work intelligently together in a common universe, in a world of Truth, that they expect to be taken seriously, to be listened to with straight faces, while they go on to saw off the only limb they have to hang on? It is comical yet also tragic to see them bore holes of sophisticate and unfounded doubt in the boat which we all need to keep afloat. Particularly tragic, of course, is it to see the advocates of sheer faith try jubilantly to sink our boat of common meaning.

Obviously this point of view is mostly a mood rather than a method. It is the mood of the scientific life, the life of description.

It is a good mood in its place, a most important methodological mood within its proper field of human knowledge. Even objectively, however, it fails to do justice to the fuller use of reason, and to account rationally in any way for the origins of and within process; and existentially, as we have already seen, it is both impossible and irresponsible.

b. Instead of simply describing all there is whenever it came to be and leaving it there, we can say that all things are equally real but not equally actual. Actuality depends upon the right arrangement of things. Not all things that are, are all the time. They constantly become actual. Yet they are all the time possible. If the arrangement of things under certain circumstances is such that they are likely to become actual, they are potential. What is, is. Once actual we know that it is possible, that it belongs to the realm of things that we know. It is in this sense true. It is in this sense real. We know of no other truth, of no other reality. Nothing is the mere affirmation of the absence of something, of this or of that. It is the affirmation that this or that is not actual. We know no total or general nothingness. That is a mental abstraction. All things that we know to be here and now we also know to be equally true and real but not to be equally actual. Historically some things became actualized before others, but that does not mean that they are less true or less real than the others. Nor does it mean that their reality as such is dependent upon the others. A new combination of things produces that new actualization which as a possibility was always equally real with all else that we know. Naturally certain combinations or ingredients are necessary if a certain actuality is to be potential or to become actual. This is no appeal to an evasive, constructed whole. Yet this position answers the problem of becoming by keeping the reliability of rational discourse. It does not say that something came from nothing at any one time any more than any new occurrence ever comes from nothing when it is merely actualized. And who can deny that new things, including our own experience, seem intrinsic and indubitable parts of our knowledge, as certain as our knowledge itself?

We may compare this with our two previous points of view. The

first we may call *evolutionary materialism*. That reduces everything to the earliest inorganic level. There was a time when there
was no water. There were, however, hydrogen and oxygen. Wetness
is, therefore, mere appearance, a chance combination of oxygen
and hydrogen. Water as water has only a seeming reality. The
original elements in so far as we can isolate them are the ground
of all being, although that they were "there" first historically is
pretty hard to show except by inference (O, horrible word! O,
strange term, being true [?] but in no sense real!). Wetness is a
mere appearance. So is the mind that finds and interprets it. Life
is only the result of a new combination. It has no reality in itself.
It merely points back to the physical elements which underlie it
and are its reality and truth. The second we may call *descriptionism*. Water is as real as oxygen or hydrogen. Life is as real as the
inorganic realm. They were not but now they are. How they came
to be we do not know. Why, we cannot tell. Neither question is our
business. Our business is, rather, to state the truth of things as
they actually are. The third position, so far, we may call possibilism. Whatever can become actual at any time was always possible.
To find the fullness of truth is to find the fullest understanding of
what is possible. Somehow the possible or substance is introduced
as a category of explanation. All that has become possible up to
now is equally true. The here and now merely limits our knowledge
up to now, but more must be looked for, since more is surely possible, but either it is not yet here or else it is not yet understood
although here.

Materialism denies the higher new outright as to its effective
reality. The new is only sham and shadow, only accidental and incidental, only trivial from the point of view of permanent truth. It
is mere appearance. Science, this viewpoint says, need not explain
it. It need not stoop to philosophize. But actually materialism reduces description to the requirements of a limited method; it explains. Descriptionism nonchalantly evades the problem. Our task,
it claims, is to tell the truth as we see it and as we know it to have
come into actuality, not to offer fanciful, reductionist, and unreliable explanations. Possibilism, however, acknowledges the wider

problem and sets out to give an answer. It is a thoughtful position held by good scientists and philosophers alike. Why, then, is it not our answer to what is the most important and most real? Can we legitimately go beyond it?

Our real query about this position is this: What, precisely, is meant by the possibilities which are supposed to explain the becoming of the actuals? Do they exist in any sense at all except verbally? If they do, then things are more than they seem. Then facts are but icebergs hiding their deeper being and significance—particularly from the existential point of view. Then actuality contained wetness in some way before wetness was actually here in cosmic history. Actuality must then, in some way, have been full of life before life appeared on this planet. Then consciousness and love were in some way real before they became experienced in historic life. Then the most important aspects of actuality were either *supra* or *intra* actual. What matters most to us was then always "there"; only it had not appeared as yet. It makes no difference whether we say that this non-actual existence was above, beyond, or within actuality. It was in some way truly there, though hidden. The most important realm thus was once the non-actual, the intra-actual, or the supernatural. We know then that the hole of our existential seeking was once suprahistorical.

To make rational discourse complete, moreover, to make it truly explain, there must also have been enough power in, or with, these possibilities to actualize them, and enough purpose to make them organically related to the previous actuals. They are organically continuous on any level with previous actuality, and, like reason, make it more possible increasingly, the higher the becoming, to explain the previous lower levels of becoming. If this is not true, if possibility does not mean at least all this, we have a mere verbalism, a mere descriptionism with an admission tagged on to the effect that since the new and different came into history, and since mind cannot admit something coming from completely nothing—from neither purpose nor cause—there must somehow have been some antecedent in the non-actual universe to account for them. If they exist in no way at all, we have, of course, a mere descriptionism covered by the false front of verbalism. Then there is still only a begging of the question, an ingenious evasion of it.[11] Then the new is still admitted as sheer miracle, as a creation *ab nihilo,* without a Creator. If, on the other hand, they exist with enough status in both being and order to make them sufficient principles of explanation, they also affirm inseparably the existence of a superhistorical or supernatural realm, or an intra-historical and intra-natural realm (the question is not of location but of reality and of kind of reality) which existentially is the heart, mind, and soul of what we are interested in and try to explain. Since verbalism is no explanation, possibilism simply points beyond process begging for explanation. It can be the stopping point for science, but not for theology.

Some say that no actual element contained the new in any sense, but that the different elements contain such ingredients as to produce the new whenever the proper combination takes place. This is an affirmation that we have seen revolutionary changes within a short moment of cosmic time simply because new combinations have swiftly taken place. Existentially these are the most important changes. What, then, is the *fully proper combination of all possible elements,* what can effect it, and what will it be like when that is accomplished? Thus goes the process: non-life, life, consciousness, reason, growth in extensive and intensive modes of fellowship, creative life through responsible concern and co-operation. Are these appearances? Then in line with previous actualization will they once become all-pervasive and permanent appearances? Are they unknown resources within process? What will it be like when they are fully known? Or is there a whole before, or along with, process which by combining these structures and guiding these functions makes the new appear in due time? What more will it bring out? Where is it guiding us? We know that the whole has been more than the sum of its *past* parts by any reckoning. To call *that more* which to us is life and more life; life and par-

---

[11] For a spicy yet suggestive discussion, compare Joad, *God and Evil,* "Science and the Cosmos" and "God as Emergent and God as Created," pp. 106–179.

ticularly better life; life and hope afresh; life and faith self-justifying—to call that more mere appearance or incidental is most certainly to be blinded existentially by the limitations of both mind and method. The whole is, then, more than what was. That we know. Process has gone somewhere. That we know. The puzzle is then yet to be solved. The full picture is then not yet ours. Yet the process is now at the point where we can help to advance it. For process has reached a point where combinations are not only made by process as a whole. Parts of it can now also think, choose, act. The whole is still greater than its present parts, and new parts are constantly becoming known. Surely the whole cannot be equal to the sum of its first known parts since new authentic parts have appeared. It is rather far greater than the sum of its *known* parts. A reductionist mechanism, then, will not do as full explanation. Origins shatter it. Mere organism will not do as full explanation if organism is used as an evasive way of explaining away the new in terms of a mystic wholeness which is not genuinely characterized by its newest and best parts. Magic hats are for vaudeville, not for serious thought. *We know that the new has come and that the process points on.* Take it any way at all, *this much we know.*

Existentially, moreover, this position is just as unsatisfactory and irresponsible as the preceding ones. No whole-explanation is forthcoming at all to guide whole-response. All things are equally real and equally true. No person or society can live on that basis. Objectively mere possibility accounts neither for actualization nor for concretion, neither for the power to become actual nor for the organic relation of the new to the old. If this position is taken guardedly as an attitude and conclusion of science, strictly speaking, in order to maintain the validity of rational discourse, in order to preserve the principle *ex nihilo nihil fit,* in order to guard the idea of sufficient explanation from the undermining of those who either deny the new arbitrarily or accept it while refusing to all and any the right to explain, the attitude is then thus far all to the good; science can from there on leave to philosophy and to religion the further questions of the adequate explanation of possibility and process. With such a guarded attitude science is heading strongly in the right direction. Only when it becomes defensive and therefore falsely restrictive, only when it makes itself directly or indirectly into a metaphysics or a religion, does it become false to truth and destructive of man's highest welfare. The problem is thus not only objective, as above, but also existential. Existentially there are no two ways about it. To call all actualized possibilities equally real and to stop there is definitely to fail to fight, whether ignorantly or perversely, in man's deeper struggles for freedom, truth, and co-operative creativity. Our crucial questions are what is the most important and the most real, and how the two are related. It is no answer to anxious whole-response simply to say: "anything and everything."

B. We have considered the disjunctive use of the here and now as the standard of truth. We are now to think through the conjunctive use of process as the content which constitutes the criterion of our existential ultimate. This, again, comprises many shades of thinking, but two can be taken as typical. Both interpret process coherently by means of the most ideal and inclusive principle of interpretation within it. The first, however, holds the whole of process, the whole of the here and now, the sum and substance of rational knowledge, to be the standard of truth. The most high is as real as process shows it to be. God may be perfectly good, for instance, but the power or the wisdom of His goodness must be judged by the nature of the process. The second position holds that although the most high is the most real it is permanently limited by the nature of a process which includes finite freedom.

Both of these, moreover, rise to the level of explanation in a vital sense. They accept the fact that process has become radically altered by the emergence of all that is existentially important. The fact even of description is, of course, that process becomes and that it goes somewhere. Whether we deny the reality of the new, evade explaining it, or try to explain it by reference to possible existence, the fact is that what matters did come into history and, as time goes, has come into it as a blitz-emergence leaving us gasping. Both of the views that we are to consider try to account for the appearance of the significant new in terms of adequate grounds of explanation. The first of these holds that God is finite and grows with the process. This makes more of process than the other view, in which advance within process, even though accountable only by reference to the most high, is yet only temporary and incidental.

a. This view holds that religion "is concern about experiences which are regarded as of supreme value."[12] But "it always involves a set of beliefs about reality"[13] as well. Religion is chiefly concerned with the most high. It wants to see it as much real and as much realized as possible. Yet how much real and realized it is can be judged only by the standard of coherence in the sense of rational knowledge. The facts of process must judge to what extent that which is of supreme value in the universe is also in control of the universe. The fact of evil, particularly of needless evil, of natural evil, makes the full synthesis of the most real and the most high impossible. God is all good but limited in His power. He is thwarted from within. Power is a problem even to God. Process shows this to be true. Were He perfect in every sense He would have made a better job of creating the world. God as well as man is working out His salvation in fear and trembling. God struggles with evil, which is out of His control. Such a position is empirically adequate in the sense of being based on what we know now to be true, no "surd evils are ascribed to the will of God,"[14] it maintains the clear-cut distinction that we need between what is good and what is evil, and is "an inspiring challenge to eternal coöperative moral endeavor, a coöperation between God and man."[15] It also holds out the hope of an increasing and perhaps final solution of the problem of evil. The writer was once so deeply convinced of this position that he strongly felt that anyone who did not acknowledge it as true was either stupid or insincere. Time teaches both patience and humility, if we will only let it! Although he still be-

[12] Brightman, *A Philosophy of Religion,* p. 17.
[13] *Ibid.*
[14] *Ibid.,* p. 314.
[15] *Ibid.*

lieves it to be one of the most adequate and morally noble points of view, he can no longer hold to it. Nearly every view seems to number among its upholders great and good men. That makes us most humble and calls for open minds and hearts. It makes us increasingly look less at people and more at positions, and less at the exact positions of people and more at the central affirmations on which the positions themselves are based. Only in the great and good and in the most adequate positions do positions and people coincide. That happens most seldom. Be that as it may, a puzzle in life, why must we look beyond this position for an adequate content for our existential ultimate?

In the first place, since the viewpoint which makes the coherence of the actual central appeals to the highest within the actual for its most inclusive principle of explanation, why does it not also make this its standard of truth? Why make reason, for instance, a principle of interpretation and then subject this to the test of the whole of the present process for its truth? The day before yesterday, cosmically speaking, reason was no part of any actual that we know; today it is here; what will it be like tomorrow? Why make today the standard? If yesterday were made the standard, reason would have no truth at all. Then truth itself has flashed like lightning from out the black night of nothingness. That actual which contained no reason was not made a standard of reality; why should this? Why not tomorrow? Why should the totality of present process be more true than its higher instances when the only reason that we can interpret truth at all is that reason itself has appeared? Why should we freeze process at this point? Is it because truth has to be limited to our knowledge? Is it because we must feel secure, and cannot do so unless truth is our possession? Is not this position Ptolemaic? Does it not make us too central in process? To make the totality of process one with our knowledge is only right. That is what we now know, or rather might know. But why equate it with truth? If a cosmic second ago we had subjected God to that test He would not only be finite but in no important sense at all would He even be. Why, then, make this our limited knowledge of a swiftly moving process the content of our existential ultimate? Why make it the criterion of our existential faith judgment?

We know that time and eternity are a puzzle for any view. There can be no complete explanation of our own given. The form of truth can never be legitimately substituted for its content. At least we know of no way to explain the historical in terms of any non-historical or superhistorical which does not leave some problem. There is a defiance offered by the sheer new to the very nature of reason. The basic function of compelling reason is neither to postulate nor to posit but to interpret what is given in experience. Our next volume must wrestle with the problems of concrete contents. Perhaps the actual is soon to see a new light that will solve powerfully that key puzzle. Until then we must explain as fully and as suggestively as the evidence will allow. Even then, moreover, the solution must be reflexively superspective. We must always, too, end in a whole-response that is a faith judgment—or else we should be the infinite knowing itself and all its parts from within. Else were we God. Our faith judgment, however, must be based as fully as possible on accurate and adequate whole-reason. From this point of view present process seems nearly absurd as the content of our existential ultimate. Why, out of the billion billion sidereal years raised even to the five hundred and third power, should the last little second of half a million years, or so, be so important existentially as to be made the standard of truth? Why should human history in a recorded sense be such a tiny fraction of a cosmic eyewink? Why should we as a human history be less than the tiniest tick on the smallest billionth of a second hand on the universal clock? Why this cosmic swoosh of history? Why this blitz-emergence? We are dazzled by the speed of advance and its incredible acceleration within the last cosmic second. What will happen in the tiny tick of the next million years of human history? So much has happened within ten thousand years! All of civilization. Less than the littlest measure ago, it seems, Jesus interpreted God to be a Responsible and Self-giving Concern who guides every bit of process. Even now his teachings gird the globe. How will they be received within such a small section of time as the next hundred thousand years? What has happened technologically to widen our human horizons within one hundred years, within these last decades? What has happened within the last few weeks for cosmic good or ill? Will control of the atom control us constructively or will it declare our doom? Who can see even five hundred years ahead? Has the cosmic driver put the accelerator down to the floor board? Or has He just now barely leaned His foot on it?

The point is that present process is such a mere passing point. From its point of view, the time when there was nothing, or nothing existentially important, and the time since there was do not go together. For adequate explanation we must appeal to a different dimension. There must be cosmic differentials. Someone has shifted the gears. Our driving is mostly in the deep dark. While the molecules spin in the car the driver covers the vast distances with a different aim and a vaster outlook. While the ants crawl in the car the car speeds on. While the baby plays in its basket in the back seat the car hurtles on. How poor those figures in comparison to Reality! Could we only be big enough to sit in the front seat and see through the windshield! We can only surmise. The truth is larger. There must be countless other histories. The vast times and the vast spaces that we know—and what is that?—have little meaning in relation to our time and to our part of space unless a vaster purpose uses them in ways differing from our understanding or holds them in readiness for new kinds of development in new kinds of existences or by new kinds of life. To freeze present process and to make its totality the standard of truth may one day come to be seen to have been worse than Ptolemaic, far smaller than Lilliputian. Truth can be of process and yet point vastly beyond it. Faith can grasp it. We are part of Reality. Purpose has appeared in process. We can both know and share meaning and purpose. That is essential. The full process may be reflected in our process; it may be seen as an ocean is seen in a drop of water. We can know truly and yet only bit by bit. Truth, however, belongs first of all to the ocean, the truth of the whole. Perhaps we see a bit of bay. But the whole of what we know is not the whole truth of the ocean. The drop, or the bay, we see is of, but is not, the ocean. Present process is of, but is not, the whole of all Process. It is best seen in the most high within it. The reality of it must not be limited either by or to the drop. Yet even this figure misleads. For impurity in the ocean would be reflected in the drop. Our figure is static; truth is dynamic. Our present process is under the pressure of swift and radical change, cosmically speaking, because the better is working from without as well as from within. The present is thus not a drop like the ocean but more like an unfinished work which will be made like its model. The seed, to use an organic figure, grows according to its nature, but there are also the sun and the soil. The fruit represents the tree better by ripening, by being changed. The imperfections of our process do not symmetrically report imperfections in Process. The systematic interpretation of present process as an inclusive whole, or rational knowledge, is not the most adequate standard of truth. The selective ideal-actual is more true than the totality which is set up to judge it.

Then also "God as cause of the world would be real even as the world is real."[16] If the totality is itself the standard of truth rather than merely of our knowledge of it, then we know of no truth to explain the coming of the new, the advance of process, the arrival of significant emergence. If, however, we can see how arbitrary it is to freeze process, to equate knowledge and truth, if we can see that knowledge points beyond itself by being only an actual among actuals, a point in a moving process, then we can know of truth beyond process to change process; we can know truth anticipatorily through a selective ideal-actual, which is itself more real than the totality of the process; we can know that whatever existential decision alone can satisfy our lives and make for a good society is more than a matter of subjective preference, for it is also based on as much knowledge as can be had dynamically. Thus, while existential truth outstrips knowledge it is yet consistent with the best indication of the truth that we have from knowledge. The existential is thus beyond the theoretical; but not contrary to it except as it posits itself as the truth, except as it

[16] Hocking, *The Meaning of God in Human Experience*, p. 305.

becomes existential, or religious content. Whenever that happens the two clash with much vigor and vitality. If the ultimate is adequately to explain, however, it cannot be reduced either to mere description or to any fuller interpretation of the actual which is based on the knowledge of what has taken place up to now within the borders of our competent observation. The now of knowledge falls far short of the future fullness of truth which can be "known" only by faith, "known" because it is based on what is before and beyond process. Process, if it is growing, if it is adding new, different, and higher ingredients, cannot be explained by process. Process must be itself explained by something from beyond itself, however truly this may also be within itself. That which explains cannot be totally different or it would not be known. It can only be selectively actualized within process. When the full realization has taken place there will be no need for explanation. Then the temples of interpretation will be torn down and God himself will be the temple thereof; our little suns and stars will give way to the Source of all lights.

Who, then, or what then, made the process grow beyond itself, and so suddenly? If God is as real as the world, to be judged by the process as a whole, who gave Him a terrific shot of vitamins so that all of a sudden He began to grow, and from practically an embryo to shoot up beyond reckoning? If God, on the other hand, is considered greater than the world, why should He be judged by it? Why should the process in that case be a measure before the results are in? Why should we taste the green fruit and then pronounce the tree to be not fully good? Two problems must, of course, be kept apart: (1) Why should the fruit ever be green and not be fully good from the start? (2) Should we judge the goodness of the fruit by the greenness of the fruit in the early summer? The first problem is not for this volume (cf. *Evil and the Christian Faith*). The truest test of the worth of the tree, however, is surely the ripe fruit. If we had seen no change, no ripening, we ought to test the tree by what it keeps bearing; but our process, cosmically speaking, grows faster than sprouting oats in the warm oven—incomparably faster.

Then, too, the God who grows with the process is hardly the

God to trust and to worship, at least, serenely and without qualms. We can admire Him, sympathize with Him, co-operate with Him, treat Him as the friend who bears our infirmities and who understands. Yet is He even perfectly good? How He became so, so suddenly, and when, is a mystery. Why the problem is simply with power and not with wisdom and goodness as well is hard to guess. From the history of our process is this plainly indicated? If He is as real as process and is to be judged by it, do we know that God is fully, even though not effectively, love? How can goodness and wisdom be established apart from being, power, existence? Is not Kierkegaard right in saying that in the light of this world it is precisely that God is love that is so hard to believe?[17] If He is to be limited by the process known through the totality of our present process and its past history, why is He not limited all around? Is this belief in His perfect love, but not in His perfect power, not an illegitimate separation of value and existence, of thought and being, of the ideal and the actual? Is this not highly and abstractly speculative? If He is to be judged by the process as a whole, why is He not as bad as the worst in it as well as as good as the best in it? We see, of course, that He is improving rapidly but is He now better than the world is good? On what grounds? Is He the answer to our deep quest for authority and motivation? Can we trust Him even as Jesus did and found both personal peace and power and the Resource through which the world can be evaluated, redirected, saved, and changed? Do we know that He will not have a tantrum worse than the most horrid picture of Him in the Old Testament, demanding vengeance on women, innocent children, and even cattle? Do we know, if He is as frustrated as our process, that He will keep mental sanity? Out of the blackness of night like a meteor His creative activity shot forth; can it be that He will weary and return to His rest? But can He choose? Was He not rather created by nothing rather than the conscious creator of something? Here we have a human history which is less than a reflex of His muscles. Perhaps it rose to the level of whim. A God which is as finite as process now indicates that He is neither enough to explain our

[17] Cf. *Fear and Trembling*, pp. 40-41.

present process nor enough to offer practical help to our world. He is adequate neither objectively nor subjectively. He falls far short of the full answer needed for adequate whole-response. He will satisfy neither reason alone nor the full man. He is not the God of whole-thinking. He is not our existential ultimate.

Yet how can we avoid arriving at a finite God if knowledge has any relevancy? How can the most high be truly the most real in the light of the evils of our actual world? Can we combine value and existence outright without winking at evil, or at least without making light of it? Is this not the reason why great and honest thinkers must hold the doctrine? After all, are they not simply bowing to the facts that underlie all knowledge, that must be accounted for in every worthy and compelling world-view? To this problem we must devote our final chapter of the next volume. It is the deepest problem of religion. If there were no evil there would be no problem for religion. Religion is negatively man's struggle with the problem of evil both personally and socially, both practically and intellectually. The finite God, however, offers no adequate solution to this problem. He merely describes a situation. This is true both practically and intellectually. He explains neither the beginnings nor the ends of process. He is the God of the possible, of our hopes, but not of either adequate vision or full faith. He is not the God of truth as the most organic synthesis of knowledge and faith. It may, of course, seem presumptuous even to try to solve the problem of evil from the tiny crevice of our perspective. How far beyond us the full truth is. Yet try we must. When we have given religion concrete content we shall discuss the problem of evil in the light of the reflexive superspective, challenging as best we can many arbitrary presuppositions, dismissing many inadequate levels of solution, and finding in the most high itself a key to the problem that will unlock many doors. Through them we may look out on new and broader vistas. Although we may not even so see the edge of our historic horizons, we hope to see them recede. We hope to see the weather clearing in the direction in which we are going. The god of rational knowledge based on our present process and its possibilities is, in any case, not the answer to the deepest anguish either of our minds or of our whole selves with respect to this central problem for all existential thinking. This much can be said even now, moreover, that some of us who have struggled personally long and deeply with the problem have found that right religion, by undercutting the usual standards of "human wisdom," by sidestepping the shallow understanding of the natural man, by refusing to think in terms of our natural wants rather than in terms of our deepest needs, has provided us with a way of living and of seeing that has become woven into the innermost fabric of our lives. No answer to this question will ever do that is not both satisfactory to our best thinking and also at the same time through and through existentially adequate.

b. The second conjunctive form of the here and now as the basis for truth is that which identifies God in all respects with the most high and the most real in their fullest combination as far as He Himself goes, but holds that imperfections and evil are *perpetual* parts of process. God Himself is perfect, but His perfection is compromised in His work necessarily by finite freedom. Human beings are never either perfectly good or perfectly wise and, therefore, since they are parts of process, process itself is never perfect. Yet a perfect God is responsible for it. He can be perfect and yet also responsible for an imperfect process because that process be is better than that process not be. He is a God who cares, who cares enough, indeed, to let men alone to make their mistakes. Their very rebellion indicates God's humility. Their very sins show Him to be the savior who keeps taking into His own life men's sins while willingly leading them on, trying to persuade and lift them to better levels of life. God is absolute in some respects, but relative in some; absolute with reference to Himself; relative with reference to the world. This, roughly, is the view of Charles Hartshorne in *Man's Vision of God*. The intelligent and alert reader will open-mindedly and open-heartedly ponder this work. It is robust and competent enough to speak clearly and strongly for itself. In this instance, like the last, the argument can be completed, of course, in so far as we now can and have opportunity, only when the final chapter on the problem of evil and last things has been written.

Our problem is not primarily that of the absolute and the relative. That cannot be discussed formally with much significance. The content of the absolute must be the key to that problem. Our concern with this position is rather the statement that there can be a synthesis of the most high and the most real which is perfect in itself but which is continually accompanied by an imperfect work. Even if the imperfection is attributed to the creatures, these, too, are the work of the creator, and indirectly He participates in their work and in the responsibility for it. Obviously we have a far stronger view of God in this view than in the one preceding. He is a real principle of explanation. That fact stands. Actually, however, far too little is made of the process in its character of a blitz-emergence. This history has no one goal toward which it is moving. The arrow of process no longer points. The superspective is static and not reflexive. God is continually creating and He always has been. God as creator is consequently to be judged by the process as it is rather than by it as it is headed. Since this is so, we cannot accept the idea that this is a full synthesis of the most important and the most real. That synthesis is, in fact, prevented by the making this bit of process a true indication of God's workmanship.

This general approach makes too little, then, of the basic fact of process in its swift unfolding. Like the previous position it makes too much of the present segment. The previous position described God in terms of the best here and now; God Himself, consequently, becomes limited by that description since what is best here and now is obviously thwarted by what is here and now fully actual. Yet there is great hope. God has grown hugely of late, and who knows, if we help, how much more He can grow in the next cosmic second. In this position, on the contrary, God is permanently limited in His relations. He cannot outgrow His difficulties ever. His work remains eternally imperfect. It must be said, of course, that in neither position is God wholly responsible inasmuch as He does not create afresh but with some prime stuff whether of a limited self or some material other than Himself. In either case this prime stuff offers resistance. Plato's receptacle is still with us, in whatever form.

The position that God is perfect but rules an imperfect world is powerfully suggestive from many angles. Particularly impressive is its denial of the reality of progress by the process as a whole in an eternal sense. Progress is a matter of the fluctuations of temporary conditions as human beings accept or reject God's purpose. Progress of process has for itself no eternal goal, meaning, and reality. Yet this position is not based on our best knowledge. We do not know that God is, or always has been, creating. How can we know it? We know no myriad creations before, or other than, our cosmic history. All that we know is a cosmic comet speeding to a suggested end. All that we know is a cosmic process pushed and pulled through rapid momentous changes, existentially speaking, cosmic second after cosmic second. In the case of such knowledge, of such a process, God must be judged more by the form of the flux than by the nature of it. Or if He is to be judged by the nature of process, the nature forming and reforming is more important than the presently formed nature. We cannot afford to dismiss as irrelevant the main thrust of the evidence.

If we infer from God's nature that He always creates, we must infer from the nature of this process to His general way of creating. We cannot freeze this stage of process and make that the proper example of His general work. We must rather use the history of our whole process as the indicator of God's eternal creativity. God does not eternally create green fruit, but He creates fruit that ripens. He does not eternally build scaffoldings, but cathedrals. He does not rear infants, but maturing children to share fully in the family life. If this world is God's best work, in any case, we definitely have no right to conclude that God is the good tree, the master-builder, the perfect Father. Such a God can be believed in only when we follow the evidence dynamically and fulfill knowledge by the necessary and appropriate act of faith.

Is it then said that although God is perfect, any possible world including finite freedom must be imperfect? Let us reply at once and unhesitatingly that no Person is perfect whose product must *ever* remain imperfect. You cannot judge the whittler when he first slices off a few chips from the rough wood, but you can judge him by his masterpiece. You cannot judge the painter by the first daubs on the canvas, but his best finished painting must measure his capacity. But are we not forgetting the matter of finite freedom? No! That God is greater who can make his creation come out right than he to whom it must ever be a problem child. That father combines better love, wisdom, and power who can give his son the maximum freedom and opportunity consistent with his growth and thereupon proceed to guide that freedom both by severity and by goodness until the son willingly does and likes to do the best, than does the father who fails to bring up his son for the best because of his freedom. A perfect God can both use and control freedom to his perfect ends. The means, moreover, cannot be judged except in the light of the ends. Much difficulty has clouded the problem of evil because we have not dug deep enough in our understanding of the meaning and nature of perfection. In any case, Purpose must be judged by the ends of process.

From the evidence presented by our process, moreover, as basically being rather than basically becoming, we have no right to believe in a perfect God. This actual world contains too much evil, far and away too much evil, to allow us such luxury of mind and emotion. To claim such a God, if our kind of process is permanent, is to lose moral sensitivity. What of the many evolutions that went wrong? What of animal suffering? What of the idiot? What of the suffering of the innocent? This world is full of more suffering, seemingly *hopeless* suffering, than we like to think. Unless the present process will eventuate in conditions so utterly good that praise can find no bounds, *for each and every life in it throughout its whole history,* and unless this process of gradual growth is necessary to full freedom, God simply cannot be all-good, all-wise, and all-powerful at the same time. Choose we must. Either a staggering faith beyond our wildest imagination, *centered in God,* or else the darkness of description, explaining nothing. No perfect God can be responsible for all the horrors of this world, most of which are not faced by well and normal people, if this present stage is a true indication of God's general and permanent creativity.

For him to whom life is mostly good, it is obviously possible to produce such a theory as this, but the moral sensitivity of the former view, and of all the sincere thinkers who hold to still lower levels of interpretation, often because they cannot wink at the depths of the problem of evil, is far more acceptable. If love be love and happiness responsible, the whole earth has no right to be happy at the expense of one sufferer; and the more sensitive we become to others, the more we must suffer with them. The less possible, therefore, it becomes for the whole world to be happy while one is suffering. The ninety and nine sheep are left—and that in the wilderness—by the good shepherd in order that the hundredth sheep might be brought in. No one can be deeply and responsibly happy in a world like this without a staggering faith. Depths of happiness cannot be achieved at the expense of moral sensitivity. We can be happy in the deepest sense only if we believe that we and all are in the strong hands of One who cares for each life unto this last, and that to its perfect end, an end which is really no ending, but only a fulfillment. Happiness is itself perhaps a superficial word. Blessedness is better. Blessedness is being already part of God's redemptive activity whereby we know through faith even now that the final end is so indescribably good that a perfect God can let us go through these evils for His love's sake, for our sake, that we might share forever His own life and joy. Blessedness is living now in the peace beyond this world which we know shall transform all suffering into endless praise. Yet this is anticipating our content of right religion. The evils of this world, in any case, if that as it is now be a sample of God's creativity, forbid us to believe Him perfect. Only if what we see is the green, green fruit and not the ripe, do we have a right to judge the tree to have a perfect nature. We must always remember that this is but a passing point in the swoosh of cosmic process. That basically conditions all evidence.

No manipulation of the ontological argument, furthermore, can change this statement. There is something fascinating about it, to be sure. The older forms of Anselm and Descartes were mostly definitional. Perfection by definition has all positive predicates there are. Therefore existence must be one of them. To exist is more than not to exist. Aquinas and Kant, among others, examined this approach and found it wanting. This older argument was built on too formally rational lines where thought and being were too easily equated. A solution in thought is after all basically only a solution in thought; it is dominantly analytical. This is true even of necessary or ultimate being, as far as knowledge goes, if our reasoned experience contradicts the solution. Then, by knowledge, we cannot attain to a perfect God. In our day men like Hocking and Hartshorne have done much to bring in empirical elements, to connect organically the possible with the actual. These men have rendered such immense and important service to our day that they deserve careful reading.[18] The ontological argument is greatly strengthened and enriched. The old idea, we repeat, is fascinating. How can we know the idea of the perfect, than Whom nothing better and more real can be thought, unless He be real, unless He truly exist? Is not the simplest and truest explanation of this idea of the perfect God the fact of God? Yet, on the other hand, is not this idea mentally warping and morally dulling when men can hold it, as many theologians have, along with a belief in an eternal hell, or better but still horrible, along with a belief in this world as a fair example of God's general work?

Hocking has fortunately never accepted the argument except against a dynamic background and Hartshorne has introduced the idea that the perfect cannot be surpassed except by himself, that is by his improvement of history which is his very body. This improves the position somewhat by making possible a better world. Practically that is to the good. In respect to what God eternally is in himself, then, he cannot, in this view, be surpassed, but with respect to his creative activity, he can. This idea we not only ac-

[18] Hocking, *The Meaning of God in Human Experience;* Hartshorne, *Man's Vision of God,* and "The Formal Validity and Real Significance of the Ontological Argument," in *The Philosophical Review,* May, 1944.

cept, but must make central in our understanding of God. Only because history can be changed, only because God's realm can be perfected, only because there can be growth in line with a perfect purpose to a perfect end, can we believe that God is perfect. Unless we can honestly say in the light of our reflexive superspective that this process is perfect for its purposes, we cannot legitimately believe God to be perfect. We cannot believe so, that is, in whole-response including whole and right reason. We can, therefore, only fully combine the most high and the most real if the ontological argument is dynamic rather than static. If the idea of the perfect is with us, is in history, it is not only possible, but also that much actual. In this Hartshorne is right. The possible has meaning only with reference to the actual. "To conceive a thing in two alternative states, actual and possible, is to conceive something common to these two states, as well as something different."[19] It cannot be known by us except as existing beings. That far, at least, and in some form of actuality or unactualized potency, it must be organically related to our history.[20] It can, therefore, never be purely formal. Truth is always a synthesis of form and fact. Yet actually God can be *known* only as *possible* in the fullness of perfection. For the rest He must be believed, or as Richard Kroner has suggested, grasped by the religious imagination.[21] The religious imagination, however, must be dynamically anticipatory. Knowledge that cannot be verified by reference to both form and fact is not full knowledge. Rational adequacy includes actual demonstration of some kind. God cannot be so demonstrated as a perfect being. An imperfect process can suggest by its nature, but never prove, a perfect God. He can be inferred, postulated, reasoned to be such, but He cannot be known to be such, in the more strict and careful use of the term.

He can, nevertheless, with reason be believed to be such. Truth is ever a synthesis of knowledge and faith. Truth is dynamic.

[19] Hartshorne, *Man's Vision of God,* p. 309.
[20] Cf. "The Formal Validity and Real Significance of the Ontological Argument," in *The Philosophical Review,* May, 1944.
[21] *The Function of the Religious Imagination.*

Truth is from within the flux of process to the reality permanently beyond as well as within it. The ontological argument can become existential. In that case not only is the possible actual in so far as it is thought, but perfection to be the standard of existential truth must find besides some concrete content within historic experience which illustrates it. That is a wrong way, however, of putting it. The existential ultimate must be a selective actual fully as much as a selective ideal. The best is existentially defined by a concrete historic event. We must begin with history. Existential thinking never starts with abstract ideals. It starts with the selective ideal which is at the same time fully actual. The most high must be the most high of history. We know no other most high except as the speculation of part-thinking. The perfect must somehow be defined in terms of the interpretation of actual experience. It must be a reasoned whole-response. The perfection that we see is then the advance point of process pointing to the reflexive superspective. The perfect is already an event, a true historic occurrence. Faith is based on selective knowledge, itself actual and besides both intellectually and practically, most importantly and inclusively related to all the rest of actuality. The decisive event may not characterize the whole locus of any whole-responses, of any person, but it must dominantly and increasingly, in steadiness of vision and power, and conclusively characterize that life. The perfect we start with must be historic perfection; it must be incarnational. Else we have only the idea related as a possibility to the actual, or actualized only in the part-response of speculative thinking. Perhaps also in part-living, but part-living is not whole-living, not dominant whole-response.

The ontological argument fails as a merely formal intellectualism. As the vision of truth by faith and reason in dynamic interaction, however, the truth of Who is and what is to come, and what now is in that light, as such the ontological "argument" is at the very heart of religion. God then becomes "the unity within the universe which gives the sense of holiness and the sense of supreme guidance towards the best possible."[22] Beyond that, too, is the full

[22] Whitehead, personal conversation.

assurance that the best possible will be attained in God's time and in God's way.

Although God cannot be known to be perfect, then, the pointing of process nevertheless suggests it. Existentially, moreover, such a God satisfies our deepest needs, and only He. This will be our line of thought throughout, from now on. Man cannot do without Him. As Frank says suggestively and existentially: "The real proof of God is the agonized attempt to deny God."[23] Or Augustine:

> And if I say to thee "Is God changeable or unchangeable?" thou wilt answer immediately, "Far be it from me either to believe or imagine that God is changeable: God is unchangeable." Thy soul, though small, though perhaps still carnal, could not answer me otherwise than that God is unchangeable; but every creature is changeable; how then wert thou able to enter, by a glance of the spirit, into that which is above the creature, so as confidently to answer me: "God is unchangeable"? What, then, is that in thy heart, when thou thinkest of a certain substance, living, eternal, all-powerful, infinite, everywhere present, everywhere whole, nowhere shut in: When thou thinkest of these qualities, this is the word concerning God in thy heart.[24]

Suggestive are such statements and worth pondering. Yet God cannot be known as perfect, particularly so when His goodness is stressed, from within the frustrations of process. He can be believed to be such with reason, and our lives and our history as a whole can more and more prove our faith to be right. Until the very end of process, however, we have to be satisfied with some statement like that in the Epistle to the Hebrews: "For in that he subjected all things unto him, he left nothing that is not subject unto him. But now we see not yet all things subjected to him. But we behold him—even Jesus."[25] We can see the blueprint and we can know to a great extent the power of building—yes, we can even see the building under construction—but we see not yet that building which alone can attest the skill of the perfect master-builder.

[23] *Op. cit.*, p. 43.
[24] "On the Gospel of St. John," in *The Nicene and Post-Nicene Fathers*, Vol. VII, p. 10.
[25] Hebrews 2:8–9.

3. The third possible explanation of process is the most high as the most real. This means that the most significant novel emergence in history best accounts for the process as a whole. The most significant emergence meets most fully the needs of whole-response, including right knowledge. This highest emergent indicates which way the water is rising. This most ripe part of the fruit foretells the way the fruit will ripen and indicates the nature of the tree which bears it. This selective ideal-actual which alone can explain the why of the process as far as it has gone by now at the same time points to the position toward which the process is going. This regulative pattern which shapes the process, however recalcitrant that process may be, shapes it into an arrow which points beyond and ahead.

We take this point of view for several reasons. In the first place, the highest can be explained in no terms less than itself. Unless reason had emerged, for instance, we should not now be interpreting the process at all. Reason can be explained in no terms less than itself without absurdity. Obviously to deny the competence of reason, which must be based on its reality and truth, is also to forfeit all rights to be listened to publicly. Nothing is trustworthy that is not true, which is not the conformity of appearance to reality. Reason must be a real relation indicating the nature of reality. Yet reason finds a content which is even greater than itself. Reason is but a living part of a living whole. Even whole-reason is rooted in whole-response, in a person who is such by virtue of his constant interaction with the world in which he lives. Yet persons differ. Whole-responses are more or less true, more or less adequate, more or less rightly conforming to reality. Thus the highest novel emergence is that whole-response which can most fully satisfy man's deepest needs: the need for solid yet dynamic truth; the need for full and increasing life in creative freedom; the need for co-operative community; the need for faith in the future based on authority and motivation ultimately capable of solving and overcoming the evil which so easily and widely besets life. This deepest need indicates organically the nature of the womb that bore us and the home that rears us. This greater content which reason finds, as we shall see later, can be explained by nothing less than itself. The stream rises by itself no higher than its source. If this highest emergence, which gives meaning to life and process, which makes possible science, philosophy, and the highest religion, and which also makes ever more creative vision and constructive action possible, is to be explained, and without it there can be no inclusive explanation. It can be explained by nothing less than itself.

The highest can be explained in no terms lower than itself. If it could, then that would be the highest. Then that would more deeply meet our fullest existential needs. The ultimate can, of course, never be proved. No reason can be given for its existence since it is the very ground of existence. It constitutes the highest unity of meaning ascertainable from any actualized event. Barth is, therefore, quite right in one sense in affirming that theology can never be founded on any scientific or theoretical structure. That is, it must be an "act of faith."[26] Theology cannot, at least, be proved true and still be "the science" of the ultimate. The very fact that it cannot be explained by any other event or by any other chains of events is indeed its strongest proof. That is the very nature of the ultimate. Yet the highest must, oppositely, be able to give the most meaningful answer to the why of all things. It must be able, in fact, to provide living meaningfulness since life is the very center of meaning. It must be able to satisfy even our deepest existential meaning, explaining all things, as far as human beings can, all the way from the depths of our whole-responses to the lowest level of inorganic being. The highest must answer our quest for the why of things from the meaning of life and death to the meaning of the very soil we till. Not whats and hows but whys constitute the inner stuff of the meaning of meaning. This is the existential crux of our situation.

Naturally the ultimate can be grasped, whether by faith or by knowledge, only in some relation to our actual world. It cannot be simply nothing or totally other, provided rational discourse have any meaning. Given any particular at all, we can never arrive at a universal negative. Being must be as positive at least as what

[26] Cf. *Die Kirchliche Dogmatik, Erster Band*, pp. 1–23.

we know. If we give up all rational discourse, if we surrender all transfer of reliable meaning, we become exiles from the common lot of humanity and indeed from our own natural and normal selves. Nor can it be wholly other. That which is ultimate is all-explaining. It must include our world. To say that this world has no reality, that only the ultimate has, is to include ourselves as unreal in every respect and therefore to deny all relevant meaning; it is to abandon all public discourse. For small zeros to talk about a large Zero is time wasted. The wholly other can be known exactly in no way at all. It cannot even be meaningfully intended except as a contradictory denial of all meaning, theoretically; or as an attempt to escape completely from all life and responsibility, existentially.

The most high is, furthermore, inadequately present within process to be explained from within process. This is true partly because it once came into our process. It was not always there. Since the most high is the ground of explanation, and cannot be explained by what came before it in the process as we know it, we know that there must have been a superhistorical or supernatural realm. Yet if that realm were now equal to what we know of the most high, it would not be equal to explain our great cosmic and practical problems. If the supernatural had by now become completely actualized, we should still lack an adequate principle of explanation. The most high constitutes an adequate principle of explanation for process chiefly because it points beyond process. That is the other reason that it cannot be explained from within process. There is ever more meaning for us to find along the same line while this meaning is also ever craving to be realized. This superactual is even now in control of the actual, even of the conditions of man and of his freedom, in such a way that more of this living meaningfulness must become actualized. The most high must not be frustrated but fulfilled by man's freedom. The most high is thus, in its immensity, indescribably higher than the process. The most high must be basically known through the reflexive superspective. From this point of view, that of transcendence, the most high can be and, we shall see, is, radically and dominantly other than the totality of the process. The most high is both completely for the process and yet dominantly other than the process. The more the selective ideal-actual differs from the general nature of the process in its actuality, while yet fulfilling it the most possible in its essential potentiality, the more the most high is seen to be beyond the actual process. It is because of this incommensurate "more" that it can constitute both an adequate principle of explanation and a source of the world's salvation.

The most high cannot be explained, then, by anything less than itself and yet it can explain the why of all else. Beyond that it cannot be explained either by itself as a given within the process, partly because it has come from beyond the process and partly because its power to explain and to transform the process from within its own measure of actuality is incomplete. The most high can explain mostly as a blueprint and as a scaffolding. The building has scarcely been begun by now. The truth of the most high is therefore not only not explainable in terms other than itself but also not explainable in terms of its own actuality. It points beyond itself like a live wire to its source. It must be by the nature of process a dynamic truth. The truth must be a combination of pointing and of going that way. It must be a synthesis of faith and reason. It must be a matter both of growing meaning and of the realization of meaning. It must be a dynamic relation between realization and realizability wherein, though the most high be ever so much seen to be the most real, it must nevertheless also become increasingly known as such. Truth is thus both beyond, yet relative to, process. Something of this both fixed and active nature of truth is caught by Schleiermacher:

> If a system of propositions can be understood from their connexion with others, then nothing supernatural was required for their production. But if they cannot, then they can, in the first instance, only be apprehended . . . as parts of another whole, as a moment of the life of a thinking being who works upon us directly as a distinctive existence by means of his total impression on us.[27]

[27] Schleiermacher, *The Christian Faith*, p. 50.

Only the highest emergence is able to explain the relation between continuity and discontinuity. Life is not non-life, whatever way the two are otherwise related in either becoming or being. Non-life gives no reason in itself why we should expect life. The description of what was could not lead to what became. Yet, given life, we can see both how life depends upon non-life and why life should need an environment. The two were organically related as soon as the second appeared. Given non-conscious nature there is no reason that we can see why consciousness should appear. Yet when consciousness does come and particularly when it rises to reflective interpretation we can see how non-conscious nature is necessary to the development of consciousness, both individually and socially; and especially, we can see how without it we should be left either with an uncontrolled finite freedom or with a divine determinism. Antecedent to the coming of the new it cannot be predicted; consequent to its coming we see that the old and the new are related. Meaning, therefore, is from the top down. It is from the highest to the lowest level. All the machinery in the building is directed from the top tower and only by understanding something of that room can we see how all the operations in the building go together. It makes no difference if the coming of the new is fast or slow. Climbing a mountain from below we cannot see what is on the plateau ahead of us. Yet when we climb over the edge we can see both what is there and what is below. It makes little difference whether the climb up is steep or gradual, direct or winding. Not even if we hire an airplane and fly as swiftly as a bird can we see what is on top of that plateau before we are that high. From there we can see both the way we came and where we are, no matter how we came or how fast. Because there is continuity in process we tend to think there is only causal continuity and to reduce everything to it. Yet to get to mere causal continuity we must read both back and out. We must read back the continuity that we can see from our present perspective, and we must read out as unreal or incidental all that has been added to the original continuity.

The most high, too, can give us adequate doctrines of actualization and concretion. By actualization we mean the power to become actual according to one's nature or kind. By concretion we mean the actualization according to organic order and purpose. Suppose all is energy. What is energy? We know no pure energy except as an abstraction. The energy of physics and of life may be at bottom the same. Yet if energy is intrinsically of such a nature, or of such a power, as to become no more than hydrogen, there is no reason that man should be a possible form. If the original energy, however, is of such a nature and direction as to make the creation of man possible, he is accounted for. There is, then, a true, eternal continuity of adequate source. The source is adequate, however, only if it is as high as its highest stream. If, moreover, that stream is rising and forcing ever new changes we know that the source is still higher. If this stream thunders down the times, furthermore, or forces itself with enormous power even beyond the obstacles and inertias with which it has to contend as the original impetus is spent, then we know that the stream is still higher than we thought and still feeding mightily the stream of process. Man and history are possible to process because the original energy is according to their nature or power of being. It is conscious, willing, seeking to create value, striving to create fellowship and creative satisfaction of a high order. Whatever upward power and arrival are in the process are also in the source. The lower inorganic forms of being can be accounted for as instrumental to the main purpose of the process. Possibility, we remember, is a mere verbalism unless it be equal in power and purpose to its actualization. Possibility means the capacity, illustrated in actuality, for the original energy to individuate, to adumbrate, to give of itself, to produce of its kind, to be truly creative and productive. The ultimate mysteries of creation are beyond man as far as the how goes, for we are ourselves part of that creation. We know, none the less, that the original power must be equal to the result, else have we thrown away the basic continuity of rational discourse. The stream must rise no higher than its source. We must have an adequate doctrine of actualization.

By an adequate doctrine of concretion we mean that actualization is according to the degree of organic order and purpose, at least, that we see. The universe hangs together remarkably, far fuller, we have reason to believe, than we yet see. The inertia in it, the disorder in it, the evil in it may all be accounted for as the stream becomes purified, becomes aerated, later on in its flow. Even now, however, the process as a whole flows together; the separate streamlets and crosscurrents are understandable only in relation to the main flow. The universe that we know simply cannot be accounted for except in relational terms. Even "accounting for" is a term of relation. On the lowest levels we have causal continuity; on the higher, continuities of purpose. Freedom, of course, introduces an interruptive element into the universe. "The existence of personality presupposes interruption; it is inexplicable by any sort of uninterruption; it is inexplicable by any sort of uninterrupted continuity."[28] Berdyaev should have added, however, "except itself." Personality, or its purpose, is the most inclusive continuity that we know which can include even itself, particularly when this Personality has an all-embracing purpose. The eternal personality has a continuity beyond our process by means of which we can see whatever unity is here and now actual and also the prospective unity of undeveloped or perverted parts. The organic relations that we do see in process are so utterly embracing and intricate that there must be a ground for them. This is necessary since these relations have most importantly and enormously been added to from outside actuality. The new relations, moreover, come prefashioned to fit our actuality. The new must therefore come from the same ground as the old. The developing organic nature of process points beyond itself to its Purpose. "All ultimate reasons are in terms of aim at value. A dead nature aims at nothing."[29] "Apart from a complete metaphysical understanding of the universe, it is very difficult to understand any proposition clearly and distinctly, so far as concerns the analysis of its component elements."[30] "God is the ultimate limitation, and His existence is the ultimate irrationality. . . . No reason can be given for the nature of God, because that

[28] Berdyaev, *Slavery and Freedom*, p. 21.
[29] Whitehead, *Modes of Thought*, p. 184.
[30] Whitehead, *The Function of Reason*, p. 54.

nature is the ground of rationality."[31] To hold that the unity which we do see in the process is not basic in essence and that all the new that has come into history fits organically and fulfillingly into it by sheer chance is not a high faith and not an admirable mental honesty, except perhaps most ignorantly and unreflectingly; it is rather an absurd and most probably defensive credulity.

Yet more important than all these reasons of knowledge are the two which are basically existential. They accord best with the nature of religion. Buddhism and Christianity, for instance, have had, and have, such power over men because they are by nature deeply existential. Both have been weakened by the development of speculative systems which fail to make central the original intent. Idealistic philosophy is not New Testament theology, and consciousness-only (Vijnanavada) is a cousin once removed of the direct existentiality of Gautama's teachings. We can rationalize religion so as to destroy its power. Usually such rationalization proceeds from the inside out because some other religious content has already subtly taken the place of the more adequate profession. A religion is rationalized whenever reason becomes identified primarily with part-reason and with knowledge rather than with whole-reason and with faith. The rationalizer has already given his heart to another religion or else he has never accepted the deeper one with his whole heart, mind, and strength. His acceptance has become more conventional than personally compelling. Within the circle of right religion the most high must be the most real, beyond our best knowledge, primarily on existential grounds. What are these two existential grounds?

Whenever we get too far afield speculating and think that we shall find truth that way, we need to be brought up sharply by the fact that truth-thinking is whole-thinking. It is basically existential. It requires the deepest passions, as well as intellect and will, of the whole man. We must throw all we have and are into it or we are not digging for foundations that will last when the storms come and the rains fall. We need to have something of Gautama Buddha's impatience with mere speculation, so vividly illustrated by

---

[31] Whitehead, *Science and the Modern World*, p. 257.

Hindu thought: "Whether the world is eternal or not, whether it is limited or not, what is certain is that birth, old age, death and suffering exist."[32] Yet no foundation will last unless the existential reason has sincerely seen and surrendered to all available knowledge. Tillich has well stated this truth:

> If rational truth, with its contributions to the different realms of knowledge, is excluded, Christian faith necessarily becomes sectarian and exclusive. If existential truth with its practical bearing on religious and ethical activity is excluded, Christian faith becomes relativistic and sterile. Only by a proper union of the two can the intellectual needs of our present world situation be met.[33]

One of the basic existential grounds for the most high's being the most real is our need for an adequate authority and motivation. This is a depth-need indicating the call of the cosmos. This is an organic need on a basic level revealing the urge within us that we ripen according to the nature of the tree. Ritschl, who is currently under a cloud in many circles, particularly among the existentialists, felt this: "In every religion what is sought, with the help of the superhuman spiritual power reverenced by man, is a solution of the contradiction in which man finds himself."[34] His contradiction was chiefly between spirit and nature, but not wholly that. What he experienced basically was the contradiction we are in. This contradiction itself is our existential situation. To solve it we need a compelling faith, neither arbitrary nor artificial, but rather consistent with strict, honest thinking when that means adequate whole-thinking, when that means thinking without artificial or arbitrary methodological limitations. To become whole as individuals and as society we need a saving faith that is grounded in truth, in the truth of that which envelops and carries us on, of that with which we hang together, of that to which we must react, but by which in the end we are determined, in terms of which even our choices have their final meaning and are heavily freighted with fate.

[32] Champion, *The Eleven Religions*, p. 22.
[33] *The Christian Answer*, p. 33.
[34] Ritschl, *Justification and Reconciliation*, p. 199.

Our authority and motivation must apply equally to interpretation and action. Our whole lives must be moved by the truth that compels us both by its power and by its rightness. It must interpret our lives and our history and it must change, yes, save our lives and our history. The content of right religion must, as Reinhold Niebuhr rightly maintains, be "final not only as a category of interpreting the total meaning of history but also as a solution for the problem of the uneasy conscience in each individual."[35] No idea can do that. No ideal can do that. Only the full truth can do that. Truth must do it, a truth that is actual, that is of the stuff of history, that we have seen applies directly to life. The truth that saves must come out of some actual whole-response. It must be existential. It must be something to which we must bow because it grips us with the intensity of a mystic intuition, subduing us. "Must" means here no primarily external compulsion. "Must" means rather the compulsion of insight which is based equally on what need be, what is best for us, and the nature of things the way they really are. Value and existence join hands inseparably in real authority and motivation. To deny truth to that selective actual which goes beyond our general actuality and can save it is to be traitors to our own true destiny. Freedom can spurn it under conditions. Freedom cannot escape those conditions. To spurn is to go away from life. Jesus on the cross is better off than Judas with the silver. Suffering has always a joy set before it when it is the following out of that authority which leads to life. Even as it faces the worst it can give the peace that the world cannot ever have. This most high must compel our whole self. It must compel our thoughts. We are always up against it. Sometimes it deeply frustrates us and we live shattered lives. Sometimes we run from it into jaded nerves and into the fevers of life. Sometimes we hide it in our depths, becoming like groves with gay flowers and soft breezes above, and seemingly as happy as the sunny skies over the cemetery, while all the time we decay within. No life escapes the compulsion of depth truth. Sometimes, however, it saves us. It always will if we let it. Then all of life becomes freed from our lifelong

[35] *The Nature and Destiny of Man*, Vol. I., p. 143.

slavery to fear—particularly the fear of death. Then order and creative zest begin to characterize our whole life. "Something has happened which compels our faith and which requires us to seek rationality and unity in the whole of our history."[36]

The most high compels our actions, too. It demands whole-response. Nothing less is right response to whole-truth. It compels even our faith. Faith when it is deep is not merely belief, nor even moral decision. It is full surrender in whole-living to that above us which we acknowledge to have a right to command us unconditionally and which we consequently can trust implicitly. "A belief that believes only in itself is no longer a belief. For true belief transcends itself; it is belief in something—in a truth which is not determined by faith, but which, on the contrary, determines faith."[37] This depth compulsion cannot, in any important sense, be analytically described or even conceptually known. It takes hold of us below the level of the division into such functions of the self as feeling, thought, and will. It works directly on our whole-self. "Even though it were possible to express the whole content of faith in conceptual form, it would not follow that one had understood faith and how one had entered into it and how it entered into one."[38] Understanding still leaves us baffled by the mystery of its working and its reality. Nothing but the most high as the most real can thus compel us. Such compulsion comes certainly not from any intellectual analysis whereby we find that no lower level of knowledge can satisfy our intellectual problems. We need such analysis, but we are licked before we start if we stop there. Such an analysis by itself leaves us much as we were before; perhaps much worse. Thought can become a substitute for the real thing. The idea can separate us from reality as well as bind us to it. The idea can become the counterfeit which makes us think that we are rich. All ideas are counterfeit, or are made such, whenever we become interested in them for their own sake. That often happens and we miss being paid. Such ideas circulate without the ring of reality in

[36] Richard Niebuhr, *op. cit.*, p. 139.
[37] Frank, *op. cit.*, pp. 42–43.
[38] Kierkegaard, *Fear and Trembling*, p. xiv.

them. They look right on the surface but sound wrong. Their purchasing power is poor because in their depth responses men are shrewd and canny. Even the best checks are only a piece of paper until they are presented in the bank. Men must be sure of the bank.

Only whole-response, whole-surrender moment by moment in full trust, can ever give us the experience of the power of the most high as the most real. Only lives which so live can demonstrate the power of that authority and motivation. When we examine the content of religion we must ever be on guard to keep distinct the intellectual and even practical suggestiveness of the most high, from our own actual opening up in whole-response to its truth, beauty, and power. When the most high is believed through whole-response to be the most real we have an adequate authority and motivation. When life is lived for anything less, our problems become many and vexing. For our own day, we need desperately, humanly speaking, such authority and motivation.

The most high as the most real, in the second place, is alone sufficient to solve the problems of our process existentially because it faces, fully and victoriously, the end of our process. It faces ahead resolutely. The most high as the most real means necessarily the ultimate victory over the problems of evil which beset us. From our present stage they seem unconquerable. The short view scares us. We seem to be pinned down by gigantic forces of destruction and evil. Not only evil wills but ignorance and inertia threaten to overwhelm civilization; and our own lives are touched by them on every hand. As far as knowledge goes, we saw in the discussion of the last few positions that if we make the ultimate too much like our present process, it fails to explain it. Existentially, too, such a negative measuring of the most high by our present process certainly fails to give us the full assurance of ultimate victory. If, on the other hand, we make God perfect while the process is always imperfect, thus falsely separating the two, we also get little hope for a radical victory over evil. If we are to get both an adequate solution of the problem of evil in terms of knowledge and an adequate solution in terms of existential decision, we can never rest until we reach the point where the full religious synthesis has been accepted. Then our problem is already prospectively solved. We have a reflexive superspective in the light and power of which we can work. Then we can face the future with faith and vigor. We need this sense of the sovereignty of the highest good. Why has such a great proportion of religious thought been deterministic? Has it not been due to this depth truth in man? Determinism is right, if by that is meant the ultimate control of the good, conditioning and controlling even man's measure of freedom.

Such ultimate determinism makes freedom all the more precious and practically real. Without all law freedom is anarchy. It is ever some combination of necessity with spontaneity. Do the Marxists work any less because they believe that the nature of things is controlled ultimately in their favor? Do the strict Calvinists abuse their freedom more than others because they believe in predestination? Are the strongest Moslems the most easygoing individuals religiously because they, like the Calvinists, stress the sovereignty of God as the determining, central reality? When religion is both real and right it is all the stronger because of its unassailable conviction of the ultimate victory of the good. Man's freedom is real but never beyond the measure of God's ultimate sovereignty. When religion is a rationalization the ultimate victory of the good is rejected because if the good is so utterly and certainly in ultimate control, the scorner and the dillydallier are out of step with the ultimate and are bid on the certain pain of consequences to repent and to reform. Really right religion takes the pleasure clean out of foolish and selfish irresponsibility. Real and right religion faces a compelling future. The most high is the most real and is the finally determining factor in the universe. Man has no ultimate choice. He cannot escape if he rejects "so great a salvation." He has only the immediate choice. And wrong choice is always fraught sooner or later with painful consequences. When man is free only within the law of what is ultimately right and good, his freedom cannot be an excuse for any breaking of that law. He is free only to break and to be broken. To be healed he must return. Behold the severity as well as the goodness of God! True goodness is always and utterly severe with all evil and self-indulgence. It is never sentimental. That is why it can heal, make whole, and set free.

Those who make the most high less than the most real are not facing the full future of process. Some look a bit ahead at some better stage—that cannot come, for that matter, without the Best. Some look at the present; some look back on the way that we have come. None of these approaches will do if we are to solve with full vigor the problems of our process in deed and in truth. The first is a blunted hope. The second is a case of arrested development. It is a refusal to grow in line with the process, as directed by Purpose. It is a mere standing still. Or it is a false seriousness. It is trying to move the world from within the world. It is believing that the progress of process is left mainly to human power. God has no feet but ours, they say. What a problem He must have to walk in one direction in that case! No wonder they despair of God's power to help! The third approach, the looking back on process to find truth, is existentially a revolt from our responsibility under God for the future. It is a trying to return to the irresponsibility of lower levels of existence. It is psychologically a regression. It is infantilism. We shall not solve our problems by denying them. We shall not overcome our evils by refusing to believe that moral and spiritual categories have any truth or reality. We shall not be victorious over evil by means of its description, however accurate. The best explanations of it in terms of rational knowledge may find the door, perhaps even the keyhole. But they have no key that turns. They cannot open the door to sweep clean the house. Existentially we must face the future not only with courage and with good intention, not only with the maturest human wisdom, hoping that we shall all learn to choose the truly good rather than evil possibilities. We must face it with the power of salvation. We must face it with a wisdom beyond our own, beyond where we now are, with a wisdom which is rooted in the utmost reality. We must face it with irresistible convictions that evil can be overcome, with convictions that arise from our personal contact with a power beyond process that has helped us to bear and conquer our own evils, and whose resources we have hardly begun to tap. Religion, when it is right, faces the future of process with all confidence and power to overcome evil. Religion in the wisdom of the world is absurd. It believes the impossible. But the measure of its faith is the truest measure of the possible, for with God all things are possible. Religion is the hanging together with that power in the universe Who is already the victor over evil and awaits without a doubt our eventual victory, knowing both our resources and those of the enemy.

Religion, if it is real, is no opiate. It is no escape from the unpleasant facts of life. Religion is the facing of the future with God so as to see all the more clearly our present evils in the light of his judgment and so as to overcome them by His grace and power. Our knowledge at best is slight. "The impassable gulf which necessarily separates the best-established human knowledge from the sight of the very foundation of knowledge measures precisely what is lacking to our full satisfaction.[39] We must get the best knowledge we can. What we really see, too, is veridical. Yet beyond that knowledge, and far, far deeper in ourselves where we are related to the very Source of our being, we must face responsibly the evils which confront us with the assurance that no matter how hemmed in and defeated we may momentarily seem to be, yet immeasurably stronger is He that is with us than any power for evil in the world. The hope of religion when it is based in faith in the most high as the most real can never, and will never, make us ashamed. That is the right depth-response of full religion. Right religion is the unconditional will to the victory of the good and the experience of this victory both presently and anticipatorily. Right religion faces the future without fear. It knows, as Werfel points out, that "skeptic always rhymes with septic."[40] It knows the power that casts out all fear because fear is grounded in the existential ignorance and rejection of the most high as the most real. Right religion is the celebration of the victory of life in the midst of its battle with death. It is the enjoyment of the future before and as it comes into being because God is already there and He is able.

[39] Gilson, *The Philosophy of St. Bonaventura*, p. 387.
[40] *Between Heaven and Earth*, p. 51.

Depth-thinking is existential thinking. It satisfies the needs of the whole man. It seeks the fullest knowledge possible in terms both of description and of explanation. Yet it does not stop there. In knowledge man is still in a sense the center of his world of truth, at least by his judgment of it. Existentially that knowledge may come with dire judgment on his life. Then, however, it is already more than knowledge. Depth-thinking in a world like this should surely lead to whole-reaction which is whole-surrender. *Islam*, "surrender," must be a basic element in every right religion. The profound self soon wearies of its deepest thoughts and finds its best understanding to be but shallow groping. What he sees may be mostly true, but oh, the piercing mysteries that baffle his soul. He knows all too well the truth of the old Chinese proverb that one cannot draw water from a deep well with a short rope. The depths of eternities overwhelm him. He feels utterly empty and superficial. Except for faith and his being held by divine hands he would turn a complete cynic. His deepest needs outrun his best ideas. He matches his faith and wisdom against the total needs of the world and confesses in utter humiliation that only God will do and that only God's time is the right time. He can do no less because his consciousness and conscience have become bound up with the world and his private satisfactions burn within him as selfish and irresponsible except as they are of such a kind as to give God glory and the world help. Only if his joys are the demonstration of truth and reality which shall be to all people can he find it in his heart to allow them. He knows that the very needs of his own life speak of realities which are the more mysterious the more he ponders them and the more deeply he tries to live them. Yet he knows also that though his knowledge cannot ever reach down as far as his deepest longings, though it cannot satisfy his most basic redemptive relations to the world to which he reacts, he can yet use it. He honors it, without worshiping it. He knows that it can at least be used in him as he comes to rest on that truth which holds him as soon as he stops trying to hold it. Depth-thinking in whole-surrender has let him float in that very endless ocean in which he was drowning as long as he strove to keep himself by his own effort above its surface. When he lets himself float, too, he can swim and get somewhere, do something. As long as he struggled to keep himself afloat by his own effort, however hard, he was merely wasting his effort. And in that way lay death.

Only the full surrender to the most high as the most real far beyond our own attainment and understanding can compel our lives wholly and give us the sense of truth that sets us free from fear and free for creative living.

The Circle of Science we can draw. Its circumference holds in the logico-empirical realm. The Circle of Philosophy we can draw. It holds in all rational knowledge based on present process. The Circle of Religion we cannot draw. No human compass is large enough for that. It includes the most critical and adequate science and philosophy available. It uses with thankfulness all the efforts of science and philosophy to get at the truth according to their natures and within the areas of their proper efficacy. Yet the Circle of Religion cannot be drawn from there. It includes knowledge but is not centered in it. Its center is the most high in history. It is the highest selective event that most fully and meaningfully lights up all else. Yet that center is also our greatest mystery of being both for what he is in himself and for Him beyond process to whom he points. This center, moreover, is itself a moving point. It is not static. It is dynamic. It must be personal since it is our most adequate actual whole-response. Yet it points immeasurably far beyond human personality. It both points and leads like a strong current of energy beyond itself, beyond all the process that we know. All the rest of the process is less than that event. He mediates reality at its highest. He fills our deepest needs—only to enlarge and refill them. The center satisfies us only to make us the more spiritually hungry. He is our highest discontinuity, our truest difference from the preceding process. The question of quality, degree, and kind we can leave for now till the volume reserved for it. Yet who can live with Him day by day and not either revolt against Him or else surrender to His claim to be different from general humanity by being Himself the uniquely emergent message in history which fulfills, not in syllogisms but in life, not in theory but in grace and truth, all other messages.

The wheel of the process rolls on. Its axis moves toward a goal. The spokes grow longer as history fills out. The wheel gets weaker and stronger. The rims of process wear out and are changed. But He remains the axis. We know no better center. He is our given fact. We must have an actual event for our center of existential truth. The Circle of Religion, nevertheless, can never be drawn for there are no limits to it. No human being, at least, can understand the depths and the outreaches of that Reality with whom we hang together. No compass of human thought can draw that infinite circumference. Out beyond science. Out beyond philosophy. Religion is inescapable. Religion we must have. Every heart is necessarily a church, as an old proverb has it, though God does not always preach the sermon. He is not allowed to. False priests are hired. But the church cannot be closed. The service must go on. Religion we must have; yet we cannot possess it. Our reaction is at best a feeble faith held in by the incommensurate Greatness. The strongest human faith is like clay in comparison to God's strength. Even if the center were static rather than dynamic so as to allow us to put the point of the compass there, no circle drawn by human mind would be big enough to do more than discourage us. Religion is endlessly creative because its truth is infinite. The circle must be drawn around us far beyond our understanding.

To be right we must be defined increasingly in terms of the area of the circle. The circle cannot be defined in terms of our position. Knowledge we must have. More of it we already have than we use to advantage. Nevertheless the circle of knowledge must be swallowed up in the endless circle of faith—the circle that we draw is incommensurate with the circle that must be drawn around us.

Beyond knowledge lies our existential decision. Doubt and fear of the Most High as the Most Real lead to disintegration and defeat. Faith and love in that truth lead to life and life more abundantly. Unto us frail creatures of time is given the privilege and the great honor of choice, a choice albeit heavy with responsibility. Before us is set death or life, darkness or light, fear or faith, weakness or power, division or love, self-imprisonment or fellowship, self-idolatry or God-worship. Unto us frail children of time is given such choice. This choice is not theoretical. It is not verbal. It is no vicarious drama. We cannot decline to choose. The choice is as real and as necessary as our very lives. We can choose temporarily the frustrating weakness of cosmic irresponsibility. We can choose lastingly a strength not our own and a love that passeth knowledge. For creative living as individuals and as society we must make the choice of right religion. Religion is right, moreover, only when our normally necessary whole-response is to the Most High as the Most Real.

Faith and Reason

In a recent attempt to survey the future of religious inquiry, John Bennett has suggested that the major problem still confronting religion is the relation between faith and knowledge[1] This assertion finds ready response in all thoughtful religious circles. Scientists and philosophers, in increasing numbers, have become unafraid to use the word faith. They declare that we must have faith in reason, faith in democracy, faith in man, and even occasionally faith in the religious foundations upon which our civilization has been built.[2] But just as the need for faith is more widely felt, so also is the conviction, at least in many quarters, that at this time especially we can by no means afford to forsake reason as our guide. We must have a rational science, a reasonable philosophy, a reasoned religion. Just how closely faith and reason are related can be seen by the fact that men ask us to trust reason and to have a reasonable faith, to trust the scientific method to solve our problems and to have a scientific religion with which to meet them, and to trust philosophy and to have a philosophy in which we can trust. What, then, is the relation between faith and reason?

From their usage it appears that they are neither direct opposites nor essentially the same. Our first task, therefore, is to give definitions of both that will neither cut off each from the other nor absorb one into the other. Such definitions, for instance, as "Reason

---

[1] "The Outlook for Theology," *Journal of Religion*, Oct., 1941, Vol. XXI, No. 4, pp. 341 ff.

[2] Cf. for instance Birkhoff's presidential address at the one hundred third meeting of the American Academy for the Advancement of Science; or the First or Second Symposium of the Conference on Science, Philosophy and Religion.

is but faith clarified" or "Reason is the handmaid of faith" on the one hand; or on the other, "Faith is the extension of reason" or "Faith is believing what to reason is absurd," although they all contain truth, do nevertheless also miss the real point and tend, besides, to prejudice an adequate inquiry into their respective natures and relations. Instead we hope to suggest how and in what sense faith and reason are both necessary to religion and to each other by our viewing them in their actual functional interdependence.

As working definitions we therefore suggest the following: Faith is essentially the affirmation that some ideal (ideals) is ultimately more real than our average actual world of experience and has the power to transform it. Faith is thus suggestively akin to C. I. Lewis' idea of significance as belonging to the pragmatic *a priori* and not to the empirical actual:[3] "The significance of knowledge depends upon the significance of possibility that is not actual."[4] But to faith that significant possibility has a reality eminently prior to actuality itself with the power ideally to transform it. Reason, again, sees what actually is and what is possible in terms of that actuality. Faith, consequently, is *primarily* grounded in the ideal while reason is primarily grounded in the actual. Faith is basically a will to believe while reason is basically a challenge to belief. Faith says: "I see that which is more real than the actual and can change it." Reason replies: "Show me that what you do see is more real than the actual and that it can change it." Between them there is a running debate which in the very nature of things can never be settled by argument or counterargument. Yet faith and reason need each other, for without faith reason fails in courage and social concern, while without reason faith fails in vision and application. As long as the conflict between the ideal and the actual lasts, faith and reason can never be reduced to each other without the deadening loss of creative tension in the intellectual life of the world.

---

[3] "It is the *a priori* element in knowledge which is thus pragmatic, not the empirical." *Mind and the World Order*, p. 266.

[4] *Ibid.*, p. 142, note.

I

The Existential Aspect of Faith. Only as long as we yearn to change our actual world, our world bespotted by fear and selfishness, by envy and suspicion, by hardness of heart and misunderstanding, by possessiveness and pretension, by decay and death, in short, by all the evils which beset our finite and sinful selves, only so long has faith vital meaning. Faith is a demand on the best we know by what is best in us that both we ourselves and our total world be changed into its likeness. Faith is a living affirmation, by a self struggling with sin, that the ideal which it sees is ultimately more real than its own attitude and condition. Faith is an assertion by that self which cares deeply and steadily for people in all their troubles and sorrows that there is a better order in which these can be overcome. William James affirmed that two factors were common to all religious experience, namely, the feeling that there is something wrong about us as we actually are and the belief that we are saved from this wrongness by our making "proper connection" with higher powers.[5] Unless we understand this basic nature of faith and unless we ourselves are struggling both for a better kind of personal life and for a better world, we have no unity of experience and consequently no unity of discourse in terms of which to discuss the relation of faith and reason; for in the end, "a unity of experience is the precondition of a unity of discourse."[6]

The real dividing point both in life and in thought, therefore, as Calhoun has observed, is "between those who put primary stress on things that are seen and those who put primary stress upon things that are not seen."[7] The difference between the perspective of the actual and that of the ideal is "decisive." This difference, moreover, is not first of all a descriptive difference. Albeit different total views are described, these views are not totally different. The

---

[5] *Varieties of Religious Experience,* p. 508.

[6] Dewey, *Logic,* p. 68.

[7] Calhoun, "The Dilemma of Humanitarian Modernism," in *The Christian Understanding of Man,* pp. 68 ff.

basic difference between faith and reason is, rather, a living decision. Faith is not static, but dynamic. It is not speculative, but personal. It is not theoretical, but existential. The difference between faith and reason is definitely not between reason as seeing and faith as refusing to see, but between reason insisting on what is and faith used to describe a world which ought to be in the light of some selectively actual ideal which is taken by it to be real beyond what here and now is observed as aggregatively actual. Without faith, for example, there can be philosophy but no religion, for religion is never, to use a phrase by H. R. Mackintosh, "the optimistic acceptance of the actual," Religion and faith spring alike out of man's inescapable decisions concerning his ultimate meanings and values. Naturally only positive decisions regarding the reality or, at least, realizability of the ideal are properly called faith, for such is unmistakably its deepest connotation. Christian's definition of religion as "interest in what is regarded as most important in the universe"[8] (and here faith and religion are synonymous) contains a vital truth which, however, is weakened by the neutral connotation of the word "interest." Faith is truly far less a matter of general interest or even of explicit and specific decisions than it is a matter of total positive commitments and basic affirmative attitudes. St. Thomas had a deep insight along this line in his observation that "grace takes possession of the root-unity of the soul below the distinction into intellect and will."[9] Faith is primarily an existential judgment entailing a different dimension as a changed perspective.

Faith as existential decision may be analyzed into many phases.[10] The first is the experience of the wrongness of our actual situation.

[8] Christian, "A Definition of Religion," in *The Review of Religion,* May, 1941, Vol. V, No. 4, p. 412.

[9] Cited in H. Wheeler Robinson, "Revelation" (privately printed); read before the London Society for the Study of Religion, Dec. 1, 1931, p. 6.

[10] Naturally this analysis aims only to exhibit an essential element in vital and significant faith. Since knowledge is by nature a social act, both genetically and co-ordinately, the analysis is logical rather than primarily psycho-chronological, is focused on the consciousness rather than the content of faith, and is more concerned with the general than with the individual consciousness.

James, as we have seen, called this a common element in all religious experience, and Royce wrote that "dissatisfaction is the universal experience of every temporal being."[11] Whitehead, in fact, thinks of consciousness itself as arising in the "affirmation-negation contrast" between the physical feeling "in fact" and the propositional feeling "might be," between an actual nexus and that nexus as differently related to a complex eternal object, i.e., to an ideal situation.[12] From his point of view faith is an essential ingredient in all creative consciousness. Faith is not only the vision of the better that is seen as a desirable mode of operation but is also the effort of aim at value or ideal self-decision needed to sustain and realize that vision. Faith is always a "creative adventure" because it can never be tested by what is already actual.

Faith thus begins in a relation between the vision of the ideal and its consequent challenge of the actual. This first phase of faith has been well described by Heim:

> The question whether, and how far, the actual deserves to be maintained or to be abolished is precisely the question which my will has to decide; whenever, therefore, an act of volition takes place, the whole existing state of the world is laid in the balance, and a decision must be come to regarding what elements in it are worthy to endure, and what elements ought henceforth to be fundamentally altered. The fact that something is there is in itself no sufficient reason for supposing that it ought to be maintained or repeated.[13]

The second aspect of faith places stress increasingly on the ideal as objectively real and decreasingly on the independent power of the man of faith; for the more he tries to realize the ideal, and the more of it he tries to realize, the more he begins to see himself in his true proportion to the whole world and its unfathomable needs. Pratt has observed that "religion involves and presupposes the acceptance of the objective";[14] for experience shows that a sub-

---

[11] *The World and the Individual,* Second Series, p. 382.
[12] *Process and Reality,* p. 407.
[13] Heim, *God Transcendent,* pp. 196–197.
[14] Pratt, *The Religious Consciousness,* p. 3.

jective ideal, known to be such, lacks not only objective reality but even religious value, since even psychologically it cannot constitute an object of genuine belief.[15] Those, in any case, who have struggled earnestly and patiently to change the world have discovered how woefully little they can do in their own power and how great must be that ideal reality which can change the actual in rightfully desirable directions. Hopeful human idealism is good at the beginning of faith, but if it continues to be no more than such hopeful idealism it is either ignorant or complacent, for it has surely never come to grips with the deeper and eternal aspects of man's spiritual conflicts. Unless despair or bitterness sets in, the idealistic phase of faith ought therefore to be fulfilled by the losing of its easy optimism, its complacency, and ignorance, in order to open up increasingly to the cosmic resources for world-transformation which are known only to and through faith.

In the third phase, instead of man's merely finding an ally in ultimate reality, he confronts its absolute demand upon him and upon his world. This experience may take many forms, for example: mysticism's infinite demand for purgation and union; the demand by the categorical imperative for the fulfillment of the moral law by the good will; the demand by the eternal Thou in the Incarnate Word for human compassion and constructive concern. Whatever the form this demand may take, the man of faith comes to feel that both he and his actual world are irretrievably in the power of a Reality which decisively controls his life and efforts. Since he now knows that he can achieve little permanent good except in line with this Reality, he begins to make himself its channel rather than its source, its servant rather than its master, its follower rather than its leader. Faith begins to mature when the finite self feels himself in the grip of the great mystery of life which he did not choose and which he can never master, with interests, dreads, hopes, and dreams far beyond his control, and when he comes to the knowledge that the span of his life is shorter, even in terms of the length of time that he can think, than the whiz of a passing car. Faith thus tends to mature from optimistic ideal-

[15] *Ibid.*, p. 7.

ism to objective trust in the ideal powers which control human destinies and values, and finally to an understanding and willing surrender to that (Him) upon which (whom) all depends.

Faith, however, does not stop with the mere recognition of the objective reality and demand of its ideal, but goes on to explain the actual itself in the light of that ideal. Since faith holds that the ideal can and ought to transform the actual, and since the highest ideal is taken to be most real, value and power are intrinsically joined. In existential commitment they are felt to be of one ultimate cloth. The selective ideal thus becomes a determinative motif or a regulative pattern which gives a new meaning to actuality. What is, is seen in the light of what ought to be, not only in terms of value but in terms of reality. Lotze's basic metaphysics, for instance, is largely religious, and for this very reason. One of his most climactic assertions comes almost at the end of his *Metaphysics* in the words: "I seek in that which *should be* the ground of that which is."[16] Faith never denies the actual *for what it is*, but sees it within a new context of meaning which alters its status from a standard of reference of final truth to a standard of contemporaneous actuality. Because faith sees all things in the perspective of the highest ideal, it is selective seeing as opposed to aggregative seeing. The coherence of the actual is accepted for precisely that, and that coherence, of course, includes the measure of ideal realization that we now see; but this coherence it is precisely which faith refuses recognition as a standard of ultimate truth and reality. Faith consequently demands an honest and critical philosophy, for in order to change the actual it must know it correctly. Faith declares its highest ideal to be most real and systematizes all things in terms of this its regulative pattern. But this is faith at its highest, faith as the conviction of things not yet seen.

Precisely here, however, lie the dangers of faith. Faith starts with the desire to change the actual. As it grows, it then roots in objective reality its conviction that the actual can be changed in rightfully ideal directions. It finally accepts this ideal as most

[16] Lotze, *Metaphysics*, p. 536.

eminently real and compelling, forcing actuality to be viewed in its light. But as it grows two subtle snares also threaten it. Faith may become counterfeit either by denying or by neglecting the actual. The first counterfeit, that of denying the actual, takes the form of saying that history is not real and that we must therefore be delivered from it. Reason and actuality are thus both denied in the supposed interest of the ideal. If evil is not real it is hardly worth while to contend with it. In the second instance, the believer becomes so engrossed in what ought to be that he forgets his responsibility for what is. He dreams about the ideal, worships its selective realization, and gazes at its superhistorical fulness, but neglects to change the actual into its likeness. In either case the tension between the actual and the ideal is gone and there is now no desire to change the actual. Thus real faith has become counterfeit. The identification and participation with and in the ideal which is necessary in order to transform it are gone so that the man of faith has been delivered from his complacency with the actual only to land in the complacency of an unrealized ideal. Thereupon prophets who are still in faith's creative tension arise to denounce faith as the opium of the people. Faith is thus misused and abused. For the prophets who thus denounce and renounce faith in the objective ideal themselves land in the quicksands of subjective idealism.

To avoid this danger, the ideal of faith must always be defined from within the tension of life. The prophet must always be "the mystic in action."[17] Worship saps the vitality of religion unless it continually expresses itself in work. By the fruits we always know real faith. The writer of James may have been much misunderstood on this point. Even though our works are naturally not our faith, we must show our faith by our works. But work is more than the result of faith. It is also a stimulus and food for faith. For faith is a living decision affecting the whole man. There is a fresh, fruitful wind blowing through Macmurray's concept of religion as intentional activity, the organic synthesis of contempla-

[17] Hocking, *The Meaning of God in Human Experience*, p. 511.

tion and action.[18] If he, however, errs on the side of subjectivism, Przywara's *Polarity* gives a profound analysis of the religious consciousness as strong only in the balanced tension of striving *for, in, and under* the ideal. Faith is part of life. It is a dynamic tension between the actual and the ideal, in which the ideal is affirmed as more real over and against the actual.

II

The Theoretical Aspects of Faith. We have taken up first the existential aspect of faith because faith is first of all a living decision. From a purely theoretical point of view faith has no meaning except for the fact that living people have had and have what they call faith. Faith goes beyond descriptive reason for it is the conviction of things not seen, *as faith sees them.* Reason as sight sees what actually is and what seems possible in that light. Faith as a commitment to the highest ideal known, as most real and true, is absurd to reason to whatever extent it goes beyond available evidence in the realm of what actually is. Faith's total context of meaning cannot by its very nature be wholly validated because as yet it is not. The actual is what it is and can be roughly tested or experienced as such. The ideal, however, is so exceptionally and fragmentarily realized, especially as it approaches its fullness, that only an act of faith can designate it with assurance as ultimate reality. This element of personal decision makes inadequate the distinction between reason as sight and faith as insight. To whatever extent reason is rooted in what is, and can be proved by it, while faith is what is largely not yet, and cannot therefore be proved in terms of what is, there is a clear-cut existential gulf between faith and reason, and the two can neither be reduced to each other nor be proved false by each other. There is no court of final appeal to settle the claims of faith *versus* reason and vice versa, except the future. As long as we are human, and as long as there is need for religion at all, so long the tension between faith and reason is unresolvable, but precisely in this creative tension lies our

[18] Macmurray, *The Clue to History.*

greatest hope. To surrender to actuality, on the one hand, or to be doped by an unrealized ideal, on the other, is to lose the zest for a better life and a better world.

This functionally irreducible difference between faith and reason has led many to fix an absolute theoretical gulf between them. This is a mistake. Faith and reason have congruent theoretical aspects. "All reason, involved in the acquisition of 'knowledge,' is leavened with faith,"[19] while faith, as we shall see, is decidedly not without rational justification. This is certainly no place to examine the limits of the purely theoretical reason, if such there be. Many modern philosophers, especially after Kant, have done that. Whitehead, for instance, has shown in recent years how untenable is any narrowly rationalistic or empiricistic system. We can agree with Hegel's stricture on Kant's method that even the examination of reason is an act of reason and takes its validity for granted. Reason is sorely tried in the modern world, and it certainly is true that "it would be folly to cast away our most trusted weapon because some have cut their fingers on it."[20] But to many of us it nevertheless seems true that there is not a sufficient measure of empirical or theoretical knowledge to deal adequately with the deepest values and meanings of life, especially if we include the central problem of motivation, namely, the empowerment of our wills to affirm, appropriate, and achieve the highest ideal as the most real demanding to be made actual. There are, of course, limited areas of investigation in the realm of formal and material knowledge that are open to a high degree of exact, objective verifiability and inclusive communicability, but in these very fields the prior question of the ultimate relation between method and metaphysics is being more and more seriously raised. In the overwhelmingly large areas of workable and meaningful knowledge, moreover, faith plays an ever more important role. Birkhoff seems right in his assertion that all intellectual investigation is surrounded by "an aura of faith."

Faith, on the other hand, has no organ and no content except reason. Remsberg is right that "faith tells us more about God than

---

[19] Tennant, *Philosophical Theology*, Vol. I, p. 299.
[20] Brightman, *An Introduction to Philosophy*, p. 17.

reason can. Reason tells us more about the world than revelation."[21] But faith does not go beyond all experience and reason. If so, we could *know* nothing about it. Faith is not the knowing only of negations. It is rather, as we have seen, a selective reason which uses the ideal as a distinct perspective or principle of explanation. We have defined reason as rooted in actuality because in relation to faith our interest must be primarily in the final criterion of truth and reality. Mere consistency is obviously an inadequate standard in a dynamic world where the real struggle is between the aggregative and the selective seeing. Neither formal consistency nor material consistency per se, or both together *in loco actualis,* can adequately judge the truth of faith. Consistency there ought to be, to be sure, within the realms of both faith and reason; but the latter thinks of it as coherence with what is actual, while the former thinks of what consistency the ideal motif requires. Notwithstanding there are common areas. Since actuality, for instance, is no fixed reality but is rather itself subject to change, faith is not, even theoretically, completely arbitrary in its insistence that there is an ultimate truth beyond the consistent aggregative interpretation of the here and now that is best seen in terms of the selectively highest ideal. What is becomes. Actuality is dynamic. Transformability is a truth of reason as well as of faith. The faith that the ideal can change the actual is not merely a desperate determination of will, or of wishful thinking, but partly an observation of the actual itself. Not only is actuality transformable, and thus not fixed as an aggregative actual but open to the increasing actualization of some part of it, but, besides and moreover, faith is seen to create new facts. The will to believe, as Perry has observed with regard to James's philosophy, is not only truth-finding but truth-making.[22] Hocking writes: "It is the nemesis of an imperfect realism that its illusions become its effective reals."[23] Faith matters. It makes a difference to actuality. Thus reason can ob-

[21] "The Relation of Faith and Knowledge in Luther and Aquinas," in *The Lutheran Church Quarterly,* Jan., 1942, p. 14.

[22] *The Thought and Character of William James, passim;* or James, "The Will to Believe," in *The Will to Believe, and Other Essays.*

[23] *Thoughts on Death and Life,* p. 217.

serve and report the important fact of the relation of faith and actuality and confirm that faith is not altogether without reasonable evidence in its claim.

But here we need a strong caution; for even if faith can transform the actual in ideal directions, and even if reason can record and attest this fact, faith cannot, nevertheless, claim in the court of reason that the ideal is more real than the actual except to whatever point the transformation has been actually achieved, or at the most, seems from our present perspective readily achievable.

Faith, besides, is not completely arbitrary, even from the point of view of reason. In addition to the fact that actuality is by nature changeable, so that faith conditions dynamic reality, the ideal of faith must both apply to the actual and have some power to transform it. The relevance of the ideal for the actual is a rational check on faith. Just as faith judges the aggregative actual by the selective ideal, demanding its own realization, so reason judges the selective ideal by its significant relevance to the aggregative actual. Faith and reason thus both challenge and check each other. The ideal cannot be a mere matter of abstract speculation or of wishful thinking, for then it would be devoid of both applicability and transforming power. The ideal which is most needed to transform the actual would naturally have the highest degree of reality for faith. But if reason found this ideal impossible of even gradual attainment, it naturally would be no relevant ideal, and consequently no true ideal even for faith. The religious ideal, therefore, must be not only applicable to all of experience and thus rationally realizable, but it must also have become sufficiently a part of history to bear concrete witness to at least its partial actualization. Faith's claim that the ideal is more real than the actual can thrive only in some encouraging relation, in the depths of experience and history, between realizability and realization. Faith is thus again not totally arbitrary from the point of view of reason but is rather an affirmation of things not yet fully or sufficiently seen. Faith lives in some having and in much hoping. Our faith grows out of our intelligent affirmation of our concern for the world. It must consequently live on the assurance which is nourished by growing insight and experience through both subjective commitment and objective efficacy of the reality of its ideal.

Faith also lives on the knowledge that its highest ideals have come to be known and experienced within historic time. They were not always actual, even in human ideals. That we know. Man's highest ideals have been slow to emerge at all and slower still to mature in the general social consciousness. The reason for this is importantly that since the ideal above the present self-attainment judges the self that sees it, it is hardly welcome to anyone whose concern is not increasingly for the world. The ideal demands a surrender to it which is offensive to the actual self. That explains, in part, the slow actualization of the ideal. But since man's highest ideals have, nevertheless, come *into* history, faith has some reasonable right to claim that they had an adequate source beyond it. That the highest ideals are mere self-creations or haphazard happenings without intrinsic relation to the whole process and the meaning of that process into which they came is at any rate an affirmation without adequate reasonable evidence. Faith holds that these ideals show what ultimate reality is better than anything less than they. This interpretation seems more likely than that they were caused by some configuration of natural energy or even arose from some non-purposive protoplasmic irritability—unless, of course, reason commits itself to the proposition that the lower always explains the higher, or that seen succession is a better principle of explanation than seen significance. Such a commitment, however, is an *a priori* acceptance of the actual as most real and seems unduly anthropocentric and Ptolemaic. Besides faith holds that since so much of the ideal has become known and cherished even within our little drop of historic time, it would be Ptolemaic, indeed, not to believe that we may stand on the threshold of some new epoch of ideal realization.

To the changeable nature of the actual, the fact-making power of faith, and to faith's ideal relevancy to the actual is thus also added the significant consideration of the historic emergence of the ideal into the actual. These and similar considerations illustrate how the nature of the actual itself, and especially that of history, is an important bridge between faith and reason with common territory immediately on both sides. Faith is no jump in the dark over an unknown river but rather an adventurous existential leap across from actuality to the land of the ideal by means of unfinished theoretical scaffolding.[24]

III

To sum up, our thesis is that faith and reason both need each other. They come in conflict only when each tries to usurp the function of the other. Faith and reason, religion and philosophy, must not be confused. Both are needed in a constructive society. Faith is the vision of the ideal and the affirmation and discovery of spirit that this vision is ultimately true. Reason is the careful observation, systematization, and appraisal of man's historic experience as a whole. Faith must not deny reason for in the neglecting, denying, or falsely interpreting the actual lies the danger of its own death. Reason must not deny the challenge of faith but must let the spirit launch out daringly beyond what can be proved true by the actual. Faith must abide by reason's demand for relevance to the actual and for demonstration of its power to change it in ideal directions. Reason must open up, beyond its proper and vital task of truth, to the demand of the spirit for the good. There can thus be a reasonable faith and a faith-filled reason that co-operate for the common good without ever confusing their distinctive natures, functions, and fields.

This approach to the problem we hope will commend itself to those who have struggled with the history of the relation of faith and reason. Sometimes philosophy has been deeply influenced by religion and in the great classical tradition not only are thought and being but also goodness and being largely equated. Those who at this point think of Plato and Plotinus can almost as well think of Aristotle, for his system, too, is dominated from the top. From the side of religion, on the other hand, the equation of the good and the rational with ultimate being is obvious, to be found not only

[24] Since writing this the author has come to see that what is most unfinished is the practical scaffolding, the realization of Purpose by process.

with the Platonic Augustine but also with the Aristotelian Aquinas. One of the very weakest links in Aquinas' long and strong theological line of thought is, in fact, his easy argument that being is also good, else were men's desire for perfection vain. That, he held, would be an unreasonable assumption.[25] Hume and Kant, therefore, did both religion and philosophy great service by their rigid criticism of the theological arguments for God. Hume saw how much religion depends on faith and Kant realized that its main arguments hang on the ontological argument, which as a sheer rational-empirical proof is deficient whether it is taken to be an analytic or a synthetic judgment. It was Lotze who saw how emotional in nature, or we should say existential, is the ontological argument. It is truly good that much modern philosophy is critical of overextended arguments for religion. Faith and reason can then be seen in their true relation. We have no right to say, of course, that philosophers should not usurp the place of religion by becoming existential, but we can say that it is *as such* obviously no longer philosophy as the systematic interpretation of the actual. We can say, moreover, that such philosophy, as far as it involves faith and decision, is religious in nature. Nor have we the right to forbid teachers of religion to adopt the rational, empirical, or pragmatic method, which are all chiefly philosophic in nature. We can say, however, that coherence with the actual, correspondence to the actual, or workability within the actual can never be adequate standards for religious faith. They are important to religion to test its relevancy and power, and are therefore partially religious standards, but religion can never limit its truth to the actual. Its power and perspective are not primarily of this world.

Faith can act as an irritant and a vitamin to philosophy. It can remind philosophy that the totality of our temporal existence here and now is changeable, that faith does produce new facts, that its ideals have come into history within an amazingly short time, and that the world is young and "groaning for redemption" in order

[25] Cf. *Summa Theologica,* Vol. I, pp. 53 and 122 (Question V, Art. 1, and Question XII, Art. 1). These are really an emotional form of the ontological argument.

that philosophy keep free from premature and negative conclusions as to the nature of reality based on its systematic observation of what is now actual. As such faith is an irritant. As a vitamin, however, it can help philosophy concentrate on those human problems, both inner and social, which mankind must tackle in a spirit of resoluteness and hope. It can ask of philosophy that it be not optimistic beyond what the facts warrant but that it dare to see and tell the truth. Seeing the truth, faith can come as courage and stamina and concern to all men who will have it and thus help to remove from the actual its sting of despondency and fear.

Reason, at last, can keep faith to its proper task. Bixler's insistence that our faith in another world must not contradict what we know of this is healthful to faith so long as it does not limit to the actual its scope and power. Reason can be both a check and a challenge to faith, keeping it in line with an applicable ideal that can show its power to transform our world. If reason and faith are both accepted for what they are and used by humble and compassionate spirits as well as by critical and disciplined minds, both can co-operate in that common task to make the Kingdom of God come on earth as it is in heaven.

Reason Must Become Religious

Our times are confused. So much new building material in terms of knowledge and techniques has piled up that the very structure which we are raising is obscured. An especially acute problem is our general confusion about the relation of reason and religion. This question is ever basic to thought and action, but in our age it has become inflamed. It must be faced frankly. Religion and reason are both indispensable aspects of life and upon their right relation in theory and practice depends the health and wealth of life for both the individual and society.

Religion means our necessary relation to the universe in its ultimate nature. Our word comes from the Latin *religare*, "to bind." Religion is our boundedness by the universe in our intrinsic dependence upon it. From within and without, from beginning to end, our lives are fixed by the way we hang together with Reality. Religion is not optional but necessary. Even though religion contain options these themselves are rooted in the necessity of the ultimate nature of things. Religion is our unavoidable reaction to that ultimate Reality upon which we all depend and which is always acting upon us. React we must. As to that there is no choice. Our freedom to react, which is primary experience, is an opportunity and responsibility rooted in Reality and eternally fixed by its nature.

Our reason is our capacity for intellectual response to Reality.

Our response is relative both to our ignorance and to our rebelliousness. Reality demands that we change to fit the requirements of its purpose for us while our natural response is to wish that Reality change to meet our wants. Although our reason cannot change Reality in its ultimate nature and demand, we can hide from it, we hope, by interpreting it in the light of our own desires. Much that poses as religion is nothing but man's rationalization. Right religion is right response to Reality; right reason is the right interpretation of it. Right religion and right reason go together. Without right reason there can be no right response; without right response reason is under heavy pressure to distort what it sees to accord with the response. To find salvation we must therefore have the increasingly constructive, interactive co-operation of reason and religion.

At this very point, however, we need to be exceedingly cautious, otherwise we arrive at a smooth theoretical solution which belies the actual situation in which we are. The easy co-operation of reason and religion is interrupted inevitably within our actual situation by two unavoidable conditions. The first is that actually we are dominantly self-seeking. That is, our natural response to Reality is self-centered and calculating. Such a response distorts reason in that we naturally try to justify our response by means of a false interpretation of Reality. We tend to make it less demanding and more to our liking. This drive to distortion even largely precedes our actual seeing, preventing the free function of our reason, by means of an original self-regard which infects all the mental processes that deal with our relation to Reality. Still man must react to Reality and sees enough of its real truth to leave the self fearful and restless in its rationalizations. While thus aiding our escape from Reality, reason nevertheless also recognizes that the response *is* an escape and remains dissatisfied.[26]

[26] Paul Ramsey has objected to my assertion that reason can help to correct itself. He holds that the unrest is rather completely of the spirit, reason being simply its instrument. After careful reflection I must still maintain, however, that reason be used in a more inclusive sense, as having concrete contents yet restless with them all unless they are perfectly coherent throughout; and that is impossible, history being what it is. Even coherence

Right religion and right reason thus go together only in so far as the response to Reality is right, namely, the decision to be changed in accordance with the demands of Reality. Such a change involves the self's being broken and remade. We are changed from being primarily selves to being primarily sons.[27] The self naturally dreads being broken, for it rightly treasures being a self; but being remade into a son it dreads also its reverting to a self as its primary status. The only right response to Reality is faith, for faith is the surrendering of self to Reality in order to become and to be remade and enlarged from selfhood into sonship. Right religion and right reason therefore find constructive co-operation only in faith.

The second caution is to the effect that Reality does not present itself to us with a clear countenance. That Being is also wholly good, a completely creative and self-giving concern for all, can never be directly observed in our history even when the right response is made. Evil is a basic fact of existence—of both experience and nature. To ignore, minimize, or throw it off with easy explanations is to court moral blindness and spiritual superficiality. Even the solution, "I believe therefore I know," is disastrously misleading if it involves ignoring the reality of evil. By seeing Reality and making the right response to it and vice versa we can, to be sure, arrive at a source of explanation which affords us principles for interpreting man, history, nature, etc., and which will convince us of the total meaningfulness of life and of the goodness of God beyond the present attainment of our historic process. But the ends of that historic process are still to be realized

with God's perfect will leaves reason in restless clash with the actual. Thus while faith can free reason from basic anxiety it can never rest it in any complacent solution. Naturally spirit is basic and finally determinative. Yet reason has, nevertheless, laws and relations of its own which influence the spirit, contents among which spirit must keep choosing. Reason thus used is the eye of the spirit. The eye may see; the spirit may choose not to see and look away. Or the spirit may choose to keep seeing what the eye has found. Then, too, the spirit can turn its eye more toward or away from the light.

[27] This thought was suggested to me by the reading of Blakney's *Meister Eckhart,* p. 78, first paragraph.

and evil is still frustratingly real. Faith must, therefore, mean more than the right response to Reality in which religion and reason are constructively co-ordinated. It must also mean a trusting beyond present attainment. It must mean the assurance of the ultimate unity of God and the good, based both on the experience of the right response and on the increasing vision of how the two are in fact seen to be united by the very meaning and nature of the historic process. Right religion thus demands right reason and entails an absolute demand for loving God with all our minds, an intellectual task which obviously no man can ever fulfill.

I

Our present limited task is merely to indicate three kinds of rationalism and three kinds of antirationalism and their respective relations to religion. Naturally the most we can do is to open up a few paths for further reflection along the lines indicated. By rationalism we mean the theory that the reason of the natural man is the final criterion of truth. By antirationalism, accordingly, we mean the denial that our natural reason constitutes our final criterion of truth. The word "natural" is important in that it means our reason in the normal service of our actual nature.

The first kind of rationalism is the classical doctrine that the mind is itself the determinative source or channel of truth. We mention a few varieties of this theory to remind those who already know and to suggest further lines of study for those who do not. There is, for instance, Plato's doctrine of knowledge by recollection. In a higher, former existence the soul knew the pure ideas and therefore comes to know them in this life by simply recalling them, or by bethinking itself, at the prompting of the broken forms which are exhibited by the constant flux of historic change. Or else we may recall the innate ideas of Descartes whereby we know by certainty in proportion to the clearness and distinctness of the ideas themselves. Kant's universal and necessary forms of consciousness in general (*das Bewusstsein überhaupt*) also make the mind principally primary in the construction of all knowledge. An interesting modern similarity to Plato's theory is Freud's depth psychology where, as for instance in *Moses and Monotheism,* not only dispositional inclinations but also actual noetic content is inherited in the depths of the subconscious memory and exercises a strong conditioning role in later thinking and acting. Interesting, too, are modern social pragmatisms where *a priori* principles of interpretation, though themselves social products and not objectively necessary, yet constitute the general categorical presuppositions for our thinking along those lines.[28] Only a careful and extensive discussion would reveal the similarities and differences of these varieties but they all qualify illustratively under our definition by containing definite *a priori* contents or principles which exercise a determinative role on knowledge.

How does this kind of rationalism relate itself to religion? Knowledge is here basically self-knowledge. The Socratic maxim, "Know thyself," is thus entirely appropriate. So is the fact that "the subjectivist bias" came with Descartes. In Kant this subjectivism was universalized and a strong modern cry is for pre-Kantian approaches to truth. Psychologism and social relativism are similarly part and parcel of our "acids of modernity." Whatever truth this kind of rationalism may have outside religion, and it has considerable, religion is response to Reality, not to the self, or even primarily through the self. The actual self, in any case, is basically evil and our potential self, the image of God in us, does not become the dominant response in us apart from God's grace in history and to the individual. The knowledge of our actual self must itself be judged by the highest historical revelation and by the Holy Spirit. By discounting God's direct work in history, past and present, this rationalism never allows for more than a benevolent deism and, as Whitehead maintains, such a hypothesis is quite superfluous.[29]

The second kind of rationalism is the one which makes reason with a small *r* correspond to Reason with a capital *R*. The microcosm finds truth by its proportionate or harmonious relation to

[28] Cf. C. I. Lewis, *Mind and the World Order,* p. 228.

[29] Cf. his *Science in the Modern World,* p. 111, for a good explanation of this assertion.

the Macrocosm. Coherence is the test of truth. Inclusiveness and consistency, wholeness and integration, are the final criteria of truth. Even the good itself is defined in these terms so that truth and goodness tend to be equated outright. The coherent is the reasonable and the reasonable is the good and the true. We recall Hegel's famous statement to the effect that the whole is the true (*das Wahre ist das Ganze*).[30] His *sich entwicklendes Wesen* (developing Being) which followed *die kalt fortschreitende Notwendigkeit der Sache* (the coldly proceeding necessity of the situation) was the Whole which was both the reasonable and the real so that the warm, graphic language of religion was merely a matter of *Vorstellungen* (pictorial representations) which must be reduced to the *Begriffe*, the cold concepts of the logical reason. Today Brand Blanshard has given us an able presentation of the kind of rationalism which we are considering: *The Nature of Thought*. "How are we to conceive," he asks, "of the necessity in which thought can ultimately rest?"[31] "Is all necessity relative to a whole which in the end is *the* whole?"[32] And his answer is, "Coherence is our sole criterion of truth."[33] By coherence he means, too, the whole of experience which is accessible to "our immanent and common reason."[34]

What are we to say of this kind of rationalism from the point of view of religion? Our answer is rather obvious. "Our immanent and common reason" is just our actual reason which we know is distorted in line with our actual response to Reality. Man's reason cannot be equated with God's Reason, microcosm with Macrocosm, simply because such an equation fails to take realistic account of our natural state of sin. It presupposes the natural goodness of man. The harmony between reason and Reason can come about only when man's response is that of surrender to Reality whereby through faith, grace, gratitude, and obedience he increasingly finds his reason truly seeking and being instructed by God's Reason by

[30] *Phenomenologie des Geistes*, p. 16 (*Werke, Zweiter Band*).

[31] Vol. I, p. 654.

[32] Vol. II, p. 427.

[33] Vol. II, p. 259.

[34] Vol. II, p. 519.

means of both historic revelation and the Holy Spirit. In the second place, the coherence of experience as a whole is after all nothing but the coherence of our actual total world of time and space. And that is but a drop of purposive process, a parenthetic creation among countless parentheses, within the creativity of Reality. Such coherence, when made an ultimate religious criterion, confuses God's time with our time. God's time is, rather, best to be seen in the highest, selective, historical revelation which always judges the coherence of the actual. Nor can such a coherence of the actual equate Being and Goodness without either denying the reality of evil or making God finite. And such conclusions root back in an inadequate religious method, not in the nature of Reality.

A third kind of rationalism is that which holds that truth can be reached only by pushing explanation to its utmost limits,[35] and then proceeds to limit explanation by certain inadequate tests of truth. Consider, for example, the use made of the modern scientific method. Some make science into a metaphysic and tell us that the scientific reason finds all the truth that can be found. They even speak of scientific theology. The whole problem of the incompetence of our actual reason to interpret Reality is simply ignored. The deep insight contained in Kierkegaard's assertion that "truth is subjectivity"[36] is rejected in favor of an inapplicable objectivism. The scientific method is good in its place, but how can it possibly deal with existential ultimates? Its very nature and use give almost exclusive emphasis to the areas of actuality which can best be objectively tested and publicly verified. The whole weight of the method therefore tends to reduce the spiritual to the psychological, the psychological to the biological, the biological to the chemical, etc., not because the lower levels are more true but simply because the lower they are the better they can be tested. The spiritual realm, on the other hand, that of freedom,

[35] Whitehead, *Process and Reality*, p. 232. Few have done more than Whitehead to combat this kind of scientific rationalism.

[36] Cf. for instance *Samlade Vaerker*, Vol. VII, p. 228. See also Berdyaev's excellent discussion in *Spirit and Reality*, pp. 4 ff.

decision, and personal relations, cannot be handled at all adequately by this method. The more religious reason is the less by its very nature can it be tested by any category within actuality apart from the highest selective revelation, which, just because it is selective, cannot be judged by the aggregative, but rather judges it by its organic relation to it and possibilities for it. Religion has its own field, method, and criteria, and it is simply woolly-mindedness to forget this primary fact. Science cannot deal with religious motivation, absolute authority, and existential ultimates. The scientific method, if used as a criterion of ultimate truth, faces the dilemma that the more meaningful and rich anything is the less it can be proved to be true, while the more meaningless and thin it is the more it can be proved true. And the fault lies with the method, not with truth. This kind of scientific rationalism can get meaningful truth back into thought and life only by increasingly disregarding its own method and tests. Scientism in religion is thus a reductionistic rationalism which prevents vigorous religious response and reason.

II

In contrast to these rationalisms we wish also to indicate three kinds of antirationalism and their bearing on religion. The first kind is logical positivism. This holds that philosophy is but the "deduction of the relations of equivalence from the rules of entailment."[37] Reason is limited to the finding of necessary relations within logical structure, but this logical structure has itself no necessary relation either to actuality or to Reality. Actuality can be known only probably as the stuff of sense is interpreted and tested by science. Ethics, theology, metaphysics—all are literally nonsense. Whereas the above theory made science the sole test of truth and then tried to stretch the scientific method as far as possible, logical positivism is vigorously critical in its severe shearing of reason. What bearing does this kind of antirationalism have on religion?

Since it makes room for faith by destroying reason, many conservatives are hailing it as a philosophic savior. It does make

[37] Ayer, *Language, Truth, and Logic*, p. 87.

short shrift of science as metaphysics and of all reductionist rationalisms. In this sense it is an ally. Religion has suffered severely from the fact that we have been philosophically uncritical and continually succumbed to reductionistic metaphysics. Logical positivism ought to teach us to become competently critical within the realm of reason itself; for after all both rationalism and antirationalism use reason as the means whereby they may establish their own theories! On the other hand, logical positivism makes faith entirely arbitrary nor can faith dispense with reason. Reason in religion is the continual criticism of our response to Reality. Even though it tends to be distorted in line with the characteristic response of our actual nature, it also suffers from its knowledge of this distortion and restlessly calls for the truth. Right religion must always include in its response to Reality better reasoning, a more adequate interpretation of all that it sees. Reality is organically related to actuality as its savior. Reason can see this truth, making it eager to know more concerning this relation; and even though those who try to evade Reality may deny our reasoning, they are peculiarly disturbed in the depths of their lives by what they unpleasantly feel to be the truth. Right religious response must include our being increasingly able "to give a reason for the faith that is in us."

A second kind of antirationalism is that which makes feeling, decision, or action the final test of truth. We contact Reality through a feeling of complete dependence upon it and all knowledge is decidedly derivative. Sometimes knowledge is even held to be a barrier to the right contact with Reality. All "systems" of truth, all set interpretations of Reality, "come in between" man and God and hinder the experience of immediate confrontation. Every kind of reasoned continuity thus stands in the way of true religion where man stands naked before God without merit and without the possession of truth. Certain aspects of Barth's theology fall under this heading of exclusive contact of God through immediate decision. There is an antitheological trend, too, which has been holding that man's actions are his faith and are the only thing which really matter.

What is the relation of this kind of antirationalism to religion? It does contain the truth that reason is only one aspect of religion and not the primary one at that. Personal response includes conation, affection, and cognition, but it is greater than all three put together. As a protest against all rationalisms which make themselves the primary category of religion, the stress of this kind of antirationalism is indeed well taken and sorely needed. When, on the other hand, it makes affection or conation, feeling or will, primary, it is surely equally at fault. Religion is whole-response to Reality and nothing less than that. It is man's necessary response as a total being to Reality as an unavoidable ultimate. To make feeling or action more important than reason is to distort the truth that religion is whole-response to Reality. Then, too, no response can be right unless it be intelligent, for intelligence in religion is precisely the right interpretation of Reality. And how can the response be right without cumulation or growth of interpretation? In this sense religion is eminently reasonable. It is hard, nevertheless, to say that reason has primacy, even as a part of the reaction. For the whole is indivisibly involved, including both the will to respond, the way the self feels about that to which he responds, and the interpretation of that whole action and reaction. But even as the will and the feelings inform reason about the nature of the object and thus keep conditioning it strongly, even so reason by its growing interpretation heavily modifies the will and the feelings. Reason has a right and necessary place in the response which, based on the recurrence of experience and the consequent growth of interpretation, tends to give both light and steadiness to religion. Without reason there could be neither true conversion nor true nurture in religion.

The third and last kind of antirationalism which we wish to consider is that of revelation. This openly declares that the natural reason is by itself incompetent to constitute the final authority of truth. There are chiefly three kinds of revelational antirationalisms. The first takes the point of view that the natural reason in the sphere or religion is positively misleading. Revelation alone shows us God and salvation. Reason shows us idols and false paths that lead to death. God's special revelation must be kept completely distinct and never related to general truths of reason, for such relations always become distortions, in natural reason being corrupt and constitutionally incapable of bridging the gap between the special revelation and general and fallen creation. This school can in general be identified with men like Paul, Tertullian, Bernard of Clairvaux, Pascal, Kierkegaard, and Barth. Its deepest insight is desperately needed, namely, that if revelation is ultimate truth (if Christianity, for instance, is really ultimate, a first principle of explanation), it cannot logically, by the very nature of the case, be verified in terms of anything else outside itself, because in the very attempt at such verification, its basic claim is denied. The ultimate can never be proved by anything less than itself. Yet many have hankered for a proved religion. We must grant, too, that this kind of antirationalism is not necessarily negative, deny-ing like logical positivism that man can know what to believe and what to do, but can be vigorously positive with steel convictions that gird solidly the meaningfulness of life both for the individual and for society. At its best it combines deep faith with creative insights and with moral and cultural sensitivity. Pascal may serve as our example. In this view there is, nevertheless, an artificial arbitrariness that lends itself to fanaticism. Even though revelation is primary and cannot be ultimately tested by reason, it can yet be tested in a secondary sense by its organic relation to all life, its capacity to serve as a social ideal, and by the power which it can make available for individual and social transformation. The reason that this antirationalism lays itself open to fanaticism of different kinds is that it has no organic relation between revelation and general creation. Even though our actual reason cannot and will not see the light in its own power, it can see and use the light when it has come into the world and as it lets the light flood its own darkness. And even those still in the dark can see the light, however much they may turn from it and refuse to see it. Even though revelation fulfills reason unexpectedly, it yet fulfills it.

The second kind of revelational antirationalism is that which believes revelation to be the extension of reason. Consider Thomism. The unaided reason can by itself know that God is, what he is not, and by analogy certain general things about His nature, such as His infinity, unity, etc.; but revelation is necessary to disclose God's fuller nature, to make effective man's salvation, and to disclose God's ultimate plans for man. Even though this school of thought has often been commended for its reasonableness, even been upheld as having provided the best solution of the relation of reason and revelation, we nevertheless call it antirationalism because the natural reason is not the final criterion of truth but is rather decisively unable to discover the basic truths which affect man's salvation. Since revelation, moreover, contains all the necessary eternal truths for those who cannot master reason, reason, too, becomes rather superfluous. There is also no full organic connection between the disclosures of revelation and those of reason; something otherwise unknowable is simply added; the discontinuity of revelation thus becomes for the most part arbitrary, external, informational. Revelational knowledge is not primarily a matter of response and of a new perspective of both eternity and history from within actuality itself. The synthesis is, in fact, mostly an able compromise between the growing prestige of the Aristotelian philosophy of the thirteenth century and the traditional dogma of the Catholic Church. It has served well as a strong makeshift and we must be thankful for it. But even given this revelation which is the extension of reason, there is no abiding, comprehensive necessity or intrinsic unity of discourse between reason and revelation in which all thought can feel a gripping security. This fact stands out in spite of St. Thomas' gallant and generous efforts in his *Summa Theologica* to provide just that security.

III

The third kind of revelational antirationalism is that of the Augustinian-Anselmian *credo ut intelligam*. "I believe in order to know" can, of course, be interpreted in at least two ways depending upon whether we emphasize the first or the last part of the sentence. There are some historical grounds for maintaining that the tradition itself stresses the latter part. In that case faith becomes the means to a glorified philosophy. The end is to know rather than to believe. "Our faith," says Augustine, "will become truth."[38] If, on the other hand, we stress the former part of the sentence excessively, *"I believe* in order to know," we rob reason of its rightful degree of functional autonomy within experience, and tend, in fact, to turn true faith into a thin fideism. The right emphasis, however, we suggest is on both parts of the sentence, though the stronger stress must still fall on the first part. The formula thus accented we believe to be the clue to the solution of the relation between reason and religion. It satisfies the definitions of our opening discussion, particularly the two requirements that the whole-response of religion be understood as the basic determiner of our rational perspective, and, secondly, that even if we could forget the eternal necessity of faith as existential decision, our existential situation, by the reality of evil, demands a seeing beyond present realization of historic process.

If "believe" is taken to mean an active response requiring the whole person, and if knowledge is taken to be primarily dynamic and personal rather than primarily empirical and evidential, then "I believe in order to know" does constitute the locus of our solution. This is so since the whole-response to reality in terms of faith means a surrender to it, a freeing of reason from the pressure of self-centered natural man. This response is based on trust in Reality. Such a response depends for its content (which we are not considering in this inquiry) upon the highest historical revelation truly available to the responder, the general grace of creation which accounts for our very natures, and the immediate co-operation of the Holy Spirit. There is thus one real sense in which Aulén's strong stress that God is the subject of faith is right.[39] "I believe" is always a false statement unless it involves the experience of the immeasurable priority of God. We may secondarily create an idea of God. When we confront the real God, He compels us. "I believe" for a Christian means that he has experienced the

[38] "On the Holy Trinity," in *The Nicene and Post-Nicene Fathers,* First Series, Vol. III, p. 81.
[39] *Den allmänneliga kristna tron,* p. 35.

judgment of God's incomparable love, found his natural self condemned, and accepted the goodness of God which leads to repentance, forgiveness, and faith.

Yet God is not the subject of faith in the sense that we are not willing to believe. Religion is our response to Reality. Our new self came to be, even as the actual self, seeing the suicide of its own ways, accepted God's grace, which strengthened the image of God in the former self into a dominating position against the old, natural self which formerly ruled as the whole self deciding. This is a response to Reality by the whole self, the self seeing, willing, feeling God, but by a self which was itself *made whole*, was born, made a new creature, even as its primary response took on the nature of a surrender to Reality which was also an empowerment of the image of God in man, the actualization of man's deepest essential self into the new creature for which he has been created. The isolated self of the natural man, the self of possessiveness, pretension, will to power, the dissatisfied self that draws a circle of self-interest around itself and yet longs to break out of the very circle it draws—this old self loses its dominating power by the response of faith which is the willing acceptance by the self, too weak to escape its own imprisonment, of help to be set free by a power not its own. This very response is an eternal necessity for it is the only right response to Reality by the very nature of that Reality, for God is always God and man the dependent creature. Even though, therefore, man's response is genuinely his, if his reason is to be right, his whole-response must be the response of faith.

This relation between religion and reason also solves encouragingly the relation between Reality, realizability, and realization. We saw that part of our historic process is evil and that there is no use denying or minimizing that fact. Yet if faith shows us God and His purpose for man; if history, freedom, nature, and human nature all conspire to fulfill that purpose, however much frustrated and baffled we may then be within our own brief historical situation; we know Whom we have believed and we see increasingly what His ways are and how they are working out. Our hearts are stayed in God and our minds are satisfied by His mighty works. No matter how real, dire, and threatening evil may be now, we have seen God through faith and in His light and strength we see suggested the full final solution.

This brief sketch has been primarily concerned with the functional relation between religion and reason. We have tried merely to suggest some interrelations between religion as whole-response to Reality and reason as the ensuing interpretation. Another important task waiting to be done is to fix the relation between this functional interaction between religion and reason and the criteria for testing the concrete historic contents of religions. In this sphere reason is both cautiously critical, tending to insist on continuity of both insight and commitment, and critically creative, urging forward the interpretation of primary religious responses. It is both an organ of novelty in the search for the ways of God and the organ of continuity between creative discontinuity and critical continuity, demanding of both adequate application to life as a whole. Our stress here has rather been on the primacy of religion as whole-response to Reality over reason which can function at its fullest efficacy in the vital spheres of life only when it is definitely religious.

Individually and socially we must react to Reality. There is no escape. Neglect is simply the inadequate reaction of the natural man. Our times are too critical for mere theory. Religion itself is response, but we need the right response. We cannot be right before we have surrendered our isolated and inbent selves and found genuine fellowship in heaven and on earth, functioning through freed reasons and the creative power of faith. Our reason can be right only when it has been set free from the distorting power of the stifling pressure of self-encirclement. The challenge we face is momentous: to be deeply enough religious to become vigorously and creatively intellectual. We need reason in all spheres of life and of human endeavor, but the reason freed, lighted, and empowered by faith. Reason itself must become religious.

Index